FAMILY
TERROR
NETWORKS

DEAN C. ALEXANDER

CONTENTS

INTRODUCTION

An Unlikely ISIS[1] Wife

It was a short, unexpected romantic episode. Daniela Greene was a Czechoslovakian-born, fluent-German-speaking former FBI contract linguist with a top-secret clearance. Her suitor was Denis Cuspert, German ex-rapper (Deso Dogg) turned ISIS propagandist and fighter (Abu Talha al-Almani). Things did not turn out well for either of them.

In June 2014, Greene submitted a falsified US government Report of Foreign Travel form, FD-772. In that document, Greene stated that she planned to visit her parents in Germany. She lied to her FBI supervisor and chief security officer at the Indianapolis FBI office regarding her pending travel arrangements. In reality, she intended to travel to Turkey. From there, she sought to live with Cuspert in Syria.

Greene purchased a round-trip ticket from Indianapolis through Chicago to Turkey. Her return flight was scheduled barely one day after her arrival. She did not proceed with that departure. Rather, less than a week later, she purchased a one-way ticket from Indianapolis through Toronto, with a destination of Istanbul. From Istanbul, she reached Gaziantep, Turkey, less than twenty miles from the Syrian border. From Gaziantep, a Cuspert contact aided her in crossing into Syria. Once there, Greene met Cuspert and warned him she worked with the FBI and that the agency was investigating his activities.

In late June 2014, the pair married in Syria. They lived there until August 2014, when Greene left Syria for the United States. Soon, she comprehended her mistake in marrying an ISIS operative she had investigated. At the time of her travel to Syria and nuptials with Cuspert, Greene was already married to a US soldier.

Days after her return to the United States, Greene was arrested for violating 18 USC section 1001, making false statements to the federal government in relation to international terrorism. Greene pleaded guilty to that charge. She received a two-year sentence rather than eight years, as allowable. The US Attorney's Office recommended the reduced sentence as Greene had cooperated and substantially benefited the government.

Greene was released from prison in summer 2016 after having served her sentence. Subsequently, Greene worked as a hostess at a hotel lounge in Syracuse, New York.[2] In January 2018, German authorities disclosed that Cuspert was killed while fighting for ISIS in Syria.[3]

What Happened in Vegas

Amanda Woodruff met Jerad Miller at a flea market in Lafayette, Indiana. Before they met, Jerad was incarcerated for drug offenses. The pair married in 2012, despite the opposition of Amanda's father, Todd Woodruff. Woodruff was particularly concerned about the couple's nine-year age difference. He recalled, "I begged her not to marry him. I begged her not to move to Las Vegas. He was into all this Patriot Nation and conspiracy theory stuff, and the next thing I know, her phone was getting shut off, and she was getting isolated from us. The whole world was against him [Jerad], and he was just, he was just nuts."[4]

As a couple, the Millers delved into a host of extremist ideologies. Among the radical tenets they followed were white supremacy, sovereign citizenship, and militia themes. The Millers' neighbors in an apartment complex in Nevada said the couple talked about killing police officers. The pair also handed out white-power propaganda to residents there.

The couple spent time at the ranch of Cliven Bundy, a Nevada rancher who, along with supporters, had an armed standoff with government agents over grazing rights. Bundy ranch representatives asked the Millers to leave the homestead, as their ideals were too extreme. Jerad was captured on a video at Bundy's ranch threatening law enforcement: "I feel sorry for any federal agents that want to come in here in and try to push us around or anything like that. I really don't want violence toward them, but if they're going to come bring violence to us—well, if that's the language they want to speak, we'll learn it."[5]

In a June 2014 posting on Facebook, Jerad wrote a pseudo-manifesto, noting in part, "Those of us who know the truth and dare to speak it, know that the enemy we face are indeed our brothers. Even though they share the same masters as we all do. They fail to recognize the chains that bind them. To stop this oppression, I fear, can only be accomplished with bloodshed."[6]

There were threats of violence in a 2011 Facebook posting, Amanda wrote, "The people of the world" are "lucky I can't kill you now but remember one day I will get you because one day all hell will break loose and I'll be standing in the middle of it with a shotgun in one hand and a pistol in the other."[7]

In June 2014, the couple shot and killed two Las Vegas police officers. The murdered lawmen, Igor Soldo and Alyn Beck, were eating lunch at a Cicis Pizza restaurant. Jerad shot Soldo in the head and Beck in the throat. Amanda then joined in shooting and killing Beck. Next, the Millers covered Beck's body with a yellow Gadsden flag ("Don't Tread on Me") and swastika. Additionally, the Millers pinned a note on Soldo's body: "This is the beginning of the revolution."[8]

After removing the officers' guns and ammunition, the Millers shouted that the attack was the "beginning of the revolution."[9] The Millers then entered a nearby Walmart and yelled, "Get out. This is a revolution. The police are on the way."[10] Joseph Wilcox, a shopper with a concealed weapon, confronted Jerad. However, Amanda intervened and fatally shot Wilcox. Subsequently, the Millers exchanged gunfire with police at the Walmart. During the firefight, the couple was wounded, Jerad fatally. Amanda shot herself and later died at a hospital.

Cousins in Crime[11]

In late 2014, an undercover FBI employee posted a Facebook friend request to Illinois-based Army National Guard Specialist Hasan Edmonds. In January 2015, the pair communicated on multiple occasions. Hasan explained that he and his cousin, Jonas Edmonds, wanted to go to Syria and join ISIS. Hasan also revealed that his cousin's prison record might impede his travel overseas. If so, Jonas would send his family to Syria prior to his launching a martyrdom attack in the United States.

If restricted to remain stateside, Jonas would use Hasan's military identification to access a military installation in northern Illinois where Hasan worked. Once there, Jonas planned to commence an attack with others. Jonas foresaw he would kill between 100 and 150 persons. Prior to the projected strike, Hasan would travel to Syria. The Edmondses interacted with undercover FBI employees online and met face to face with another undercover FBI employee. The Edmondses believed that they were conferring with ISIS operatives.

In March 2015, Hasan was arrested while seeking to fly from Chicago's Midway Airport to Egypt, while Jonas was detained at his home. The cousins, both US citizens, were charged with conspiracy to provide material support to a foreign terrorist organization, ISIS. By December 2015, they pleaded guilty to the conspiracy charge. Also, Hasan pleaded guilty to seeking to give material support to ISIS. Likewise, Jonas admitted lying to police in relation to an international terrorism offense. In September 2016, Hasan was sentenced to thirty years in prison. Jonas received a twenty-one-year prison sentence.

What are Family Terror Networks?

The cases of political violence just shared—Cuspert/Greene, Millers, and Edmondses—are illustrative of an emerging and troubling threat, family terror networks. Prior to expounding on the latter term, it is conducive to define families. Families[12] comprise individuals who descend from the same ancestor, as in shared blood (consanguinity). Families have affinity resulting from marriage and adoption. They encompass the range of spouses, siblings, aunts/uncles, cousins, parents-in-laws, and brothers/sisters-in-law, to name a few.[13] Families include kin based in one nation or several countries. The family is one relationship or social bond that can serve as a terror node.

Family terror networks (or alternatively, family affiliated terrorism) involve two or more people from the same clan who support the threat or use of terrorism. Kin terrorism has appeared across diverse views from religiously motivated precepts to national liberation, and from hate-based ideologies to other viewpoints. Family structures enable higher instances of conversion to radical beliefs given the imprimatur of credibility and trust that attaches within the family unit as opposed to unaffiliated networks.

This subset of terrorists comprises a full range of socioeconomic, racial, religious, ethnic, national-origin, and foreign-affinity ties. Terrorists aligned with hierarchical and network groups and unaffiliated cabals are represented in this form of terrorism as well. Family affiliated terrorists include group leaders, operational cadres, active supporters, and passive supporters.[14] They use terror tactics including bombings, suicide bombings, and gunfire, among others, with variances in operational stages.

Patriarchs strongly influence their kin to become terrorists. Wives and other females may sometimes embrace violence. The "Black Widows" of Chechnya are the most notorious of such radicals. These women had husbands in Chechen jihadist terror groups. Their spouses were killed by Russian forces or died during a terror attack on a Russian target. Also, the term is often used more expansively to include women whose other family members were killed by Russian forces in the Chechen conflict.

Family networks afford exposure to terrorist ideology, recruitment, funding, training, and operational opportunities more easily than those outside the familial structure. From their private setting, family members disseminate doctrine, culture, and grievances to their kin. These trusted family voices might engender cohesion and unity of purpose while inciting hostility against external threats. The family's animus might be targeted at government, industry, nonprofits, nongovernmental organizations, the public, or a segment thereof.

There are many factors affecting the susceptibility of individuals to becoming terrorists, including: socioeconomic factors, geography, real or perceived victimization and marginalization, infatuation with an extremist ideology, personality traits, mental health challenges, and influences of technology. Analogously, criminologists proffer that "low self-control is associated with higher levels of deviance and criminality irrespective of the strength or weakness of one's social bonds."[15] Social network analysis also demonstrates that, to some, nonfamilial influences can hasten participation in terrorism.[16] Contributing to involvement in extremism are "the contacts, ties, and connections of the individuals in the network."[17]

Still, the belief system, values, power, control, and capabilities based in a family can afford member participants achievable, though sometimes measured, terror operations. Abandonment of terror plans in a family cell is less likely because it brings shame and dishonor to the family member. These conditions greatly contribute to radicalism being disseminated and maintained absent other factors.

Family terror network attributes may include self-sufficiency, autonomy, and flexibility. These might not exist when family members take direction from a non-family terror network. A family's informal and decentralized structure is conducive to successful terror operations. Families have an ingrained resiliency as challenges are often encountered fervently.

Many people embrace extremism despite not being introduced to such ideas at home. Yet this book proffers that family terror links appear in radicalism more willingly and thoroughly than those without kinship. The core argument of this work is that family structures are very influential in potential terrorist participation. This volume addresses terror networks developed within families and shares strategies to withstand this dynamic threat.

Family Terror Networks: An Increasingly Prominent Type of Terrorism[18]

In the United States, as internationally, families have been cajoled by Islamic State propaganda. For instance, in 2014–2015, a Mississippi couple (Jaelyn Delshaun Young and Muhammad Oda Dakhlalla); a Texas family (Michael Wolfe and Jordan Furr), comprising a husband, a wife, and their children; and three Illinois siblings (the Khans), including two minors, were apprehended at different airports while trying to join the self-declared caliphate in Iraq and Syria.

In 2014, German authorities seized the two Farah teenage sisters from Colorado and their female schoolmate after they arrived at Frankfurt Airport. The trio was en route to Turkey intending to reach the Islamic State. In 2015, Syed Rizwan Farook and his wife, Tashfeen Malik, killed 14 persons and injured scores in an ISIS-inspired attack in San Bernardino, California.[19] In that same year, brothers Alaa and Nader Saadeh and three others conspired to travel to Syria and enlist with the Islamic State.

Other noteworthy family-linked terrorist attacks in the United States include Boston Marathon bombers Tamerlan and Dzhokhar

Tsarnaev and two sets of brothers who performed as hijackers on 9/11. A set of brothers were on two different flights during the September 11 attacks: Wail and Waleed al-Shehri (American Airlines Flight 11) and Nawaf and Salem al-Hazmi (American Airlines Flight 77). Additionally, three cousins participated in the 9/11 incidents: Ahmed and Hamza al-Ghamdi (United Airlines Flight 175) and Ahmed al-Haznawi (United Airlines Flight 93).

Also, family affiliated terrorist actions have taken place globally. The cabal involved in the 2002 Bali terror bombings plots included three brothers: Ali Ghufron, Ali Imron, and Amrozi Nurhasyim.[20] A fourth brother, Ali Fauzi, spent three years in prison for terror offenses unrelated to the Bali attacks.[21] More recently, French nationals and brothers Brahim and Salah Abdeslam participated in the November 2015 Paris attacks. Brahim conducted a suicide bombing at a Paris restaurant. Salah rented a car that brought a group of attackers to the Bataclan concert hall. Salah abandoned his plan to conduct a suicide bombing that evening. Subsequently, Salah fled to Belgium, where he and several coconspirators eluded authorities for months. Ultimately, he was captured in Belgium and extradited to France.

Salah had served time in prison for armed robbery with the mastermind of the Paris attacks, Belgian Abdelhamid Abaaoud. Abaaoud and other members of his cell, along with his female cousin, Hasna Aitboulahcen, were killed in a police raid following the November 2015 attacks. Abaaoud recruited his thirteen-year-old brother, Younes, to move to Syria and join ISIS.

Other contemporary instances of family connected terrorism abroad include the August 2017 jihadi terror cabal in Spain consisting of multiple sets of brothers[22] and terror family links in the jihadi-inspired May 2017 Manchester suicide bombing.[23] In May

2018, two jihadi-aligned families were responsible for a series of suicide bombings in Surabaya, Indonesia, targeting churches and law enforcement.[24]

The dynamics and instances of domestic and international family terror networks brought to the forefront this terror phenomenon. Its attributes have profound effects on the nature of terrorism and counterterrorism. Consequently, a work addressing this theme is long overdue.

Why Family Terror Networks are Important[25]

Family terror networks are important for multiple reasons. Households are an integral part of traditional social networks. This paradigm allows radicalization and recruitment to occur in a setting of trust, confidence, and privacy. The family unit has a greater level of legitimacy than the outside world. Even after detection of a kin-linked terror cell, deradicalization and disengagement programs may not succeed as family members may impede participation.

Competing or incompatible opinions have trouble piercing the family network's ideological wall with outside viewpoints. Trust ties arising from friendship, religious institutions, and schools are less sustained than family ties. It is improbable that kin will abandon their terrorist activities when extremism was sourced at home. Frequently, vocalizing concerns about engaging in terrorism is barred within a familial terror cell.

The zeal and skills gained through a family setting are magnified more than otherwise. Household members can teach the best practices of extremism to others. Parents or other kin may intimidate household members to support radicalism or even carry out a martyrdom operation. Often, the bullied family member agrees out of duty, honor, or fear. This radicalism exploits the trust and security features that exist in households.

Attracting terror prospects from within a family provides a close source of personnel. Keeping a terror cell limited to kin enhances security as only trusted individuals take part in the cabal. A paucity of numbers may limit the scope and severity of the cell's intended operations. Yet, given their growing prevalence in terror operations, police would benefit by regularly exploring radical elements within households. Yet family loyalty characteristics sometimes make such determinations difficult.

Households are usually the initial and dominant thought sources for their members. Strong, trusted ties engendered by lengthy interactions are indicative of household extremism. A family member can proffer that violence is normal behavior and necessary to achieve the goal of a terror group. The capacity to instill these ideals in one's children, amplified during adolescence and beyond, enables kin-linked extremists to indoctrinate subsequent generations.

Families enhance sharing and confirming extremist doctrine. Likewise, a family member can have a strong effect on decision-making, especially in a patriarchal structure. A mother's support of radicalism is another path of influence on her children. Household elders have a perceived trustworthiness and wisdom that emanates due to age and experience. Also, social isolation can lead to the efficacy of a family member's influence and leverage over another family member. These factors assist in creating resiliency against counter narratives. Few chances for extirpation from extremism exist in households.

A family member may show radical propaganda available online to a child, sibling, or nephew. A family member may introduce his kin to extremist doctrines communicated at religious institutions, schools, and community events. Likewise, kin members may entice recruits outside the family. Previously unknown persons found online or elsewhere are prone to suspicion. After all, persons external to a household could be informants or undercover agents. Interestingly, terror groups can purposely target families as a whole for recruitment as in Turkey, where the "DHKP/C recruits new members from left or radical left families, whereas the Hezbollah [Turkish, not Lebanese] recruits from right or radical right families."[26]

Still, family members can expand the social networks of extremists by introducing them to persons outside the family unit. This occurred with al Qaeda operatives Khalid Sheikh Muhammed (uncle) and Ramzi Yousef (nephew). Yousef's friend Abdul Murad joined the cabal. Murad received flight training in the United States and proposed that planes could be used as missiles. He sought to crash a plane into CIA headquarters.

In January 1995, Yousef and Muhammed planned to use liquid explosives to detonate multiple civilian airlines heading from Asia to the United States. Additionally, the Bojinka plot envisioned a suicide bomber assassinating Pope John Paul I during a visit to the Philippines. Murad's plan to crash into CIA headquarters would mark the final prong of the Bojinka plot.

Prior to this, Yousef was the principal bomb maker in the 1993 World Trade Center attack. Yousef was apprehended in Pakistan in February 1995 and extradited to the United States. He was convicted in 1996 for the Bojinka plot. Yousef was sentenced to life in prison.[27] In 1997, Yousef was convicted of masterminding the 1993 World Trade Center attack with an appending life prison sentence.[28]

Murad was captured in the Philippines in January 1995. He likewise was extradited to the United States. Afterward, Murad was convicted of participation in the Bojinka plot. In 1998, he was sentenced to life in prison.[29] Muhammed was the mastermind of the September 11, 2001, incidents. He was captured in Pakistan in March 2003 and extradited to the United States. Since December 2006, Muhammed has been in US custody at an internment center in Guantanamo Bay, Cuba.

Overview of Chapters

The intriguing aspects of family terror networks and their implications merit a comprehensive book on those subjects. This volume addresses the literature gap in this increasingly relevant manifestation of terrorism in the United States and abroad. In doing so, the work chronicles the issue of family affiliated terrorism along the following construct. Chapter 1 addresses general principles of terrorism. Chapter 2 discusses the characteristics of family terror networks. Chapter 3 shares case studies involving family terror networks across ideologies. Chapter 4 proposes a model for predicting family terror networks and its utility in combating this type of political violence. Overall, analysis of the 118 case studies of family connected terrorism involving 138 examples of kin relationships (e.g., brothers, husbands/wives, and fathers/sons) is offered. For purposes of these case studies, the term terrorism also signifies individuals otherwise referred to as extremists in the media.

Chapter 5 describes law enforcement responses to terrorism, which concurrently undermine kin connected terrorism. The epilogue provides insights as to the future of family terror networks.

The appendix offers an inventory of the cases covered in the volume by the names of family members, kin relationships, and extremist ideologies. The notes, bibliography, acknowledgments, and the background of the author are provided at the end of the book.

CHAPTER 1

General Principles of Terrorism

Introduction

This chapter addresses general principles of terrorism, including definitions, threats, and types of groups as well as radicalization, recruitment, and susceptibility to this form of political violence. Also, terrorist characteristics, porous borders, profiling, creating terrorists, women terrorists, terrorists in the economic system, financing terror, the role of corporate security, public-private partnership in combating terrorism, labor and management challenges to terrorism, emergency management/medical responses to mass casualty terror incidents, and combating terrorism are covered. These topics give the reader an understanding of terrorism and facilitate comprehension of the issues addressed in the remaining chapters.

Definitions and Statistics

As used in this volume, the term *terrorism* means the unlawful threat or use of violence against civilians and other noncombatants undertaken by individuals, groups, or nations for a political, social, or religious goal. Whatever definition one uses, the typical segments of terrorism are the act (illegal), perpetrators (e.g., individuals, groups, states), objectives (e.g., political, social, ideological), intended outcomes and motivations (e.g., cause fear, create change, force behavioral adjustments), targets (e.g., individuals, government, nongovernment entities, businesses, nonprofits), and modus operandi (e.g., hijackings).[30]

The terrorist is effective even when he produces no physical casualties. The menace of force and its psychological impact suffice. Even minimal casualties resulting from an incident can aid the organization's propaganda efforts. Terrorism must be viewed in a strategic context rather than as an irritant. Not grasping this distinction has contributed to its growth. After all, countries have inadequately applied effective policies fully and uniformly.

The US government publishes a list of foreign terrorist organizations (FTOs) and state sponsors of terrorism. Over sixty US government–designated FTOs conduct terrorism internationally and threaten US national security. Most FTOs are violent jihadists from the Middle East and Asia. Homegrown violent extremism (HVE) comprises US-based individuals of whatever citizenship who are swayed by an FTO but operate freely of it.

During the Obama administration, twenty-five groups were designated as FTOs, while five FTOs were delisted. Depending on the Trump administration's viewpoints on Mexican drug trafficking organizations (MDTOs), it is conceivable that proposed measures to label MDTOs as FTOs could be resurrected.[31] In July 2014, nineteen Republican senators proposed to designate the pro-Russian separatist organizations Donetsk People's Republic and Lugansk People's Republic as FTOs. This effort will not get traction if US-Russian relations improve during the Trump administration.[32]

However, no statutory domestic terrorism organization (DTO) list exists. Apprehension to establishing a formal DTO would be rife with intense, domestic political considerations as well as constitutional challenges regarding freedom of association and freedom of speech. Still, US government agencies, including the FBI, have labeled particular US extremist groups as terrorist entities, including those associated with radical animal rights and environmental, militia, and sovereign citizen ideologies.

In 2016, the US government listed Iran, Syria, and Sudan as state sponsors of terrorism. Countries formerly specified as state sponsors of terrorism include Cuba (removed during the Obama administration) as well as Libya, Iraq, and North Korea (delisted during the George W. Bush administration). In 2017, the Trump administration designated North Korea as a state sponsor of terrorism.

According to the US State Department, there were 11,072 terrorist attacks in 104 countries in 2016. These incidents caused 25,600 deaths, and over 33,800 people were injured. Some 52 percent of the incidents were attributed to 334 terror groups. The perpetrators of the rest of the incidents are unknown.

Despite the global nature of terrorism, "Fifty-five percent of all attacks took place in five countries (Iraq, Afghanistan, India, Pakistan, and the Philippines), and 75% of all deaths due to terrorist attacks took place in five countries (Iraq, Afghanistan, Syria, Nigeria, and Pakistan)."[33] In 2016, the number of terror attacks and people killed were 9 percent lower and 13 percent lower, respectively, than in 2015. The terror groups engaged in the most strikes in 2016 were ISIS (1,133), the Taliban (848), Maoists/Communist Party of India (336), al-Shabaab (332), and Houthi extremists (267).

The terms *extremist(s)* and *radical(s)* refer to individuals or groups that adhere to ideologies supporting the threat and/or use of violence for political, religious, or social objectives. For purposes of this book, terrorists, radicals, and extremists will be used interchangeably, although in fact and law, distinctions often exist.

One type of extremism disdains others and uses force (or the threat of force) because of the person's immutable characteristics (e.g., race, ethnicity, national origin, religion, gender, gender identity, or disability). Such bias, as exhibited in criminal acts, is termed a hate crime. Lone wolves, cabals, and those formally linked to a hate group perpetrate such crimes.

Increasingly troublesome are mass casualty hate crimes in the United States. Among examples of such incidents are: Robert Bower's October 2018 attack at the Tree of Life Synagogue in Pittsburgh that resulted in the murder of eleven congregants; the October 2016 failed plot by a militia-hate aligned cabal that sought to bomb an apartment complex housing Somali immigrants in Garden City, Kansas; and Dylann Roof's June 2015 murder of nine parishioners at an African American church in Charleston, South Carolina. Other prominent hate-based attacks include: Omar Mateen's jihadi/anti-LGBTQ attack at a gay nightclub in Orlando, Florida, in June 2016 (at the time, the deadliest mass shooting in US history); Frazier Cross's anti-Semitic attacks at a Jewish community center/old age home in Overland, Kansas, in April 2014; and Wade Page's attack at a Sikh temple in Oak Creek, Wisconsin, in August 2012.[34] White nationalist rallies in Charlottesville, Virginia in 2017, and subsequent efforts in those realms nationally, demonstrate that animosity against the other shows no signs of dissipating in the foreseeable future.

In November 2017, the FBI released hate crime statistics for 2016, noting that of "6,121 criminal incidents reported, 6,063 were single-bias incidents (there were also 58 multiple-bias incidents). Of the single-bias incidents:

- 57.5 percent were motivated by a race, ethnicity, or ancestry bias;

- 21.0 percent were motivated by a religious bias;

- 17.7 percent were motivated by a sexual orientation bias;

- The remaining incidents were motivated by a gender identity, disability, or gender bias."[35]

The US Department of Justice's Bureau of Justice Statistics estimated that in 2012 there was a 60 percent underreporting of hate crimes. Hate crimes are significantly underestimated owing to victims not notifying police of such incidents. Concurrently, police departments may fail to recognize the role of bias in selected crimes.

A white nationalist resurgence—political and otherwise—may trigger other fringe elements of varying ideologies to threaten or resort to violence. An escalation of hate crimes against minorities (especially blacks, Hispanics, Muslims, and the LGBTQ communities) could produce militancy among portions of society. This is particularly so with anti-fascists movements, including Antifa, who have clashed with white nationalists at rallies and counterdemonstrations in recent years.[36]

Figures from the Southern Poverty Law Center (SPLC) reveal the number of hate groups grew from 676 in 2001 to 926 in 2008 during the George W. Bush presidency. In 2000, the figure was 602. The number of hate groups fell overall during the Obama presidency. During his administration, there was an initial expansion of hate groups from 932 in 2009 to 1,018 in 2011. Those figures dropped to 784 in 2014, prior to reaching 892 groups in 2015. Hate group numbers grew in 2016 and 2017 to 917 and 954, respectively.

Other Extremists

Those who advocate or threaten violence on behalf of single-issue themes (e.g., environmentalism, animal rights, abortion rights) have been deemed domestic extremists. Individuals and groups aligned with antigovernment movements (e.g., militias, sovereign citizens,[37] and anarchists) have been classified as American extremists as well.

Environmental and animal rights extremists may speed up their illegal acts if they perceive that the Trump administration buttresses corporate interests over their goals. Trump administration support of oil drilling (e.g., the Dakota Access Pipeline and Alaska's Arctic National Wildlife Refuge) might cause radicals aligned with environmental and indigenous interests to resort to violence. Anarchist militancy could rise due to the election of a billionaire. Yet the Trump administration's anticipated anti-globalist stance may soften such perspectives. It remains to be seen whether pro-life judicial appointments to the US Supreme Court would precipitate violence by those who are pro-choice.

According to SPLC statistics, in 2016 there were 623 antigovernment "patriot" groups. Of that total, 162 of them were identified as militias. The number of antigovernment patriot groups has declined steadily since 2012, when they numbered 1,360, to 998 in 2015.

Threats

The threats that terrorist groups represent worldwide encompass traditional challenges (e.g., bombings, hijackings, kidnappings, hostage taking, assassination) and modern threats such as super terrorism (e.g., biological, chemical, radiological, nuclear) and cyberterrorism. Terrorist threats can be categorized in two principal ways. The first pertains to threats based on the target involved. Terrorists have attacked civilian and military interests; business and infrastructure sites; and government, religious, and civic facilities. The record establishes that no segment of the population is exempt from terrorism. Terrorists do not view any target as off limits. Terrorists even justify killing innocent children in the name of their cause.

A second type of targeting concerns the modus operandi of the attacks. There is widespread use of traditional terrorist operations. Fortunately, terrorists rarely deploy biological or chemical weapons.[38] Increasingly, cyberterrorism has been used in terms of kinetic attacks as well as for supportive activities. The expanding terror trend includes resorting to suicide bombings, vehicle attacks, stabbings, improvised explosive devices, mass shootings, and simultaneous incidents.

Threats are omnipresent and global. Terror incidents can occur anywhere and at any time. Terrorists have carried out strikes against a myriad of targets by employing several tactics together. While modifications to the modus operandi are inevitable, the trend is toward eye-catching attacks resulting in mass casualties and mayhem.

Concurrently, simple attacks are on the rise, generally undertaken by lone wolves. The relative ease and frequency of uncomplicated incidents (e.g., stabbings and vehicle attacks) may impart greater fear of vulnerability to the population than large-scale strikes. Additionally, lone wolf attacks can be extremely lethal, as illustrated by Anders Breivik in Norway. In 2011, he killed seventy-seven people in separate bombing and gunfire attacks. Also, in 2016, Mohamed Lahouaiej-Bouhlel murdered eight-six people in a truck attack in Nice, France.

Terrorist sympathizers and abettors, individual terrorists, cabals, stand-alone groups, international terrorist networks, and state sponsors of terrorism carry out political violence. Domestic and international groups have attacked national and foreign targets. The deeper the collaboration between terrorist groups and their supporters worldwide, the more lethality they can exact. In turn, the higher the challenge faced by the potential victims of terrorism to prevent such threats. Collaboration between organized crime and terrorist groups further exacerbates the dynamic.

Government, business, and individuals have taken strides to be more cognizant of terror threats. In doing so, they have garnered some successes at home and abroad in combating political violence. But challenges do exist. Also troubling is the fact that each terrorist operation provides a terror group with more information with which to refine its deadly craft.

Radicalization[39]

The term *radicalization* is the process of embracing an extremist belief system. More specifically, it comprises the inclination to use, support, or facilitate violence as a way to affect political, ideological, religious, or social change. A group's propaganda is disseminated in visual, tactile, audio, and in-person forms with particular fervor to alienated or aggrieved individuals. These persons are more readily responsive to these radical messages than the general population. Terrorist/extremist groups' ideas often contrast with status quo approaches and traditional perceptions of what is right and wrong. A crucial part of this message is the permissibility of using violence to hasten change.

Extremist political goals may include establishing a pan-Islamic state through violence or neo-Nazi precepts of a white, minority-free United States forged through force; expanded gun rights for militias; less government interference inculcated with violence; and banning animals in food, clothing, medical testing, and entertainment. Once ideological goals are framed, group leadership seeks to entice hearts and minds of populations worldwide.

Individuals are radicalized through exposure to terrorist/extremist ideologies in various settings. First, radicalization can arise from the influences of immediate and extended family. In the United States, Don Black, the white nationalist leader of Stormfront.org, exposed his son, Derek Black, to that ideology. Derek served as webmaster of Kids.Stormfront.org. While in college, Derek denounced racism and ceased participation in the website.[40]

Second, radicalization takes place from exposure at secular and religious educational institutions. Such activities occur in kindergarten through university. This extremism may transpire through interactions with fellow students, faculty, staff, and student organizations, whatever their ideological bent. Failed December 2009 airplane bomber Umar Farouk Abdulmutallab discovered radical viewpoints while studying at University College London. Similar influences likewise affected Yassin Nassari, a former leader of the Islamic Society at the University of Westminster. Nassari was convicted of attempting to bring missiles into the United Kingdom in

2007. In 2018, these settings, featured globally, continue to be venues where extremists of all ideological spectrums share their ideals with the object of attracting adherents.

Third, radical tenets can permeate places of worship. At such establishments, firebrand clergy and congregants spew their venomous allure. Such exposure can manifest itself in fringe doctrine shared face to face, via audio or video, or in text, in their native tongue or in foreign languages. Instances in which radicalization occurred at religious institutions include al Quds Mosque (Hamburg, Germany), where several 9/11 hijackers met; al Farooq Mosque (Brooklyn), where a few of the 1993 World Trade Center perpetrators interacted; and Finsbury Park Mosque (London), where several of the 2005 London bombers attackers prayed. Abdelbaki Es Satty, the ringleader of attacks in Barcelona and other Spanish cities in 2017, led a mosque in Ripoll.

Particularly significant is cleric Anwar al-Awlaki, a US citizen killed in a 2011 drone strike. Al-Awlaki influenced 2009 Fort Hood shooter Nidal Malik Hasan and 2009 attempted airplane bomber Umar Farouk Abdulmutallab, among dozens of other terrorists worldwide. The Hasan-al-Awlaki interactions apparently took place only online. Allegedly, the Abdulmutallab-al-Awlaki discourse occurred face to face.

Extremist precepts are forged through referencing passages from traditional religious dogma. The terror group may misdescribe the nature of the religious text. They may fail to mention its limitation to the historical context in which it was written. Other books mesh radical ideas with operational guidance.

The publications that aided in radicalization of operatives include:

- *Mein Kampf* and *The White Man's Bible* influencing neo-Nazis and World Church of the Creator (Creativity Movement) adherents

- *The Animal Liberation Primer* (Animal Liberation Front and Stop Huntingdon Animal Cruelty)

- *The Monkey Wrench Gang* (Earth Liberation Front), texts of al Qaeda leaders and their training manuals

- Sayyid Qutb's *Milestones* and the proliferation of Islamic State electronic and printed materials

Fourth, radicalization emerges after protracted interplay with acquaintances. This camaraderie occurs whether people first meet in local, overseas, or online communities. Initial receptivity toward friendship may be shaped by a multitude of commonalities (e.g., racial, ethnic, religious, ideological, socioeconomic, geography, language, employment, education, or otherwise). Gulf War veterans and friends turned 1995 Oklahoma City bombing collaborators Timothy McVeigh, Terry Nichols, and Michael Fortier are three such examples. So, too, the Fort Dix, New Jersey, plot cabal consisted of family-linked operatives and their friends.

Likewise, radicalization takes hold through exposure to a neighbor's perspectives. Such nearby residents can persuade each other because of their closeness and regularity of contact. Similarly, one's place of employment and colleagues are additional avenues for radicalization. There, too, shared experiences and time spent together magnifies the cohesion. This connection enhances vulnerability to pursuing extremist ideals.

Further exposure to radical ideas happens during interactions with individuals at various activities, including clubs, civic and political organizations. Additional venues where radicalization takes place are sporting events, gun shows, political rallies, youth centers, gymnasiums, and recreational activities such as paintball. The individuals found guilty in relation to the stymied terror plot against the Fort Dix, New Jersey, military base undertook paintball training. This activity enhanced unity among the 2005 London suicide bombers. Similarly, radicalization occurs at youth and summer camps as well as during paramilitary training. These camps are offered in the United States (e.g., militia groups), the Middle East (e.g., Hamas and Hezbollah), and elsewhere.

Globally, prisons have been used to radicalize individuals in extremist philosophies. Abu Musab al-Zarqawi, the late leader of al Qaeda in Iraq, was radicalized in al Qaeda–related ideologies while serving in a Jordanian prison. Rachid Aglif exposed Abdelbaki Es Satty (mentioned above in connection to the 2017 attacks in Spain) to jihadism. So, too, December 2001 shoe bomber Richard Reid and September 2009 Springfield, Illinois, plotter Michael Finton discovered jihadist precepts while in prison in the United Kingdom and United States, respectively. A summer 2005 plot focused on US military and other locations in California. A largely prison-based group, the Assembly of Authentic Islam, sought those targets. Also, in the United States, right-wing hate groups (e.g., neo-Nazis, skinheads, the Ku Klux Klan) proliferate their ideals in prisons in attempts to grow their ranks.

Individuals can be exposed to extremist beliefs of government leaders, political parties, and politicians. Diverse radical perspectives are disseminated worldwide, around the clock, in different languages, and through disparate formal and informal media outlets, including print, radio, cable and satellite television, and online. Terror groups from ISIS and al Qaeda to Hezbollah and the Kurdistan Workers'

Party (PKK) have their own media outlets through which they circulate their viewpoints and disinformation. To underscore, communication methods (e.g., phone, fax, and internet) enable extremist precepts to be distributed with prospective radicals.

Predicting Susceptibility to Radicalism

According to the National Counterterrorism Center (NCTC), there are risk factors that enhance potential involvement in radicalism. The NCTC also argues that there are protective factors that reduce the prospects of involvement in radicalism. These risk and protective factors transcend individual, family, and community spheres.

The NCTC notes that the following can have an impact on an individual's risk, protective postures, and resilience capabilities:

- Experience of trauma

- Witnessing violence

- Talk of harming self or others

- Committing violent acts toward self or others

- Experiences of loss (loss of home, role, status, loved ones, beliefs)

- Expressions of hopelessness, futility

- Perceived sense of being treated unjustly

- Withdrawal from former activities, relationships

- Connection to group identity (race, nationality, religion, ethnicity)

- Degree of isolation from or connection to others (family, friends, community)

- Vocational or school integration

- General health

- Perceived economic stress[41]

Likewise, a family's risk and protection ratings and resilience capabilities are based on multiple factors, such as:

- Parent-child bonding, empathic connection

- Parental involvement in child's education

- Family members knowing each other's friends

- Family members' awareness of one another's activities

- Presence of emotional or verbal conflict in family

- Family members' violent or physically abusive attitudes toward one another

- Family members' trust in one another

- Family connection to identity group (race, nationality, religion, ethnicity)

- Perceived economic stress

- Family involvement in community cultural and religious activities[42]

Lastly, the NCTC denotes that a community's risk and protection ratings and resilience traits are:

- Trust in institutions and law enforcement

- Isolation and social exclusion, degree of insularity

- Discrimination

- Neighborhood safety

- Access to health care

- Access to social services

- Access to educational resources

- Access to recreational resources

- Degree of violence in community

- Presence of ideologues or recruiters

- Availability of self-help networks

- Cohesiveness among community members[43]

Many factors contribute to the susceptibility of individuals, families, and communities to engaging in terrorism. Similarly, multiple elements affect protective features that lessen engagement in violent extremism.

Radicalization and Family Affiliated Terrorism

Family affiliated terrorism requires one household member to enter the terrorism fold. There is no kin-connected terrorism to address absent that criterion. An example of initial kin becoming radical is Siddhartha Dhar. He is a British-born father of four who took his wife and children to join the Islamic State. His incipient exposure to extremism arose through a childhood friend. The companion was a follower of radical Islamic preachers Omar Bakri Mohammed and Anjem Choudary. Dhar was exposed to their radical precepts through this acquaintance.

By 2006, Dhar was convicted of soliciting the murder of British soldiers. In September 2014, Dhar was arrested with Choudary for supporting the outlawed Islamist group al-Muhajiroun and encouraging terrorism. By late 2014, Dhar had taken his wife, Aisha, and kids to Syria. There, he joined ISIS. In January 2016, Dhar apparently narrated an ISIS propaganda video involving five hostages. In January 2018, the US State Department designated Dhar as a Specially Designated Global Terrorism. As of that date, he is believed to be in Syria.

A terror incident arising from early exposure to radicalism was marked with a February 2016 stabbing of a police officer at a Hanover, Germany, train station. The perpetrator, a fifteen-year-old girl Safia S., conducted the attack after she was asked to provide identity papers after appearing to be suspicious. Investigations determined that Safia was of German and Moroccan descent. She was in contact with Islamic State operatives in Turkey. The ISIS members had explained to her how to carry out a knife attack.

The previous month, Safia had traveled to Turkey, intending to make her way to Syria. Her mother brought her back from Turkey to Germany. Prior to Safia's travel to Turkey, her brother went there with the hope of later reaching Syria and joining the Islamic State. Safia was also in contact with a Syrian-German, Mohamad Hasan K., who was later arrested for having knowledge of her prospective attack plans.

Before Safia's trip to Turkey, her grandmother had contacted German authorities, expressing concern about her granddaughter's radicalization. Yet it appears that Safia's parents contributed to their daughter's embracement of radicalism. After all, at age eight, Safia had appeared in propaganda videos of Salafist preacher Pierre Vogel.

Her participation in the video suggests that her parents supported Salafist teachings.[44]

The radicalization and enlistment of the first family member may arise in person, online, or both. These external forces may occur at multiple locations. Among such instances of note are educational and religious institutions; through friends, neighbors, or coworkers; and by plenty of online instrumentalities, such as social networks (Facebook), microblogging (Twitter), and video sharing (YouTube).

A family member, such as a parent, may expose a child to an extremist ideology and pursue it with vigor. At first, the child may become enamored with this viewpoint. Later, the child may reject that ideology and pursue a different radical tenet. Alternatively, the child may abandon extremism.

Future terrorists may be enticed in their youth. These phases may be spurred from within or outside the family. In 2003, Moroccan sisters Imane and Sanne al Ghariss planned to launch simultaneous suicide bombings in Rabat. The siblings were prevented from reaching their goal owing to their later arrest. Similarly, 9/11 hijackers Nawaf al-Hazmi and his brother Salem were radicalized in their youth.

A parent's sway over their children to engage in terrorism is considerable. For instance, Samantha Lewthwaite is the widow of London 2005 suicide bomber Germaine Lindsey. She later married British terror operative Habib Saleh Ghani. Al-Shabaab killed Ghani after his dispute with the group. Lewthwaite said she was proud that her eight-year-old boy and five-year-old daughter wanted to be holy warriors (mujahedeen).

In January 2015, brothers Cherif and Said Kouachi attacked the office of *Charlie Hebdo* magazine in Paris. A radical cleric, Farid Benyettou, exposed the siblings to violent jihad. Afterward, Cherif served time in prison with Benyettou for conspiracy to conduct terrorism. While in prison, Cherif met Amedy Coulibaly, who was in prison for armed burglaries. Coulibaly's onslaught at a Paris kosher supermarket was coordinated with the Kouachi brothers' *Charlie Hebdo* strike.

In 2009, Said traveled to Yemen, where he met future failed underwear bomber Umar Farouk Abdulmutallab. In 2011, Said and Cherif went to Yemen. There, the siblings obtained terror training from al Qaeda in the Arabian Peninsula. During that trip, Cherif purportedly received $20,000 to conduct an expected strike in France.

Before its territorial demise, more than 40,000 persons from over one hundred countries traveled to the Islamic State. Particularly abhorrent among those were parents taking their children to Syria and Iraq. For instance, Sally Jones, a forty-five-year-old, mother-of-two from Chatham, Kent, in the United Kingdom, and former punk rocker, married Junaid Hussain, a twenty-year-old computer hacker from Birmingham. In 2013, Jones, her son (Jo Jo) from a previous marriage, and Hussain traveled to Syria so they could reside in the Islamic State. Hussain, who was linked to many international terror plots, was killed in a coalition air strike in Syria in 2015.

By 2016, JoJo, now called Abu Abdullah al-Britani, appeared in an Islamic State video in which he executed a man in Raqqa, Syria. But for Sally Jones bringing her son to Syria, the youngster would not have become an executioner for a terrorist group. The mother's decision to allow her child to join ISIS could be portrayed as a war crime. After all, international law prohibits the recruitment and use of children soldiers. Additionally, Jones denounced the United States and United Kingdom as terrorist nations and managed multiple social media accounts in an effort to recruit individuals to ISIS. In

June 2017, Jones was killed in a U.S. drone strike along Syrian-Iraq border. That same year, it was reported that Jo Jo was killed.[45]

In May 2013, Hysen Sherifi was sentenced to life in prison for conspiring to hire a hit man to behead FBI agents and witnesses who testified in his earlier terror trial. Hysen recruited his brother, Shkumbin, and a woman, Nevine Aly Elshiekh, to arrange the murder-for-hire plot. Later, Hysen was convicted of a terror conspiracy involving the Boyd family cabal.

In April 2005, Eric Rudolph pleaded guilty to the following:

- The 1996 Olympics bombing in Atlanta, Georgia, which killed two persons and injured 111 others;

- The 1997 bombing of an abortion in Sandy Springs, Georgia, which injured seven people;

- The 1997 bombing of a lesbian nightclub in Atlanta, which injured five people; and

- The 1998 bombing of an abortion clinic in Birmingham, Alabama, which killed one person and injured another.

Rudolph was a Christian Identity movement follower. Additionally, he supported violent antiabortion and antigay activities. The Army of God group claimed Rudolph's attacks were undertaken on its behalf. Interestingly, Rudolph's mother, Pat, said of her son, "His anger, his way of dealing with this cause, is not mine; it's his. Therefore, the responsibility is his."[46] Yet Rudolph's perspectives did not arise in a vacuum. Pat took Eric and his younger brother to a Christian Identity compound in Missouri for several months before returning to North Carolina.

Terror Characteristics

Terrorists target hard and soft targets alike. Among such incidents are simultaneous assaults using alternative forms of attack (e.g., gunfire, suicide bombings, stabbings, hostage taking, kidnappings) against destinations (e.g., transportation, hotels, religious institutions).

Although underappreciated, some perpetrators of terror have engaged in traditional crime. This entrance into criminality serves as a gateway to ideologically inspired illicit acts. The 2016 Berlin truck attacker, Anis Amri, killed twelve people. Prior to that incident, he was involved in cocaine trafficking in Germany. Additionally, Amri served time in an Italian prison for arson.[47]

Brothers Khalid and Ibrahim el Bakraoui conducted suicide bombings in Brussels in March 2016. Similarly, siblings Brahim and Salah Abdeslam participated in the November 2015 Paris attacks. Both sets of kin delved into a range of traditional crimes (e.g., robbery, carjacking, drug trade) prior to their involvement with terrorism.

Terrorists leverage free, encrypted communications technologies to communicate and facilitate terrorist activities. Amri interacted with his ISIS interlocutors using Telegram. In one Telegram exchange, he pledged allegiance to the group.

Criminals and terrorists take advantage of pliable and sympathetic immigration laws of host countries. In light of expanded terror attacks worldwide featuring foreign-inspired ideologies, the accommodating posture of recipient nations is bound to be limited. In fact, the appeal of anti-immigrant political parties is increasing across Europe. This backlash is a response to Europe's admission of millions of refugees from the Middle East since 2011.

The knowledge base for making homemade explosives is widespread, growing, and available online in multiple languages. The homemade explosive triacetone triperoxide (TATP) was used in the December 2015 Paris and March 2016 Brussels attacks. Additionally, a terrorist chose that explosive in a stymied suicide bombing at a Berlin airport in 2016. Even terrorists based in the United States have built bombs ranging from pressure cooker bombs to improvised explosive devices using TATP.

Terrorists may have multiple identities, including various nationalities. Amri was found to have six fake cards using three different nationalities.[48] Amri and Lahouaiej-Bouhlel were not part of the (returning) Islamic State foreign fighters. It is expected that returning foreign fighters will undertake large-scale strikes in their home countries or elsewhere. For illustration, the perpetrators of the November 2015 Paris attacks included former French and Belgian residents who had returned from fighting in Syria.

Terror networks benefit from trust ties (e.g., family, friendship, religious and educational institutions) and operational ties (e.g., communications, logistics, organizational, financing, and training). These connections enhance cohesiveness of the cell, contributing to its strength and continuity. Yet such links may undermine the terror cell. After all, the more persons involved in a cell, the greater the chance of its discovery by authorities.

Terrorists Are Created, Not Born[49]

Political oppression, economic dysfunction, corruption, and other elements of failing states contribute to the rise in the number of economic and political refugees worldwide. Some refugees do not integrate well into their host countries. Less regularly, the settlers turn against their destination country.

Amri left Tunisia and sought resettlement in Italy. He spent time there in a refugee center. After time in Italian prisons, Amri went to Germany, where he conducted his terror attack. From the site of that carnage, Amri escaped through several European countries before returning to Italy. In Italy, he was killed during an encounter with police.

European prisons, as others in the Middle East and North America, serve in part as incubators for extremism, whether violent jihadist or otherwise. According to Amri's brother, Abdelkader, Amri was radicalized while serving a prison sentence for arson in Italy.

Likewise, persons may enter as refugees. Then they may become involved in traditional criminality. After imprisonment, they may turn into extremists. Upon discharge from prison, the neophyte extremist seeks like-minded radicals, who reinforce his decision to follow such principles. After choosing to launch an attack, the individual proceeds with his action—either alone or in a cabal. Amri was part of the Islamic State–linked network led by an Iraqi national, Ahmad Abdulaziz Abdullah (Abu Walaa), who was arrested in Germany with others in November 2016.

Porous Borders, Refugees, and Uncooperative Countries

Porous borders arise from poor monitoring and legislation permitting unimpeded travel. For instance, Europe adopted the decades-long Schengen Agreement, which largely limits border controls. Weak borders facilitate criminals' and terrorists' easy access to prospective targets. As noted, Amri took full advantage of this situation, both upon his first arrival to Italy and in visits to other nations.

Italian authorities sought in vain to send Amri to Tunisia, but that nation rebuffed the request on multiple occasions. Tunisia questioned whether Amri was Tunisian. A host country faces obstacles during attempts to return suspected terrorist refugees to their countries of origin.

Profiling

Challenges exist with "profiling" prospective terrorists. It is foolhardy to believe that just because an individual is of a particular race, religion, ethnicity, national origin, gender, or other immutable essence, that individual will be a terrorist. But depending on the ideology of an extremist or terror group, there will be a strong—if not exclusive—representation of members from a certain race, ethnicity, or religion.

In contrast, other extremist or terrorist groups may relate to an ideology that does not factor immutable characteristics. For instance, sovereign citizens embrace a variety of anti-government ideologies, none that have a nexus with immutable characteristics. Most sovereign citizens are white males. Yet nonwhites, such as those identifying as Moors, also comprise sovereign citizen members. Likewise, single-issue extremists—animal rights activists, environmentalists, and anti-abortionists—tend not to come from an exclusive race, religion, national origin, or gender.

In attempting to uncover prospective terrorist actors, it is important to take heed of the US Department of Justice's December

2014 "Guidance for Federal Law Enforcement on 'Profiling,'" which provides:

- Two standards in combination should guide use by Federal law enforcement officers of race, ethnicity, gender, national origin, religion, sexual orientation, or gender identity in law enforcement or intelligence activities:

- In making routine or spontaneous law enforcement decisions, such as ordinary traffic stops, Federal law enforcement officers may not use race, ethnicity, gender, national origin, religion, sexual orientation, or gender identity to any degree, except that officers may rely on the listed characteristics in a specific suspect description. This prohibition applies even where the use of a listed characteristic might otherwise be lawful.

- In conducting all activities other than routine or spontaneous law enforcement activities, Federal law enforcement officers may consider race, ethnicity, gender, national origin, religion, sexual orientation, or gender identity only to the extent that there is trustworthy information, relevant to the locality or time frame, that links persons possessing a particular listed characteristic to an identified criminal incident, scheme, or organization, a threat to national or homeland security, a violation of Federal immigration law, or an authorized intelligence activity. In order to rely on a listed characteristic, law enforcement officers must also reasonably believe that the law enforcement, security, or intelligence activity to be undertaken is merited under the totality of the circumstances, such as any temporal exigency and the nature of any potential harm to be averted. This standard applies even where the use of a listed characteristic might otherwise be lawful.[50]

Women Terrorists[51]

Women of all ages and marital statuses, including mothers, have taken part in terrorist operations. Female terrorists have run the spectrum of socioeconomic backgrounds from poor to middle class and uneducated to university graduates. Like men, women terrorists pursue such violence resulting from diverse elements: perceived political and economic marginalization, ideological commitment, avenging victimization of family or friends, financial benefits, a desire to improve their social status, hopelessness, and heavenly benefits arising from martyrdom. Some women have been coerced into terrorism after they have been accused of bringing dishonor to their kin through some moral infraction.

Women terrorists have been involved in a range of violent actions on behalf of groups having all ideological perspectives. Female terrorists have inflicted damage on soft and hard targets, usually enjoying laxer attitudes from government, private security, and the public, since women are typically not perceived to be involved with terrorism. This misconception is a factor in the success of female terrorists in perpetrating many attacks, including suicide bombings.

Including females as terrorists doubles the number of prospective recruits and contributors to a terrorist cause. Also, women are viewed with less suspicion than men. Women offer tactical advantages, including less frequent and rigorous searches by government authorities. Law enforcement, security personnel, and the intelligence community at home and abroad have assumed that women will refrain from terrorist activities. But these attitudes are changing with more frequent investigations and prosecutions of women terrorists in the United States and abroad.

Given the heightened visibility, lethality, and contributions of female terrorists worldwide, this underestimation of women terrorists merits urgent recalibration. The role of women in family terror networks should be considered as well.[52]

Those seeking a relationship and ultimately marriage can be enticed by a terrorist suitor. This happened with Shannon Conley, a Colorado teenager who was radicalized by jihadist propaganda and longed to travel to join the Islamic State. Concurrently, while online, Shannon interacted with a Syria-based Tunisian operative thirteen years her senior. He purportedly promised to marry her and help her engage in jihad in Syria.

Shannon joined the US Army Explorers, a career program provided under the umbrella of the Boy Scouts of America. The program provides training in armed combat, military tactics, and firearms. Shannon planned to exploit these techniques and wage jihad abroad. In case she could not fight, she promised to help the jihadi fighters while serving as a nurse.

In 2014, Shannon was caught boarding a flight from Denver to Turkey, with eventual plans to join the group in Syria. The following year, she pleaded guilty to conspiracy to provide material support to the Islamic State. She was sentenced to four years in prison.

Those who knew Shannon described her transformation as stemming from being a "bright teenager lost in middle-class suburbia,"[53] searching for meaning and a mate. Following her arrest, authorities claim they found CDs by US-born radical cleric Anwar al-Awlaki among her belongings. On her Facebook page, Shannon referred to herself as Halima. She described her work as "a slave to Allah."[54] Shannon told the FBI she was sought to defend Muslims against their oppressors.

The Islamic State actively seeks to radicalize and recruit women and girls online or otherwise[55] by disseminating the following narrative:

- Leave the decadence and apostasy of your home country, where you are deemed undesirable.

- Join the jihad and be empowered by living in a true Muslim land (the caliphate).

- You will contribute to the cause by marrying an ISIS fighter and parenting the next generation of warriors.

Interspersed in the ISIS pitch is the notion that a caliphate-based life will be exciting and meaningful. An ISIS-based life, the pitch continues, is better than what life in their home country affords.

Aisha Kadad, a Syrian woman whose first husband was killed in Homs in 2012, regretted moving to Raqqa to live in the caliphate. There, she married an ISIS fighter. Following the defeat of ISIS in Mosul and beyond, in summer 2017, Kadad and other ISIS widows claimed they were unaware of the spouses' roles in ISIS. Alternatively, the widows proffered that their husbands' participation in the group was marginal. Kadad claimed life under IS was "hell," and she regretted going to Raqqa. Such newly found widows had traveled to Syria with their husbands or found spouses there.[56]

Many children of ISIS fighters are in a precarious situation if one or both of their parents have been killed or are missing. In July 2017,

Iraqi soldiers found children, including toddlers, in Mosul and else-where who were believed to be orphans. In one instance, a Russian-speaking toddler claimed both parents had been "martyred."[57]

A policy challenge exists as to how to rehabilitate the thousands of ISIS widows and their children based in Syria and elsewhere. Determining whether such individuals still hold pro-ISIS views is a daunting challenge. For some, their allegiance to the movement will not dissipate. Their zeal for jihad continues after resettling in the West or another region. Also, discerning which individuals holding such perspectives would become terrorists is not facile.

The physical and mental harm these children suffered in the caliphate and later war zones could make reintegrating them into civil society difficult. Some youngsters might be "irredeemable" from the throngs of their troubled past.

Aqsa Mahmood established a Tumblr blog, *Diary of a Muhajirah*.[58] In it, she discussed her life as a female member of ISIS. She was born in Glasgow, Scotland, to a successful Pakistani immi-grant businessman and his wife. Aqsa was educated in a top private school in the city, Craigholme School. Friends remember her as being a Westernized girl. She later became more interested in Islam and wore a hijab. Similarly, Aqsa bought religious books, followed classes on Islam, and chatted about Islamist ideology with people over the internet.

Aqsa attended Shawlands Academy, a secondary school. Then she took a course in diagnostic radiography at Glasgow Caledonian University. She left her studies in 2013. Afterward, she reached Syria. Once there, she joined ISIS and wed an ISIS fighter.

Aqsa tweeted messages calling on others to repeat the murder of soldier Lee Rigby; the massacre at Fort Hood, the US army base in Texas; and the Boston Marathon bombing. She is believed to be a leader of the Khansaa Battalion, an ISIS female enforcer group. In August 2017, Aqsa was stripped of her UK citizenship, preventing her return.

The roles of widows and other females in the terrorism context merit further scrutiny. These survivors may undertake terror operations to avenge the deaths of their fallen kin, usually husbands and brothers. Likewise, widows in this predicament may marry again to individuals with extremist ideologies and follow their paths. Ultimately, the aggrieved spouse can support or engage in operational activities.

As mentioned earlier, terrorists who become martyrs for their cause are sometimes emulated by current and subsequent generations in that same family, such as black widows. Dozens of Chechen black widows have committed martyr terror attacks to avenge the deaths of their husbands. Often, Russian (or Russian-aligned) forces killed their husbands during the Russian-Chechen/Dagestan conflicts. Among such widows was Luiza Gazuyeva. Gazuyeva detonated hand grenades hidden under her clothes in November 2001 in Chechnya. Her attack killed Russian General Gaidar Gadzhiyev. Gazuyeva claimed the general assassinated her husband and other family members.

Aminat Kurbanova, an ethnic Russian and former actress/dancer, converted to Islam after her second marriage to a man involved in the Dagestan jihadist insurgency, who was killed by Russian authorities in 2009. Another of Kurbanova's late husbands, Magomed Ilyasov, was killed while mishandling a bomb. Before his death, Ilyasov provided terror training to another couple, Vitaly Razdobudko and his wife, who became suicide bombers. Kurbanova conducted a suicide bombing at the home of a leading Sufi cleric in Dagestan, Said Afandial-Chirkawi.

Other illustrations of such violence include the suicide bombings at two Moscow metro stations in March 2010 by two widows from Dagestan, resulting in thirty-nine deaths. The first was Dzhennet Abdurakhmanova, who married Dagestani jihadist Umalat Magomedov. In 2009, Russian forces killed him. She hit one of the transportation targets. The second, female perpetrator is unidentified.[59]

Besides killing their targets with suicide bomb belts and grenades, black widows have used explosives-laden vehicles. Such was the case of the first black widows incident in June 2000, when Luiza Magomadova and Khava Barayeva exploded a truck at a building, killing Russian forces in Chechnya. Barayeva's uncle was a Chechen militant who was killed by the Russian military in 1999.[60]

Terror group members and their supporters idolize women who have launched "martyr" operations on behalf of their organizations. This is so for children who seek to imitate female terrorists as well. Hamas member Reem Riyashi, twenty-two-year-old mother of two from Gaza, blew herself up in a joint Israel-Palestinian industrial zone in January 2004, murdering four Israelis. Palestinian Authority–run Al-Aqsa TV showed music videos in which Riyashi's four-year-old daughter said she craved to follow in her mom's footsteps. In 1996, Wafa Idris carried out the first female Palestinian suicide bombing.

Also, women have conducted suicide attacks to avenge the deaths of their militant family members. In June 2003, Hanadi Jaradat, a twenty-nine-year-old Palestinian lawyer, conducted a suicide bombing at a restaurant in Haifa, Israel. Jaradat killed more than twenty people and injured over fifty. She carried out the strike on behalf of

Palestinian Islamic Jihad to avenge the deaths of her brother (Fadi) and cousin (Salah).

Sarah H., one of three women arrested in relation to a September 2016 plot to detonate explosives near Notre Dame Cathedral in Paris, was engaged to two different French ISIS members (Larossi Abballa and Adel Kermiche). However, police killed these prospective husbands after two different terror incidents in France during summer 2016.

Terrorists in the Economic System[61]

Terrorists and their supporters take advantage of opportunities and loopholes within the economic system to further their murderous goals. Leveraging the fruits of the economic system enables terrorists to get financial, organizational, and operational help (e.g., arms, training, intelligence, and information). Terrorists and their abettors use existing traditional frameworks such as companies and nonprofit entities to raise funds, receive support, and integrate themselves into the community. Traditional and nontraditional financial systems present in the economic systems are used as well.

Perpetrators of political violence also launch a variety of criminal activities (e.g., counterfeiting currency, credit cards, and ATM cards; misappropriating and using credit card information; forging documents; identity theft; money laundering; drug trafficking; corruption; commercial espionage; general criminal activities) in violation of permissible norms in an economic framework. Additionally, some terrorists are involved in the black market: antiquity plundering and trafficking, tobacco smuggling, and machinery/equipment transactions.

Terrorists will act within domestic and international economic systems to obtain financial resources, weaponry, products, services, information, and tools that can be used against government, industry, and other segments of society. Terrorists contact product and service providers openly, secretly, and through abettors. Unsuspecting companies and individuals may provide terrorists wares for their operations. Given an enhanced awareness of such possibilities, industry is better attuned to reducing complicity with terror groups. Companies will investigate future employees, clients, and partners to lessen the chance that malfeasance occurs.

Yet the desire for profits has induced firms to close their eyes to shady deals. Alternatively, firms establish foreign subsidiaries to undertake "dirty deals" with terrorists, their sympathizers, or even state sponsors of terrorism. Unfortunately, avarice at selected companies makes such negative corporate conduct likely to continue. Expanded enforcement and modification of government sanctions, in combination with pressure from investors in such public companies, should help weaken another source of terror wares and funding.

Financing Terror[62]

Terrorist groups use an array of means—from simple to complex—to secure funds for their activities. Terror funds are derived from both legal sources (e.g., personal savings, donations, legitimate business revenue) and illegal ones (e.g., criminal acts such as drug-trafficking and financial fraud). Monies raised are distributed to terrorist groups through diverse techniques.

The tools that terrorist organizations use to fund their deadly activities include traditional and alternative financial services (e.g., banks and hawalas), charities, trading in commodities (e.g., "conflict" diamonds and gold), drug trafficking, extortion, money laundering, smuggling, securities fraud, and scams. The costs of launching terrorist attacks range from a few dollars to hundreds of thousands of dollars or more. Terrorism is sometimes referred to as "warfare on the cheap." Depending on the size and complexity of the operation, the sophistication of weaponry, and the training, the costs can vary. The 9/11 incidents are estimated to have cost about $500,000 to put together. But the attacks resulted in direct and indirect economic costs in the hundreds of billions of dollars.

The price of terror attacks increases if one includes the costs of maintaining a hierarchical terror group. The costs of operating terrorist groups range from thousands of dollars to millions of dollars if one includes funds for training, housing and general assistance, weaponry, human capital, and operational support. Money is the lifeblood of terrorism. Companies, foundations, and individuals who aid both subnational and state-actor terrorists in carrying out their criminal actions are a serious problem.

Steps to thwart terrorists from securing funds are essential in grappling with the challenge. When their funding capabilities are undermined, terrorist organizations are harmed. Therefore, it is less likely that their deadly operations will arise. If they do occur, the attacks will be less effectual than they might have been.

The Role of Corporate Security[63]

Terrorism is easy and inexpensive to activate yet very difficult and costly to counter. Business, too, is cognizant that it has limited financial means with which to curtail terrorist risks. The challenge of providing enough security without spending excessive resources has reached greater resonance. Corporations' recognition of terror dangers has compelled them to devote considerable resources to security. The time, manpower, and funding spent addressing security measures vary depending on the company's industry, size, geography, international activities, and symbolic value, as well as the probability and ease of its being targeted.

Whether industry has the products and services available to undertake preventative or corrective steps, along with the costs associated with such measures, are also relevant issues. For instance, one can consider the costs and implementation of antimissile technology on commercial jets to counter terrorists' use of shoulder-fired missiles.

Industry's security efforts are likewise influenced by whether government and/or industry mandates exist. If so, what types of accompanying sanctions attach should a firm fail to abide by government and/or industry security guidelines? A complicating security issue is that some employees do not follow company-posted security measures and contribute to weaker defenses.

The financial implications of improved security procedures are worth assessing. For example, the matter of who bears the costs of such measures is significant to whether anything is done to implement security. Analogously, should costs be designated as "security charges" (e.g., airline security fees) or subsumed within the rising prices of products and services without attribution? Businesses deemed soft terror targets (e.g., restaurants, movie theaters) might impose security charges.

Security is expected to perform a more prominent role at companies as terror threats remain. Well-known international companies exemplifying Western economic power (e.g., banking, energy, technology) will likely be targeted. Also, firms that attract many people in a concentrated area (e.g., buses, subways, train stations, stores, restaurants) are prone to being victimized. Security procedures at prospective targets will cause multidimensional responses. Using political risk analysis, traditional security products and services, risk management tools, and business continuity/disaster planning should be considered to lower the peril of terrorism. Concurrently, such steps protect company assets.

Intelligence gathering and analysis are vital pieces of effective security practices within both government and industry contexts. Additionally, the military and law enforcement are indispensable to the security paradigm.

A corporation's aim is to be profitable. One would suppose any allocation of resources that directly or indirectly undermines profitability should be avoided. In reality, counterterror measures may likewise aid firms in protecting data, preventing sabotage, and decreasing theft of company assets. Political violence can destroy a company's operations. Still, management must balance spending on counterterror efforts with safeguarding a company's scarce funds. The prospects of terror attacks enable executives to justify large disbursements on security. When the time comes that terror threats have waned (or are perceived to have done so), companies will examine once again the utility of security expenditures.

Additionally, since 9/11, the majority of US multinational companies have taken a serious approach to the terrorist threat, particularly when their employees travel internationally and visit soft-target countries. Most corporations provide risk assessments of countries visited by employees and/or where expatriates live for two-year stints.

Major concerns are kidnappings and express kidnappings (taking money from the ATMs of those employees who have been abducted).

Also, US corporations are partnering with US Customs and Border Protection with their Customs-Trade Partnership Against Terrorism (C-TPAT) programs. C-TPAT involves screening and supply-chain management of containers coming from overseas for possible weapons of mass destruction inside. Analogously, the Department of Homeland Security developed a program, the Chemical Facility Anti-Terrorism Standards (CFATS), that collaborates with chemical "facilities to ensure they have security measures in place to reduce the risks associated with certain hazardous chemicals and prevent them from being exploited in a terrorist attack."[64]

Public-Private Partnership in Combating Terrorism[65]

The interactions and support between government and industry in combating terrorism are manifested in several ways: government aiding business, industry assisting the public sector, and discord between the two. The government buys homeland security wares from companies. Through the privatization of government duties, industry gains access to opportunities that it otherwise would not possess. Government allocates moneys to companies—directly and indirectly—prior to and in the wake of terror attacks. The government may enact laws limiting firms' potential liabilities in case of a terror attack.

The public sector lends its personnel and expertise to companies before, during, and after a terror incident. These efforts try to decrease harm to a company's assets, including the well-being of its employees.

Government guides industry on terror threats and responses. The public sector aids industry by establishing rules facilitating ways to conduct business. Industry is afforded formal and informal means of communication with government officials. These exchanges enable companies to learn about new security demands and business opportunities.

The government-industry dynamic also has its difficulties. Tensions include developments in the federalization of counterterror roles juxtaposed with the privatization of government duties. Whether government or industry oversteps its bounds by entering into the purview of the other is an example of such tension. Government legislation affecting security at companies, rules affecting how business is conducted, and the transformation of government institutions have caused friction between the private and public sectors.

Labor and Management Challenges[66]

Labor and management are potential terror victims. Due to terrorism, management faces new responsibilities and risks connected with its employees. Workers are pursuing opportunities arising from counterterror activities while also being victimized due to the expansion of global terrorism. Additionally, multiple shifts in the labor market are propelled by the war on terrorism.

Terrorist incidents can damage both workers and managers. A terrorist's bomb does not distinguish between labor and management. A catastrophic terrorist incident can cause the death of thousands of employees in one industry, such as occurred with finance-sector employees on September 11. Worldwide, suicide bombers targeting mass transit or restaurants have previously killed or injured thousands within these sectors. A strike at a nuclear facility or port could severely victimize another segment of workers.

Employees can survive terror attacks by not being at work on the day of the attack due to sickness, a meeting outside the office, or travel plans. Others are not so fortunate—including workers who survived the 1993 World Trade Center attack, but not the 9/11 incidents. Fate or chance also plays a role in the potential victimization of labor.

Parts of the labor market are less vulnerable to certain types of terrorist attacks. For instance, executives flying on corporate jets meet reduced risk of hijacking. Yet senior personnel are more vulnerable to kidnapping or assassination by terrorist groups than entry-level employees.

Workers with security and business-continuity expertise are integral parts of a management team. This is especially so when a serious attack undermine corporate assets. Analogously, any incapacity or death of corporate security employees would undermine a firm's recovery and continuity.

Police, firefighters, and emergency medical technicians play critical roles during and after a terrorist attack. So, too, should private sector employees be regarded as part of the solution. After all, they make gas masks, germ detection devices, and pharmaceuticals. Defense contractors and their employees offer the government diverse products and services instrumental in combating terrorism.

Additionally, the labor market includes persons who collaborate with or support terrorists by supplying funds arising from legitimate and illegal businesses, conducting business with front organizations, or providing products and services used by terrorists. Terrorists may become employed in sectors targeted for a future terrorist attack (e.g., chemical or water treatment plants). Similarly, they may obtain roles that will not attract too much attention (e.g., "students" working at a university library or restaurant).

In this post-September 11 era, labor expects employers to play a new security-related function besides providing a job and wage. Labor envisions that employers should play a semi-paternalistic/quasi-governmental function: provide physical security, emotional assistance, and guidance in times of turmoil. For their part, executives must balance the desire to protect their workforce with conducting business under increasingly complex market conditions (e.g., rising direct and indirect costs due to terrorism).

Emergency Response Planning for Mass Casualty Terror Attacks[67]

Lessons have been learned from selected mass casualty terror attacks in Western Europe (Nice, Paris, Brussels, and Oslo) and the United States (Orlando, San Bernardino, and Boston). In particular, this section of the book touches on these terror incidents and addresses their consequences for emergency management and medical response planning.

Background

Mohamed Lahouaiej-Bouhlel plowed a truck through pedestrians viewing fireworks on Bastille Day 2016 in Nice. The attack caused eight-six fatalities and over four hundred injuries. All but one of those who perished did so within hours of the incident. Ten children and teenagers were killed in the attack. Police killed Lahouaiej-Bouhlel as he left the truck and shot at them.[68]

The March 2016 attacks in Brussels comprised three suicide bombings: two at an airport and another at a subway station an hour later. The attackers—brothers Ibrahim and Khalid el Bakraoui and Najim Laachraoui—killed thirty-five persons and injured three hundred others. Given the modus operandi, the three suicide bombers were killed instantly. Another explosive device was discovered by police at the airport and detonated safely.[69]

The November 2015 Paris attacks involved operatives separated into teams equipped with assault rifles and suicide bomb vests. The perpetrators attacked assorted targets including a sports stadium, a concert hall, a bar, cafés, and restaurants, utilizing both modalities. The incidents resulted in 130 persons killed and injuries to over 360 others. Eight terror operatives were killed during the course of the incidents. Others involved in the plot were later killed in a standoff with police, were arrested, or escaped.

The Islamic State/ISIS directed the Paris and Brussels incidents. The Nice attack appears to have been inspired by the group.

In July 2011, Anders Breivik undertook the deadliest attack in Norway since World War II. In Oslo, Breivik detonated a bomb at a government building, killing eight people and injuring more than ninety others. Later that day, he conducted a mass shooting at a Labor Party's Workers Youth League event on an island near Oslo. That onslaught resulted in sixty-nine deaths and over sixty injuries.

After a delayed response by Norwegian police, Breivik surrendered to authorities at his second target. In August 2012, he was convicted of mass murder and other related crimes. Breivik was sentenced to twenty-one years in prison, the maximum under Norwegian law. He appears to have embraced white nationalist and neo-Nazi ideologies, accompanied by anti-Muslim precepts.

In June 2016, the deadliest mass shooting terrorist incident in US history took place in Orlando. A lone gunman, Omar Mateen, attacked patrons at a gay nightclub with a semiautomatic rifle and handgun. The resulting carnage was forty-nine deaths and fifty-three injuries. Mateen was shot and killed during a shootout with police following extended hostage negotiations.

The November 2015 San Bernardino attackers, Syed Rizwan Farook and Tashfeen Malik, shot and killed fourteen and injured twenty-two others at a government office. The couple used semi-automatic weapons in their assault. The attackers also left several improvised explosive devices that fortunately did not detonate. The terrorists were killed during a five-minute shootout with police four hours after the terror incident began. The perpetrators' demise took place on a street some two miles from the attack site.

In April 2013, the Tsarnaev brothers detonated two pressure cooker bombs near the finish line of the Boston Marathon, killing 3 and injuring over 260 others. One of the brothers, Tamerlan, was purportedly killed when his sibling Dzhokhar drove over him while trying to escape from police. Dzhokhar was ultimately captured, convicted on multiple murder counts and other charges, and sentenced to death.

The Islamic State/ISIS is believed to have inspired the perpetrators in the Orlando and San Bernardino incidents. Various jihadist ideologies seem to have motivated the Boston attackers.

General Findings

Despite some commonalities, each incident posed unique challenges arising from a variety of factors, such as the number of perpetrators in the attack, the weapons used, the number of sites involved, the number of persons killed and wounded, readiness and capabilities of first responders—particularly the medical community—and vagaries such as the time of day of the incident, proximity to hospitals, and types of triage at the attack sites.

Of the terror attacks addressed above, the highest death toll (130) occurred in Paris, when multiple operatives used a variety of modus operandi to inflict damage. The fatalities arising from determined lone wolves in the cases in Nice (86), Oslo (77), and Orlando (49) demonstrate the lethality that can arise from even a single person perpetrating an attack.

Another factor to consider is whether terror incidents are one-off events or part of a larger cycle of attacks spanning multiple hours or days. As in the Boston attacks, secondary explosions may occur within seconds or much longer after a first detonation. An incident may initially comprise an active shooter situation, but improvised explosive devices can be set for detonation after the attackers leave the target area, as witnessed in the San Bernardino barrage. Active shooter situations can transform into hostage situations as in the Orlando attack and the Bataclan theater segment of the Paris incidents.

Prior active shooter drills and emergency preparedness instruction proved to be helpful in responding to high-casualty incidents. Utilizing interdisciplinary training—encompassing medical, law enforcement, emergency management, and fire services—aids in effective responses as participants become aware of what each group is responsible for during a crisis. Moreover, collaborative training—including with the private sector—contributes to forging solid social networks and confidence in partners.

Hospitals may establish an incident command center, often based outside the emergency department. Specially designated trauma centers are well equipped to deal with injuries that occur during mass casualty terror attacks. Other hospitals, too, can serve key roles in treating the wounded when such incidents strike a city.

Once hospitals begin accepting victims of mass casualty attacks, they may raise their security posture. Besides victims and their families, hospitals may contend with an inflow of first responders, the media, and the public.

Serendipity can play a role in such incidents, including having attacks occur close to a hospital, senior staff already present at the hospital during the attack, and recently completed training on mass casualty attacks. The Orlando attack took place about one-third of a mile from the Orlando Regional Medical Center and directly opposite an Orlando fire station.

The success of law enforcement in neutralizing terrorists as quickly as possible facilitates access to the victims. Some incidents allow for access to the injured within minutes. Others may take longer due to a remote location or the extended nature of the attack (e.g., a hostage situation or time in securing the area prior to reaching the victims). Helicopters can aid in bringing those wounded to hospitals more rapidly than other means, particularly when remote sites are involved. Dozens of ambulances may appear at staging areas shortly after an attack. Short transport times to medical facilities raise the chances of survival but do not guarantee it.

After large-scale attacks, cell and other telephone communications may be limited as the systems become overwhelmed. Alternative communication methods should be established beforehand (e.g., radio communications, internal networks, email), as rapid, unfettered dissemination of information is critical in such crises.

Emergency Plans

Cities that anticipated a possible mass casualty terror attack were well prepared to respond to the terror that they experienced. Emergency departments benefit from establishing procedures to respond to mass casualties. Also, backups can contribute to improved responses. In some instances, a triage tent was set up outside of the emergency department. Also, triage areas can be established near the incidents themselves so the wounded can be tended to initially, prior to transport for further care.

Following an incident, a medical facility may declare a code black, meaning only terror patients will be accepted into the hospital. Hospitals must keep the issue of security in mind as well, as the hospital could become a target of an escaping terrorist or designated as a secondary target from the onset.

The seriousness of the Paris attacks resulted in the activation of the Plan Blanc (White Plan), which called upon forty public hospitals in the city to marshal additional staff, cancel nonurgent procedures, and create space for the influx of prospective victims. In Nice, the White Plan was activated quickly once the severity of the incident was understood. The Health Regional Agency initiated an incident command base that reached out to neighboring hospitals and located available beds.

Emergency exercises, including simulations, aided medical preparedness in Nice. Such programs were undertaken after the November 2015 Paris attacks, and in anticipation of threats arising from the European Football (Soccer) Championships.

Proximity to a Target

The proximity of a hospital to an attack can be critical in getting the injured to medical care rapidly but also may create challenges to access due to spillover effects of attacks (e.g., shooters going to other locations for additional targets as well as securing the perimeter and crime scene). As noted earlier, reaching a hospital quickly does not ensure a patient's survival.

Reaching, Admitting, and Treating the Wounded

Specially trained medics may enter warm zones—areas where an active shooter might be present—with law enforcement (often SWAT personnel) to assess the status of each victim and their chances of survival. In such cases, medics may treat patients prior to the apprehension or neutralization of the perpetrator(s). The risks to such medical personnel should not be underestimated.

At pre-hospital triage, patients may be separated into immediate/delayed emergency status, minor emergencies, and dead or dying. Accordingly, patients are distributed to different hospitals for varied levels of care. Medical facilities face the challenge of treating many severely wounded individuals in multiple waves. The chaos and fluidity of such incidents may complicate the tagging and tracking of patients.

Coupling multiple terror modalities such as gunfire and explosives, as took place in Paris, provides the medical field with the challenges of treating such concomitant wounds. Against that backdrop, one demarcation setting for the wounded included the critically wounded, those needing immediate treatment, and those who could be sent home within a day. Determining which patient to treat first can prove burdensome if a high number of casualties are involved.

Depending on the location targeted, there could be a large variance in the ages of victims, including a relatively high number of children and teenagers killed or injured. In some locations, such as international airports or tourist sites, the victims may include a higher percentage of foreign nationals than otherwise. The foreigners may not be able to communicate well with emergency or medical personnel without foreign language translation. Communication with patients can also be hampered by the fact that some are unconscious, unable to speak, or in shock. Also, noise levels are magnified, making comprehension difficult at times.

Victims will arrive at a hospital after a terror attack having suffered various levels of harm, making the capacity to distinguish among them rapidly of particular necessity. Victims may arrive at a hospital by their own means or be brought by a family member, friend, stranger, or emergency professionals. Terror victims may include multiple family members. The Boston Marathon bombings resulted in the loss of limbs of many family members: Jessica Downes lost both her legs, while the attack robbed her husband, Patrick, of one leg.[70] Also, brothers J.P. and Paul Norden, who watched the race near the finish line, each lost a leg from damage arising from the homemade explosives.[71]

The Nice attack, which was not a family affiliated terror incident, did result in multiple victims within the same family. Sisters Magdalena and Marzena Chrzanowska, who were on vacation from their native Poland, died in the attack. Likewise, Frenchman Pierre Hattermann, his wife, and their child were killed in the truck onslaught. Michael Pellegrini, his mother Veronique Lion, and his grandparents, Germain and Gisele Lion, also perished in the attack in southern France. Furthermore, American father and son Sean and Brodie Copeland lost their lives in the truck attack.[72]

The November 2015 ISIS attack in Paris also resulted in the deaths of several victims from the same families. For example, Elsa Deplace San Martin and her mother, Patricia San Martin, were killed in the Bataclan theater while trying to protect Elsa's five-year-old son, Louis, who survived the attack conducted by multiple operatives.[73] Similarly, cousins Stephane and Pierre Innocenti perished while attending the Bataclan theater that evening.[74]

The growing prevalence of mass casualty attacks has spurred calls for the public to use tourniquets to reduce excessive bleeding prior to first responders' arriving on the scene. Yet others question nonprofessionals' attempting such measures. Depending on the incident, shooting victims may suffer a high proportion of head and chest wounds, rather than injuries to extremities. Mass casualty attacks may necessitate significant demands for blood supplies.

The creation of complete patient lists may take time, making accessibility difficult for concerned family members. In locales where gun violence is uncommon, treating gunshot wounds may prove more arduous than in other cities. Besides the physical injuries that victims sustain, some may also suffer negative psychological effects. Therefore, victim services, including a psychological support center, are crucial in treating such patients.

Staffing

Hospitals directly contacted their physicians, nurses, and other medical personnel, while other personnel learned of the tragedy through social media, family, or friends. In some circumstances, employees were told not to come to the hospital as adequate staffing levels were secured. Alternatively, some workers arrived at their respective hospitals upon hearing about the scope of the terror attack, seeking to contribute even on their days off.

Combating Terrorism[75]

There are generic and specific factors that affect the intensity of future terrorist challenges. Generic components that contribute to terrorism include ethnic, racial, religious, and tribal intolerance and violence; propaganda and psychological warfare; extreme nationalism; regional conflicts that defy easy solutions; intensification of criminal activities such as narcotrafficking and identity theft; the population explosion, migration expansion, and unemployment; environmental challenges; weapons development and proliferation of conventional and unconventional arms; and the growth of global mobility and sophisticated communication systems.

Specific factors and conditions that will encourage terrorism in the future include the absence of a universal definition of terrorism, disagreement over the root causes of terrorism, a double standard of morality, loss of resolve by some governments to take effective action against terrorism, weak punishment of terrorists, violations of international law and promotion of terrorism by some nations, the complexity of modern societies, the high costs of security, and disparate viewpoints on appropriate counterterrorism strategies. These contributing variables foreshadow global vulnerability to terrorism. Within the political violence rubric, family terror networks, likewise, are expected to remain a challenge for the foreseeable future.

Weakness and appeasement of terrorists will only invite more terrorism, not less. Terrorism must be combated at all levels of society. Government (civilian and military), the business community, nonprofits, nongovernmental organizations, and the public must adopt best practices in countering violent extremism, including preventing and dissuading individuals from being enticed by the throngs of terrorism—whether family affiliated or otherwise.

Conclusion

This chapter addressed general principles of terrorism, including definitions, terror threats, types of terror and extremist groups, modes of radicalization and recruitment, predicting susceptibility to radicalism, radicalization and family affiliated terrorism, terrorist characteristics, porous borders, profiling of terrorists, creation of terrorists, female terrorists, terrorists in the economic system, financing terror, the role of corporate security, public-private partnership in combating terrorism, labor and management challenges to terrorism, emergency management/medical responses to mass casualty terror incidents, and combating terrorism. These topics provide the reader with a solid background on terrorism. Such tools will enable the reader to better grasp the varied themes shared in the remaining chapters, including those addressing family connected terrorism and responses thereon.

CHAPTER 2

Characteristics of Family Terror Networks

This chapter addresses baseline principles of family affiliated terrorism. Additionally, this section covers family terror networks manifested in: patriarchs, couples, those searching for love, the role of overseas travel, terror-organized crime nexus, investigations, prosecution of kin, nonprofits, expanding the network, and financial benefits to family members of terrorists. Other themes presented in this chapter include: kin killing extremists, concerns about a child's behavior, family members' knowledge of kin's terrorist activities, family preventing terrorist activities, attempting to prevent the death of a terrorist, family supporting and condemning activities of kin, and family members killing other kin to support terror.

Baseline Principles

There are many schemes by which to analyze the prevalence of terrorists in family units. This deviancy, occurring within the rubric of social networks, is not new. Terrorism within family units is a fact that has occurred throughout history. Family frameworks enable higher instances of conversion to radical beliefs, given the credibility and trust that attach as opposed to that in unaffiliated networks. Such radicalization has materialized across diverse ideologies: from religiously motivated precepts to national liberation and from hate-based ideologies to other right-wing perspectives.

The full spectrum of familial relations has participated in kin connected terrorism. For instance, three Canadian cousins of Somali descent (Mahad, Hamsa, and Hersi Kariye; the latter two were brothers) from Edmonton, along with another cousin, Hanad Abdullahi Mohallim, from Minnesota, were killed in Syria in November 2014. The family members died fighting for the Islamic State. The three Canadians left their home country in October 2013 for Syria. Also, a fifth cousin, Abdullahi Ahmed Abdullahi, was arrested in Canada in September 2017 following a US indictment accusing him of providing material support to terrorists by conducting a jewelry store robbery in Canada to fund his four cousins and another person to travel to Syria to join ISIS. [76]

Even those outside the nuclear family can have significant effects on others to spur participation in terrorism. In November 2016, Ohio-based Munir Abdulkader was sentenced to twenty years in prison for providing material support to ISIS and trying to kill a returning US soldier, among other crimes. Abdulkader claimed he wanted to fight with ISIS. His cousin died fighting with the group. Authorities noticed Abdulkader through his tweets supporting ISIS. Abdulkader interacted with a government informant and a now-deceased ISIS operative, Junaid Hussain. Hussain had recommended several plots for Abdulkader to consider.

Besides recruiting family members to abet a terrorist group, a terrorist may decide to take his family—whether wife, children, siblings, or parents—to war zones and fight on behalf of the group. With the onset of the Islamic State in 2014, families traveled to Iraq and Syria with the goal of residing in the caliphate. The family member who instigates this travel believes that it is in the best interest of his family to live in the ISIS interpretation of the Islamic law. The Islamic State purposely portrayed the "family-friendly" lifestyle in the caliphate to attract new immigrants to Iraq and Syria.

Familial-linked operatives have been found in state-directed, state-sponsored, and non-state-supported organizations. Family participation in extremism is represented throughout the array of group participation. Some members serve as leaders of groups; others take operational roles.

Kin may also give assistance in radicalization and recruitment activities. They may offer funding, documents, and housing for the terror cell. Family members have provided their kin funding to train as terrorists. Likewise, they have misrepresented to law enforcement the culpability of their family members. The extremist efforts of family members can be unobserved until after a strike takes place.

Terror attacks have been carried out by family linked terrorists, including bombings, suicide bombings, and gunfire, with variances in operational stage (e.g., the attempt, the conspiracy, undertaking the attack, and concealing one's participation in it). On occasion, multiples family members are involved in launching the incident. While one sibling may serve as a bomb maker, another may take part in placing or wearing the bomb in a future attack. In August 2009, Yemen-based Saudi Abdullah al-Asiri blew himself up carrying a hidden explosive in an attempt to kill Saudi Arabia's deputy interior minister, Prince Mohammed bin Nayef. Abdullah's brother, Ibrahim, who also served with al Qaeda in the Arabian Peninsula as a key bomb maker, made that explosive. In August 2018, U.S. authorities disclosed that Ibrahim was killed in an American drone strike in Yemen.

Several family members engaged in carrying out some of the high-profile terror attacks worldwide: the Brussels suicide bombings (Bakraoui brothers, March 2016), and the San Bernardino attack (couple Syed Rizwan Farook and Tashfeen Malik, December 2015). Likewise, kin have participated in terror attacks that were less noteworthy. For example, in July 2016, Saudi brothers Abdulrahman and Ibrahim Saleh Muhammad al-Imir, along with Pakistani Abdullah Gulzar Khan, conducted suicide bombings at a Shia mosque in al Qatif, Saudi Arabia. The perpetrators were the only ones killed in the incident.

Sajida Mubarak Atrous al-Rishawi is the sister of the former right-hand man of Abu Musab al-Zarqawi, the one-time head of al Qaeda in Iraq. In November 2005, Sajida attempted to detonate her suicide bomb belt at the Radisson SAS hotel in Amman, Jordan. Her husband, Ali Hussein Ali al-Shamari, with whom she arrived in Jordan from Iraq, told her to leave the hotel. He then blew himself up at that site. Besides al-Shamari, two other operatives conducted suicide bombings at other Amman hotels at the same time. Both of Sajida's brothers were killed fighting US forces in Iraq.

Multiple family members have been killed during a kin's mistake in assembling an explosive. In January 2017, a Taliban commander in northern Afghanistan, Kamal Khan, accidentally killed himself and his four sons while building bombs in his home. The children died upstairs while Khan was constructing the explosives for use as roadside bombs. Family members of terrorist leaders are participants in terror attacks, including martyrdom operations. In July 2017, the eldest son of Taliban leader Mullah Haibatullah Akhundzada, Khalid, was killed while conducting a suicide bombing against Afghan security forces in Helmand province.

Family-linked extremists have targeted government, industry, nongovernmental organizations, and civilians, both in the United States and abroad. The targets of family affiliated participants have been diverse, including segments of the population (e.g., police) or the public at large. Family terror networks exist in all corners of the world, from the Americas to Europe, Africa, Asia, and beyond.

In 2008, two brothers, Ahmed and Ezzit Raad, were convicted of membership in a Melbourne, Australia, jihadi terror cell and making funds available to that cabal. The cell intended to kill thousands of people at railway stations and public places in Melbourne. In 2009, Ahmed and Ezzit were sentenced to ninety and sixty-nine months, respectively. Abdul Nacer Benbrika, who led the cell, was sentenced to fifteen years in prison. Fellow Australians Mustafa and Khaled Cheikho, uncle and nephew respectively, both trained with the Pakistani terror group Lashkar-e-Taiba. Back in Australia, the pair continued their participation in terrorism. Ultimately, they were convicted of participation in a Sydney terror cell.

Sometimes, family members may plot to attack one target, while another family member is involved with others to attack different targets. Such was the case with the Alaska-based Vernons. The husband (Lonnie) was in a militia group planning to kill federal employees. Also, Lonnie and his wife, Karen, sought to murder a judge and an Internal Revenue Agency employee.

Family network terrorism may leverage institutions (e.g., religious, educational) with which they are connected to draw adherents outside the family itself. Likewise, family affiliation facilitates introducing kin to a known extremist based outside the family unit. This arose with Mahfouz Azzam, the uncle of Ayman al-Zawahiri. Azzam served as the lawyer for Islamist ideologue and Egyptian Muslim Brotherhood member Sayyid Qutb.

Children can be exposed to radical views and activities at home. Subsequently, they may participate in a group's activities, including establishing affiliates that may appeal to young operatives. Some youths mesmerized by terrorism ultimately quit the group or condemn extremism. Family members may agree with facets of the cause without fully supporting other dogma.

Family members may not know of the extremist activities of other family members. Alternatively, family members may share extremist precepts. Others may support their kin emotionally and financially. Those who are more dedicated to the cause will take part in an actual attack or travel abroad to get terrorism training.

Siblings, along with friends, may pursue travel to failing nations so they can take part in transnational terrorism. In October 2014, the Colorado-based Farah sisters, aged fifteen and seventeen, along with a sixteen-year-old female friend, were detained in Germany and returned to the United States. Their intention to migrate to the Islamic State was undermined.

Pennsylvania-based Emerson Begolly[77] was an active administrator in the Ansar al-Mujahideen English Forum (AMEF), an Islamic extremist internet forum. He solicited jihadists to undertake violent attacks on various US targets, including police, day-care centers, and Jewish schools. During summer 2010 and beyond, Begolly called for individuals to carry out attacks claiming Allah would reward them in the afterlife. In December 2010, he solicited the AMEF audience to pursue attacks at once. Begolly also uploaded a bomb-making manual.

In January 2011, Begolly was arrested. In a superseding indictment (July 2011), he was charged with solicitation to commit a crime of violence (ten years) and distribution of information relating to explosive destruction devices and weapons of mass destruction (twenty years). In August 2011, Begolly pleaded guilty to soliciting others to commit acts of terrorism in the United States and using a firearm during an assault on FBI agents. In 2013, he was sentenced to nearly nine years in prison. Begolly's path toward criminality may have started through exposure to a variant of extremism, Nazism, as a youth. Investigation into Begolly's youth revealed his father, Shawn, exposed him to Nazism at age 11.

In September 2012, Amine el Khalifi was sentenced to thirty years in prison for attempting to conduct a suicide bombing at the US Capitol. Unbeknownst to El Khalifi, he was interacting with an FBI confidential informant and undercover agents. El Khalifi asked his government handlers to provide his Morocco-based parents $500 a month in support if he conducted the suicide attack.

Patriarchs

Patriarchs have a strong influence on the level of radicalization and recruitment of family members. This was so with Osama bin Laden. Of bin Laden's twenty-three children, several sons featured prominently in continuing the family's participation in terrorism. Initially, Saad bin Laden intended to carry the family mantle after his father. However, Saad was killed in a drone strike in Pakistan in 2009. Khalid, another son, was killed along with Osama in Pakistan during the US Navy Seal raid in May 2011. In January 2016, another bin Laden child, Hamza, called to avenge his father's death: "If you think that your sinful crime that you committed in Abbottabad has passed without punishment, then you thought wrong."[78]

In January 2017, the US State Department named Hamza a Specially Designated Global Terrorist. Five months later, he released a video entitled "Advice for Martyrdom-Seekers in the West." With his growing prominence within al Qaeda, Hamza is expected to become its leader. In August 2018, it was reported that Hamza married the daughter of lead 9/11 hijacker Egyptian Mohammed Atta. In doing so, Hamza further solidified his family terror network pedigree.[79]

The role of a patriarch in hastening involvement in terrorism was exhibited with Ahmed Said Khadr's clan. Egyptian by birth, Ahmed moved to Canada in the 1970s, spent time in Afghanistan fighting the Soviets in the 1980s, and purportedly met Osama bin Laden. He was implicated in the bombing of the Egyptian Embassy in Pakistan in 1995, before ultimately meeting his demise in a shootout with Pakistani forces in 2003.[80]

Ahmed's son, Abdul Karim, was paralyzed during the same firefight that killed his father. The following year, Abdul Karim moved to Canada for medical care.[81]

Like his father, Omar fought with jihadi forces in Afghanistan. In 2002, while only fifteen, Omar was wounded during a gun battle with U.S. forces, captured, and later transferred to Guantanamo. In 2010, a U.S. military tribunal in Guantanamo found him guilty of war crimes, including the killing of a U.S. soldier.[82] Two years later, Omar was transferred to a Canadian prison, and released in 2015.[83] In 2017, the Canadian government awarded Omar C$10.5 million after a settlement arising from a Canadian Supreme Court finding that Canadian intelligence operatives used evidence arising from "oppressive circumstances," while in American custody.[84]

Afghani forces captured another child of Ahmed, Abdurahman, in 2001. Abdurahman was suspected of being affiliated with al

Qaeda, spent time in an Afghani prison, before allegedly cooperating with U.S. forces. In 2002, he was trained by the CIA, and then spent time in Guantanamo where he alleges he served as an informant for the agency. The following year, the CIA sent him to Bosnia where he infiltrated al Qaeda recruitment operations that were sending insurgents to Iraq. By fall 2003, he stopped working for the CIA, and returned to Canada. There, he told the media that he was sent to Guantanamo, made his way to Afghanistan, and then Bosnia. The next year, Abdurahman disclosed in an interview that he had worked for the CIA. Upon that revelation, his family disowned him.[85]

Born in Canada, another son of Ahmed, Abdullah later moved to Pakistan with his family. While there, he attended a terror training camp with his brother, Abdurahman, in 1994. During the intervening decade prior to his capture by Pakistani forces in 2004, Ahmed allegedly provided material support to al Qaeda. In 2005, the U.S. government indicted him on terrorism charges, although the Pakistani government refused his extradition to the United States. Rather, the Pakistanis sent him to Canada. In his native land, he fought extradition, while being held in prison some four years. In 2010, he was released from prison following an Ontario judge's ruling that Ahmed's confession to Pakistani authorities was induced by torture. The following year, the Ontario Appeals Court affirmed the denial of America's request to extradite Ahmed, while the Canadian Supreme Court refused to hear the case.[86]

Two case studies involving hate-based ideologically linked individuals—Tom (father) and John (son) Metzger as well as Ian (father) and Nicky (son) Davison—illustrate the impact of fathers' influences on their sons. In 1990, the leaders of White Aryan Resistance (WAR), father and son Tom and John Metzger, lost a multimillion-dollar wrongful death suit brought by the family of a black man, Mulugeta

Seraw. In Oregon, members of the East Side White Pride (ESWP) beat Seraw to death. The Metzgers and WAR were found to have encouraged members of ESWP to commit acts of violent against blacks to promote white supremacy.[87]

UK–based Ian Davison was founder of the neo-Nazi website Aryan Strike Force. In May 2010, Ian was sentenced to ten years in prison for producing a biological weapon (ricin). Ian's son, Nicky, was convicted of possessing manuals helpful to a terrorist. Nicky received a two-year prison sentence.[88]

Couples

Some couples involved in terror plots met each other online. The future spouses may have held extremist ideologies before they met. Other persons are exposed to such attitudes during their courtship or afterward. Among plotters who met online are the 2015 San Bernardino shooters Syed Rizwan Farook and Tashfeen Malik (both carried out the assault) and the 2016 Orlando shooter Omar Mateen and his wife Noor Salman (charged with abetting to give material support to ISIS and obstruction of justice but found not guilty in March 2018).

Couples may commit terrorist acts. Also, they may collude with other similarly inclined people. In February 2015, a Missouri-based couple, Ramiz Zijad Hodzic and his wife, Sedina Unkic Hodzic, along with four other US-based Bosniacs, faced charges of conspiracy to give and giving material support to terrorism. The six were accused of distributing funds and materials to Abdullah Ramo Pazara, a former US-based Bosniac who traveled to Iraq and Syria to join jihadists.

Spouses who espouse extremist ideals do not necessarily take part in violent tasks. Instead, they commit crimes that align with the philosophy of the movement. More particularly, those who follow sovereign citizen ideology perceive that they are exempt from the law. Sovereigns believe they can issue fraudulent financial instruments, put baseless liens on property, and access purported federal funds for their private purposes.

Such was the situation in June 2011, when husband and wife Roderick and Amber Catrece Moore were sentenced to thirteen months and three years in federal prison, respectively. The couple was convicted of mail fraud (Roderick) and conspiracy (Amber). Roderick made a registered promissory bond note, a fictitious financial instrument, to pay over $200,000 in debt. Amber filed false liens against a US bankruptcy court and multiple entities.

Several European couples involved in terrorism are noteworthy. The terror plots of British jihadists Mohammed and Shasta Khan are mentioned initially. The case of suicide bomber Muriel Degauque and her husband, Issam Goris, who was killed by security forces in Iraq, is then presented. Lastly, the circumstance of convicted al Qaeda–linked terrorists Malika el Aroud and her husband, Moez Garsallaoui, is noted.

In 2012, Manchester, United Kingdom, plotters Mohammed Sajid Khan and his wife Shasta Khan were convicted of plans to prepare a terror attack and possessing terrorist materials. The pair sought to attack Jewish targets in Manchester. Interestingly enough, police discovered the plot while investigating a dispute between Mohammed and Shasta's father. At one point, Shasta's family informed police Mohammed was a terrorist. This tip led police to discover the developing plot while searching the Khans' home.

In November 2005, Muriel Degauque, a Belgian-born convert to Islam, conducted a suicide bombing in Baqubah, Iraq, killing five Iraqi police officers and injuring five other persons. She conducted the attack on behalf of al Qaeda in Iraq. Her second husband, Issam Goris, a Belgian jihadist of Moroccan descent, was shot and killed the same day by US forces in Iraq. The couple had traveled to Iraq from Belgium. Degauque's mother claimed Goris brainwashed her daughter with jihadist ideology.

In 2010, Malika el Aroud and her husband, Moez Garsallaoui, were convicted and sentenced to eight years in prison in Belgium (he in absentia) for heading an al Qaeda–aligned group. The group recruited persons in Belgium and France to serve as terrorists in Afghanistan. Six other persons were adjudicated in the recruitment scheme. Malika's previous husband, Abdessatar Dahmane, was an al Qaeda suicide bomber who killed a leading anti-Taliban militant leader, Ahmad Shah Massoud, in Afghanistan in 2001.

Searching for Love[89]

Radicalized individuals may leave their home countries to enter a war zone or an area controlled by a terrorist group with the aim of contributing to the cause. In doing so, they can meet a future spouse there, as they solidify their zeal for the cause. Such a circumstance developed between a former Alabama college student, Hoda Muthana, and her husband, Australian jihadist Suhan Abdul Rahman. In November 2014, Muthana left Alabama for Turkey and then Syria. The couple met and married in the Islamic State–controlled part of Syria. In March 2015, Rahman was killed after their nuptials in Syria. Despite his death, Muthana continued to recruit for ISIS through social media.

In May 2013, Nicole Lynn Mansfield, thirty-three, and two men were killed by Syrian government forces. She was fighting with Ahrar al-Sham, the "Free Men of Syria." Mansfield's family claims that she was media coordinator for one of the Islamist rebel groups. Mansfield met her second husband, a Saudi, online. He introduced her to extremist tenets. A later marriage to a man from the United Arab Emirates, whom she also found on the internet, ended in divorce as well.

Mansfield was far from the last female enticed by the jihadist message. By May 2017, over six hundred Western women had traveled abroad to join the Islamic State. In April 2014, Samra Kesinovic, sixteen, and Sabina Selimovic, fifteen, left their homes in Vienna, Austria. The pair proceeded to Syria where they hoped to become brides to jihadi fighters. Vienna-based Chechen radicals and a Bosnian Islamist preacher named Mirsad O. (a.k.a. Ebu Tejma) radicalized the two teenagers of Bosnian descent. Kesinovic and Selimovic posted photos of themselves with jihadi fighters. The girls inspired other teenage girls to join the jihad in Syria. In October 2014, the two had married jihadi fighters and were pregnant. By November 2015, Samra had been beaten to death as she tried to escape from Raqqa.

Grace Khadijah Dare is a twenty-two-year-old mother of two from South London. She also goes by Umma Isa, Muhajirah Fil Sham, and Maryam. Dare grew up in Lewisham, South London. Dare converted to Islam at age eighteen. She went to a local college to study media studies, film studies, psychology, and sociology. Dare worshipped at Lewisham Islamic Centre. Dare was married to Swedish jihadi Abu Bakr (Abdul Ghameed Abbas), whom she met online.

They moved to Syria in 2012. Bakr was a fighter with the Sunni jihadi militia Katibat Al-Muhajireen, the Battalion of Immigrants, which pledged allegiance to ISIS. He was killed in Syria in 2014.

In a video interview, Dare fired a Kalashnikov rifle while stating that she would like to fight and become a martyr. She admonished British Muslims to not be selfish, imploring them to give up their comfortable lives, families, and studies and join ISIS's fight. Hours after British ISIS executioner Mohammed Emwazi ("Jihadi John") beheaded James Foley in August 2014, Dare gloated at his execution on social media. She vowed to be the first British woman to kill a UK or US "terrorist."

After that statement, Dare became a celebrity recruitment personality for women in ISIS. Dare claimed she would not to return to Britain, even if her husband was killed. She also stated, "I wouldn't like to go back to the UK. I'll stay here, raise my children, focus on the Arabic language to communicate with the Syrian people."[90] In February 2016, Dare's four-year-old boy, Isa, was in an ISIS propaganda video. The video showed four alleged spies killed in a car bomb. Dare and Isa left Syria for Sweden to treat Isa's unresolved medical condition. The health issue remained unattended in ISIS territory.[91]

In July 2017, Iraqi forces captured sixteen-year-old, German-born Linda Wenzel in Mosul. Wenzel was discovered with other foreign-born ISIS-aligned women. Wenzel, a convert to Islam, left Germany in July 2016 after being radicalized in online chat rooms. Once in Syria, Wenzel found a jihadi fighter suitor. While predisposed to radicalism, he further enticed her to contribute to the caliphate.

Overseas Travel

Family networks transcend borders, enabling ideas, training, and resources to be shared. So, too, these transnational family networks may encourage overseas travel to the base of family radicalism. Such overseas trips may ease participation in terrorist training camps abroad. These centers offer attendees ideological and operational instruction.

Al Marri brothers Jarallah and Ali are examples of siblings who left their home country to study in the United States. Afterward, the pair got terror training with core al Qaeda operatives in Afghanistan (Jarallah) and Pakistan (Ali), in 2001 and 1998–2001, respectively. Jarallah was captured in Pakistan trying to return home to Qatar. Jarallah was transferred to Guantanamo Bay, where he was detained for over six years. Ali was detained in the United States. Initially, he was held under a material witness warrant and then on fraud charges. Next, Ali was designated as an unlawful enemy combatant. Finally, he pleaded guilty in criminal court to providing material support to al Qaeda. The brothers are presumed to be in Qatar.[92]

Occasionally, one family member travels abroad and settles in a different country with the goal of raising money for a terrorist organization. This happened with Mahmoud Kourani. He left Lebanon and unlawfully entered the United States through Mexico in 2001. Before his arrival in the United States, Mahmoud had served as a fighter, recruiter, and fundraiser for Hezbollah. Upon setting up a base in Dearborn, Michigan, Mahmoud conspired with his brother Haider to give material support to the terror group. Haider remained in Lebanon, serving the group as a military security operative. In 2005, Mahmoud was convicted of conspiring to offer material support to Hezbollah, including sending over $40,000 to the terror group. Also that year, a neighbor of Mahmoud in Michigan, Elias Mohamad Akhdar, pleaded guilty to conspiring to violate the Racketeer Influenced and Corrupt Organizations Act (RICO).[93]

Alternatively, family members may go overseas to get terrorism training and live in a conflict zone. They may travel together or in stages. Some follow soon after the first kin member goes abroad. In other instances, the family member(s) may follow years later. One household member may travel overseas to participate in terrorism. Another kin may stay in their home country due to concerns about upsetting their parents. Nevertheless, the kin who declined to travel abroad may still facilitate terrorism from his home country.

Such a scenario unfolded with UK-based Tuhin Shahensha and Mustakim Jaman. They are brothers of Ifthekar Jaman. Ifthekar, an ISIS member based in Syria, was killed in December 2014. In November 2015, Tuhin and Mustakim were sentenced to six years in prison for helping ten UK youths travel to Syria.[94]

Family members may aid in their kin's travel abroad. This arose with brothers Alaa and Nader Saadeh. In May 2016, Alaa was sentenced to fifteen years in prison for conspiracy to give material support to ISIS. Alaa purchased his sibling's flight to the Middle East with the object of joining ISIS. The other coconspirators (Samuel Rahamin Topaz, Fareed Mumuni, and Munther Omar Saleh) aimed to join the so-called caliphate. The three pleaded guilty to conspiracy to dispense material support to ISIS. Also, Mumuni pleaded guilty to attempted murder of an FBI agent.

During 2013–2014, Brighton, United Kingdom, brothers Jaffar (sixteen), Abdullah (eighteen), and Amer (twenty-one) Deghayes traveled to Syria with a friend, Ibrahim Kamara, nineteen, to fight on behalf of al-Nusra Front (ANF). All but Amer have since been killed in Syria. An uncle of the brothers, Omar Deghayes, was imprisoned in Guantanamo for several years. In 2010, the British government provided Omar one million British pounds in compensation for his incarceration as he claimed to have been held due to mistaken identity. Yet by 2017, it was alleged that Omar had given Abdullah and Jaffar money so they could attend a gym in England that was a radicalization hub.

Terror-Organized Crime Nexus

Family affiliated extremist actions may have attributes like organized criminal family networks. Family involvement in terrorism may be secondary to or of equal importance as engagement in traditional criminal activity. For instance, two brothers, Mohamad and Chawki Hammoud, were among some twenty individuals in the United States, Canada, and elsewhere who collectively were involved in cigarette smuggling, racketeering, money laundering, and other activities. Portions of the rewards of this criminality were provided to Hezbollah in Lebanon. The two brothers, who emigrated from Lebanon, reportedly had longstanding ties with Hezbollah. Mohamed and Chawki were sentenced to thirty years and four and a half years in prison, respectively.

Investigations

Kin Previously Investigated

Individuals who commit terror attacks may have kin who were scrutinized for terrorism at one point. Muhammad Youssef

Abdulazeez killed five in Chattanooga, Tennessee, in a foreign terrorist group–inspired attack in 2015. At one point, Muhammad's father, Youssef, was investigated for funding an organization that was suspected of terrorist connections. Muhammad's father was placed on a terror watch list but later removed from it.

Obstructing Investigations

Besides engaging in simultaneous strikes, family members have been accessories after the fact. For example, they have aided operational terrorists or otherwise supported their relatives in eluding authorities. Others may learn of family members' impending terror attacks or other involvement in extremism, but they do not discourage them from such actions or inform authorities. In turn, a family member might be charged with conspiracy and providing material support to a terror act, failing to inform police of the impending attack, aiding/abetting the crime, accessory before/after the fact, or lying to federal agents, among other crimes.

Initial Investigations

During initial investigations of terror incidents, government authorities often interview family members of alleged terrorists. This may lead to such family members being taken into custody for further questioning or even arrest. Later inquiry into potential family links may be resolved. Sometimes, family members in multiple locations may become another part of the inquiry.

This path is used often after a successful large-scale terror incident, as in the June 2016 Orlando, Florida, Pulse nightclub attack by Omar Mateen. The investigation included his father and wife. Inquiry into Mateen's wife, Noor Salman, led to the discovery of her possible knowledge of and assistance with the planned attack. Also, she was allegedly deceitful during interactions with authorities after the incident. In January 2017, Salman was charged with aiding and abetting in giving material support to ISIS and obstruction of justice. In March 2018, she was found not guilty on all charges.

Mateen's father, Seddique, articulated pro-Taliban sentiments in diverse media before the attack. He was investigated about his son's plot. In March 2018, the government admitted Seddique had been an FBI informant for eleven years before Omar's strike at the nightclub.

Incipient investigations may suggest that a terror family affiliated network exists. Later inquiries may show the threat is less pronounced than expected. The family may be deemed not involved in radicalism at all. In 2011, multiple members of the Khan family (Hafiz Muhammed Sher Ali Khan, the imam at the Miami Mosque, and his two sons Irfan and Izhar) along with three others based in Pakistan were charged with conspiracy to give material aid to terrorists and to the Pakistani Taliban. Charges against the sons were dropped. In 2013, Hafiz was found guilty of material support crimes and sentenced to twenty-five years in prison.

Terror Investigation Leads to Other Crimes

While one family member is involved in a terror plot, investigation of extremism perspectives of other kin may lead to discovery of participation in different criminal activity. After the December

2015 San Bernardino shootings, authorities investigated familial and other links to the married-couple shooters Syed Rizwan Farook and Tashfeen Malik. Six months after that terror attack, Syed's brother, Syed Raheel Farook, was charged with conspiracy to create a sham marriage between Enrique Marquez Jr. and Maria Chernykh, the sister of Syed Raheel's wife, Tatiana Farook. In November 2017, Syed Raheel and Tatiana pleaded guilty to a felony conspiracy and conspiracy to commit immigration fraud, respectively. In January 2017, Tatiana's sister, Maria, admitted guilt in felony conspiracy and perjury. Marquez was charged with purchasing two weapons used in the San Bernardino attacks. In February 2017, Marquez admitted furnishing tangible support to terrorists and making inaccurate statements. He faces twenty years in prison, with sentencing scheduled in 2018.

An individual may conspire to marry another person to aid the latter in getting permanent residency in a country. Such was the situation with Mohamad Hammoud's wife, Angela Tsioumas, who entered a guilty plea on conspiracy charges in 2002. Mohamed had married two US citizens to obtain US residency. In 1994, Mohamed's brother, Chawki, married an American woman, Jessica Fortune, in a fraudulent marriage. Fortune was convicted of marriage fraud in 2001. As noted earlier, the Hammoud brothers were the principals in a terrorism-organized crime cabal supporting Hezbollah.

Prosecution of Kin

Successful prosecutions of terror-linked households may result in family members convicted of the same or similar charges. Likewise, civil suits against family-linked extremists could create civil liability against multiple family members. Family members are not charged with terror offenses for various reasons: their youth, possible difficulties in convictions, or the government's perception that prosecution should be avoided as alternative pathways or outlets are accessible to those toying with extremism.

Three Chicago area teenagers planned to travel overseas and join ISIS. All three were apprehended at Chicago O'Hare Airport as they made their way to the departure gate. Of the three, only the eldest brother and instigator, Mohammed Hamzah Khan, was arrested. Mohammed was nineteen years old at the time of his arrest in 2014. The following year, he pleaded guilty to trying to provide material support to ISIS. In 2016, Mohammed was sentenced to three and a half years in prison. His brother and sister, sixteen and seventeen years old, respectively, were not prosecuted.[95]

While family members who take part in terror activities may perish, the surviving kin, a coconspirator, might be prosecuted. In 2015, Abu Sayyaf al-Iraqi, a senior leader of ISIS involved in its financing operations, was killed in Syria during a US military special operation. His wife, Umm Sayyaf, was captured during the raid. She was subsequently transferred to Iraqi custody. In 2016, Umm was charged with conspiracy to offer material support to ISIS, including providing aid in detaining Kayla Mueller. Mueller was a US citizen held hostage by ISIS. In 2015, Mueller was killed during Jordanian air strikes in ISIS-controlled areas of Syria.

In 2014, the ex-wife of Abu Bakr al-Baghdadi, Saja al-Dulaimi, and her child were arrested in Lebanon as they entered the country from neighboring Syria. Al-Dulaimi is believed to have used Lebanon to funnel money to ISIS. Al-Dulaimi had lived in Homs, Syria, then moved to the Lebanese border town of Arsal. In about

2008, al-Baghdadi married al-Dulaimi. He divorced her after three months of marriage.

Al-Dulaimi had been married before, to a lieutenant in Saddam Hussein's army, Falah Ismail al-Jasim. Al-Jasim was killed while fighting in the Iraqi resistance to the US invasion of Iraq. Al-Dulaimi's brother, Omar, was sentenced to life in prison for participation in terror attacks in Iraq. She is the daughter of Hamid al-Dulaimi from a prominent tribe in Anbar province in Iraq. Hamid pledged loyalty to the Islamic State. He was killed in Homs, Syria, in 2014.[96]

Nonprofits

Individuals associated through family networks also have been involved in helping nonprofit organizations give material support to terrorist groups such as Hamas. Such a circumstance existed with the Hamas political chief, Mousa Abu Marzook, who is married to a cousin of Ghassan Elashi, a former chairman of the board of the Texas-based Holy Land Foundation for Relief and Development (HLF). The 2008 convictions of Elashi and others confirmed that HLF had aided Hamas with fundraising in the United States. HLF was the largest Muslim charity in the United States.[97] In 2001, HLF became defunct due to its designation by the US Department of Treasury as a Specially Designated Terrorist.

Expanding the Network

Marriage can expand kin-affiliated terrorism as another family becomes potential terror recruits. Such a coupling of interests through family arose with the January 2001 nuptials of Mohamed, the son of former al Qaeda leader Osama bin Laden, with the daughter of the al Qaeda leader's military chief Mohammed Atef, who was killed later that year.[98] Indeed, "[m]arriages commonly cemented mujahedin into kinship relationships. Mujahedin and their families lived in exile because of their clandestine activities, limiting their choices of marriage partners."[99]

Financial Benefits to Family

The Palestinian Authority provides about $140 million annually to support the family members of Palestinian terrorists serving in Israeli prisons and to compensate the families of suicide bombers. "The policy of paying a stipend of sorts to the families of deceased terrorists began in 1966 as a method of helping families who lost loved ones in the fight against Israel."[100] While supporting terrorist families, such funds also encourage participation in terrorism.

In January 2017, Fadi al-Qanbar was shot and killed after ramming a truck into pedestrians in Jerusalem. Al-Qanbar killed four Israeli soldiers and injured seventeen others in his attack. His widow will receive a $1,500 one-time payment and a $760 monthly stipend from the Palestinian Authority. Al-Qanbar's sister, Shadia, said, "Praise be to Allah that he became a martyr. It is the most beautiful kind of saintly death."[101] In contrast, the terrorist's brother, Sami, claimed Fadi's brakes were faulty, and he did not intend to commit a terror attack.

Family Member Killing Extremist

Spouses or children of extremists have killed family members. Occasionally, the victim played a senior role with a radical group or movement. The murders may occur due to a family member's disinterest in extremism or for other reasons (e.g., parental or spousal abuse). In February 2017, Frank Ancona, the imperial wizard of the Traditionalist American Knights of the Ku Klux Klan, was murdered in his home in Missouri. Within days of the incident, Ancona's wife, Malissa Ann, and her son (and Frank's stepson), Paul Jinkerson Jr., were charged with the murder. In March 2017, the pair was indicted on ten charges, including first-degree murder.[102] "Prosecutors had previously said that Frank Ancona might have been killed because he had told his wife that he wanted a divorce."[103]

Concerns About a Child's Future Behavior

In July 2011, Anders Breivik, a Norwegian, undertook the deadliest attack in his country since World War II. In Oslo, Breivik detonated a bomb in a government building, killing eight persons. The following day, Breivik shot and killed sixty-nine people at a Labor Party's Workers Youth League event taking place on an island near Oslo. In August 2012, Breivik was convicted of mass murder and other related crimes with an appending sentence of twenty-one years. Breivik's mother had expressed concern about her son's future violent tendencies from the time he was four years old.

In January 2011, Jared Loughner shot and killed six people and injured thirteen others during a mass shooting at a Safeway in Tucson, Arizona. Loughner targeted US House of Representatives member Gabrielle Giffords. Congresswoman Giffords was shot and injured while meeting with constituents at the supermarket. In August 2012, Loughner pleaded guilty to nineteen counts related to the attack. Three months later, he was sentenced to life in prison.

Loughner had a history of alcohol and drug abuse. He had followed conspiracy theories regarding 9/11 and the New World Order and appeared to support selected sovereign citizen ideologies. Loughner's parents had been worried about his mental health for years. Their premonitions were confirmed when the community college he had attended denied his return absent a clearance concerning his mental state.

His parents were so apprehensive about his potential actions that they often disabled his car at night. They also took away their son's shotgun. Unfortunately, Jared, who took a cab to the site of his attack, purchased another firearm and used it in the shootings. Loughner's family issued a statement after the incident: "There are no words that can possibly express how we feel. We wish that there were, so we could make you feel better. We don't understand why this happened. It may not make any difference, but we wish that we could change the heinous events of Saturday. We care very deeply about the victims and the families. We are so very sorry for their loss."[104]

Family Members' Knowledge of Kin's Terrorist Activities

A family member who decides to launch a terror operation may tell kin of his commitment to doing so. This was the circumstance with Wafa Idris, the first female Palestinian suicide bomber. Idris carried out an assault in Jerusalem in January 2002.

Wafa told her sister-in-law that she wanted to emulate Palestinian suicide bombers. Wasfieh Mabrook, Wafa's mother, said that her family is "proud of [the attack]. I wish every man, every woman, would be the same, a bomber."[105] Wafa's three brothers were Fatah members. One of them spent ten years in an Israeli prison. The al-Aqsa Brigades, the military wing of Fatah, claimed responsibility for Wafa's attack.

Authorities are sometimes unsure whether family members knew of their kin's impending attack. Even if law enforcement believes that foreknowledge existed, the prosecution may not charge an individual since such knowledge is sometimes difficult to prove. The government did not prosecute Katherine Russell, the American widow of Boston Marathon terrorist Tamerlan Tsarnaev regarding prior knowledge of the attack. Russell lived with Tamerlan and their daughter up until the incident. But, according to the former agent in charge of the Boston FBI office, Richard DesLauriers, "I think one of the conclusions you could reasonably draw is that since she lived in that residence, she might have had some foreknowledge."[106]

Household members have told authorities about the suspected radicalization of their kin. For example, Alhaji Umaru Mutallab, the Nigerian father of December 2009 failed underwear bomber Umar Farouk Abdulmutallab, informed both Nigerian and US government officials of his worry that Umar was a jihadist. Alhaji also suspected that his son was in Yemen. These warnings apparently took place six months prior to Umar's failed downing of an Amsterdam-to-Detroit flight for al Qaeda in the Arabian Peninsula.

Alhaji was a well-respected, affluent businessman whose son became radicalized during studies at a university in London. He was radicalized further during sojourns in Egypt, United Arab Emirates, and Yemen. In February 2012, Umar was sentenced to life in prison on eight federal charges stemming from the stymied attack. He pleaded guilty to those counts in October 2011.

Family Preventing Terrorist Activities

Parents have pursued a variety of paths to avoid their family members being killed or arrested due to a kin's participation in terrorism. For instance, parents who learned their children were contemplating traveling to Syria hid their passports. Such parental interference causes the child to undergo the time, expense, and risk of discovery by authorities when acquiring a new passport.

This happened with Adam Dandach, a Santa Ana, California, resident. Adam's mother hid his passport and took the funds he intended to use to join the Islamic State. Undeterred, Adam filed a request for an expedited passport. Adam wrote he needed a replacement passport because he had discarded the former one in error. In July 2016, Dandach was sentenced to fifteen years in prison. He had pleaded guilty to giving material aid to the Islamic State and lying on his passport application.

In November 2014, French authorities took a fifteen-year-old French girl of Moroccan descent, Assia Saidi, into custody after her parents prevented her from traveling to Syria and participating in jihad. Assia had a Facebook page, which portrayed her commitment to travel abroad and wage jihad. Assia's parents looked for her after she ran away from home. They found her working at a bar in Marseille.

In November 2002, Andrew Mickel, an anti-government extremist with a history of depression, assassinated a police officer, David Mobilio, in Red Bluff, California. Mickel, a former Army Ranger and student at Evergreen State College in Olympia, Washington, leaped behind Mobilio at a gas station and shot him three times. Mickel later drove to Washington State before flying to New Hampshire. One week later, Mickel claimed responsibility for the killing on a left-wing website, the San Francisco Bay Area Independent Media Center.

Around the same time and while in New Hampshire, Mickel told his parents he killed Mobilio. His parents, both college professors, called the police. Soon afterward, police surrounded Mickel at a Holiday Inn in New Hampshire. Afterward, Mickel surrendered to police. In April 2005, Mickel was convicted of murdering Mobilio and was sentenced to death for that crime.

Family members have notified law enforcement about other family members' possible involvement in radicalism. One path of such outreach to authorities can arise after reading an anonymous terrorist manifesto. This circumstance occurred with David Kaczynski, the brother of Ted, better known as the Unabomber. After reading a 1995 anti-technology manifesto in the *New York Times* and *Washington Post*, David's wife, Linda Patrik, became suspicious of Ted's authorship of the manifesto. She then urged David to consider that possibility, and David informed the FBI. During a decade-plus period ending in 1996, the Unabomber sent or placed sixteen bombs across the United States. These incidents resulted in three deaths and twenty-three injuries. Ted is serving a life sentence at a federal supermax prison in Florence, Colorado.[107]

In 2009, Mohamed Mohamud's father, Osman Barre, contacted the FBI because of his concern his son wanted to travel abroad and pursue jihad. Osman feared his child, being of Somali descent, was delving into jihadism as other Somali immigrants had done with al-Shabaab. Mohamud discussed with al Qaeda in the Arabian

Peninsula operatives his interest acquiring terror training in Yemen and Pakistan.

In November 2010, Mohamud tried to set off a car bomb at a Christmas tree lighting ceremony in Portland, Oregon. Mohamud was convicted of those charges in January 2013 and in October 2014 was sentenced to thirty years in prison for his crime. During Mohamed's 2013 trial, Osman claimed authorities "brainwashed" his son by their use of undercover operatives during the concocted operation in Portland.

In September 2014, Boston police captain Robert Ciccolo informed the FBI that his son, Alexander, had an interest in ISIS. An ex-felon by July 2015, Alexander was arrested while seeking to purchase weapons in an FBI sting operation. Alexander said he planned to use the weapons during an ISIS-inspired terror attack in the United States. In June 2016, Alexander was indicted on seeking to give material support to ISIS and attempting use of a weapon of mass destruction.

In summer 2014, Sal Shafi was visiting Egypt with his family, including his twenty-one-year-old son, Adam. Sal informed the US Embassy in Cairo of his concern that Adam might have traveled to Iraq or Syria during their trip abroad. Following the family's return to the United States, the FBI met with Adam and later monitored him for terrorism activities.

In July 2015, Adam was arrested as he was boarding a flight from San Francisco to Turkey. The FBI claimed Adam sought to offer tangible aid to ANF. Adam had expressed loyalty to the emir of the group. Sal had assumed the FBI would enter Adam in a counter-radicalization program. To his dismay, that was not the case. As Adam's prosecution ensued, Sal said parents should not provide information about their child's extremism to authorities. Informing the government, Sal warned, would lead to a child's incarceration, rather than participation in a rehabilitation program.[108]

Family members who see extremism within their family face difficult choices. They can overlook the behavior and hope it dissipates. They may confront the person and risk alienation, further radicalization, or possibly improve the situation. Simultaneously, a parent may seek guidance from third parties who have expertise in deradicalization or psychological issues. Lastly, they may call law enforcement authorities and risk the family member being monitored or arrested.

At times, family members can prevent, identify, and counter extremist ideologies that may threaten their homes. In May 2016, Hedayah, the International Center of Excellence for Countering Violent Extremism, proposed recommendations to prevent and countering violent extremism in families.[109] The ten insights that Hedayah shared in this regard are:

- "Prioritize strengthening family-based social networks—and particularly parental influence—to build resilience to violent extremism (VE)."

- "Support and empower women—particularly mothers—as prevention protagonists."

- "Engage fathers and respected community males to gain access to vulnerable communities, and to shape existing cultural narratives, which VEs manipulate."

- "Support the development of family commitments in VE prevention programming."

- "Capitalize on the role of family relationships to rehabilitate and reintegrate VEs."

- "Focus on building family member awareness of violent radicalization signs and prevention techniques."

- "Promote interaction between families and authorities, particularly security forces, to enhance information-sharing, cooperation, and collaborative opportunities for prevention."

- "Reduce social isolation of the family—particularly women and children—to strengthen resilience to VE."

- "Tailor family-level interventions to local cultures and anchor such activities in local partnerships."

- "Make family oriented P/CVE [Preventing/Countering Violent Extremism] multi-faceted, long-term, flexible, and tolerant of short-term failures."[110]

Additionally, Hedayah noted several options in "designing and implementing programs supporting families as P/CVE protagonists."[111] Among the steps that can be taken are:

- "Building Parental Capacity"

- "Community Support for Families"

- "School-Based Approaches"

- "CVE Communications"

- "Rehabilitation and Reintegration"[112]

Attempting to Prevent the Death of a Terrorist

Anwar al-Awlaki was a senior al Qaeda in the Arabian Peninsula operative before he was killed in a US drone strike in Yemen in September 2011. Al-Awlaki's teenage son Abdulrahman was killed later that month in another drone strike, either purposely or as collateral damage.[113] In August 2010, the American Civil Liberties Union and the Center for Constitutional Rights had sued the Obama administration on behalf of al-Awlaki's father. Anwar's father objected to the government putting his son on a list of targets for assassination without a trial or judicial proceeding.

In December 2010, the district court dismissed the suit, ruling that Awlaki's father did not have standing and the issue was a political question not subject to review. In November 2010, Yemen put al-Awlaki on trial in absentia regarding plots to kill foreigners and being a member of al Qaeda. In June 2014, the US Court of Appeals for the Second Circuit ordered the release of a secret US government memo that justified the use of lethal force against al-Awlaki, noting that, while killing an American citizen without "sufficient process" is problematic, the targeted killing would be contemplated if capture was not possible and the person posed "a continued imminent threat or death" to fellow Americans.[114]

Families Supporting and Condemning Activities of Kin

Introduction

Some family members praise the terrorist activities of their kin while others condemn such actions. On occasion, there are discrepancies of opinion within the family as to whether to support or condemn such activities. For instance, in March 2011, Mohammed Merah, a French national, killed seven people in a jihadist attack in Toulouse, France, during two separate attacks on French soldiers and one at a Jewish school. Merah was killed during a shootout with police after his discovery by French authorities.

Mohammed's path to radicalism coalesced while surviving the setting of a dysfunctional family (e.g., violent father) as well as a stint in prison, where he attempted suicide and became immersed in jihadism in 2008. Additionally, France-based imam, Oliver Corel, whose followers included individuals who traveled to join ISIS in Syria, influenced Mohammed, Abdelkader, and Souad. Also, Mohammed's brother Abdelkader and sister Souad aggravated their brother's zeal for jihadism. Subsequently, Mohammed received terror training from al Qaeda and spent time in Pakistan and Afghanistan. Souad admitted being proud of Mohammed attacks since, "He fought until the end. I think the world of [Osama] Bin Laden."[115]

Abdelkader was charged with complicity in his brother's crimes, as was Mohammed's friend Fettah Malki. In November 2017, Abdelkader was cleared of being an accomplice in his brother's 2011 attacks. However, Abdelkader was convicted of participation in a terror network and sentenced to twenty years in prison. French authorities were aware of Abdelkader's radicalism since 2006. Malki admitted providing Mohammed with a machine gun and bulletproof vest. Malki was sentenced to fourteen years in prison for supplying those items to Mohammed.[116]

Mohammed's mother, Zoulika Aziri, and father divorced when he was five. Her second marriage was to a convicted al Qaeda recruiter in Iraq, Sabri Essid. Essid planned to sue the French police for shooting and killing Mohammed during the standoff. Essid alleged that French authorities could have used gas to incapacitate Mohammed, rather than using deadly force.

Sometimes a family claims to have been unaware of the impending attack of their kin. Whether that denial is truthful is based on the facts at hand. Cherif Kouachi and his brother Said attacked the *Charlie Hebdo* office in Paris in January 2015. The siblings killed twelve people during their strike on behalf of al Qaeda in the Arabian Peninsula. Cherif's wife told French authorities that she was surprised by her husband's actions.

Amedy Coulibaly, a coconspirator of the Kouachi brothers, attacked a kosher supermarket in Paris, killing four civilians. Coulibaly's family denounced his actions. Also, they claimed that the incident had nothing to do with the Muslim faith. In contrast, several days prior to the supermarket attack, Coulibaly's common-law wife, Hayat Boumeddiene, made her way to an ISIS-controlled area of Syria. Subsequently, Hayat was considered to be one of Coulibaly's accomplices. Moreover, she was suspected of appearing in a 2015 ISIS propaganda video. Too, Hayat was lauded in an ISIS publication, *Dabiq*.

In November 2011, Ibrahim al-Akari drove a vehicle into pedestrians near a Jerusalem light rail station, killing one and injuring thirteen. Ibrahim's son Hamza said he was very pleased by his father's actions. Ibrahim's brother Musa was part of a Hamas terror cell that killed an Israeli border police officer in 1992.

Family members may be reluctant to inform authorities about the apparent radicalization of their clan because of a sense of loyalty, concern about possible criminal prosecution, fear that the family will be stigmatized with a purported connection to extremism, or the belief that they can dissuade the radicalized individual without the assistance of outside persons or organizations.

Ultimately, a family member may reach out to government authorities if their efforts to disrupt the radicalization path prove unsuccessful. Likewise, this path may occur out for fear for the safety of the non-radicalized kin. After all, family members run the risk of being victimized by a terrorist in the family.

Attempts to discourage a family member's radicalization may prove successful to varying degrees. Still, the longer the kin is immersed in extremist activities, the more extended and arduous it will be to remove them from that path. Alternatively, such interventions may turn out unsuccessful. In case of such failure, the kin may aid a terrorist group, participate in a terror attack, or travel abroad to fight with a terror group.

To undermine extremism within family units, family members must observe behavior that supports extremism. In parallel with efforts to combat radicalization within the family, friends, coworkers, and other acquaintances may choose to intervene in this regard. Assessing a person's radicalization and how best to dislodge him from this situation is not a simple task. Thereby, outreach to professionals in counter-radicalization, rehabilitation, and mental status may (sometimes) prove to be the most appropriate initial path.

Condemnation

Condemnation of the planned or past terrorist actions of family members is varied. Such judgments have appeared throughout the world, encompassing terrorists of all ideological persuasions. From fall 2007, Abdulhakim Mujahid Muhammad (formerly Carlos Bledsoe) spent sixteen months in Yemen. Afterward, he was deported to the United States for immigration violations. Bledsoe claimed to have been influenced by Anwar al-Awlaki and even claimed to have met him.

In June 2009, Bledsoe opened fire at a military recruitment center in Little Rock, Arkansas, killing one and injuring one. Bledsoe, the radicalized Muslim convert, said his jihadi attack was warranted because of US military actions abroad. In January 2010, he pleaded guilty to one count of capital murder and attempted murder plus ten counts of unlawful discharge of a firearm.

Bledsoe's father, Melvin, denounced his son's attack. Melvin also expressed concern about Americans being radicalized by jihadism. Testifying before the House Committee on Homeland Security in March 2011, the elder Bledsoe stated, "We are losing our American babies—our children are in danger."[117] In a move toward reconciliation, Melvin Bledsoe and Daris Long, the father of Andy Long, whom Carlos killed in 2009, produced a documentary, *Losing Our Sons*. The video addresses the circumstances surrounding the attack in Little Rock. Also, the movie underscores the families' premonitions about jihadi recruitment on US soil.

In September 2009, Omar Hammami, a US citizen and former resident of Daphne, Alabama, was indicted on several charges of providing material support to terrorists and a foreign terrorist organization, al-Shabaab. At one point, Hammami was on the FBI's most wanted terrorist list. But despite being a well-known al-Shabaab propagandist, Hammami appeared to have had a falling out with the group's leadership. The group ordered Hammami's assassination in September 2013.

Hammami's mother, Debra, was Christian, and his father, Shafik, a Muslim immigrant from Yemen. Omar's parents were disheartened and saddened by the radical path that their son followed. Given the reality that his son had become a terrorist, Shafik remarked, "He chose the path that he did, and I do not approve of it. But, there is nothing I can do to change it."[118] Upon learning of Omar's death, his father lamented, "My own judgment is that he had good intentions to fulfill his Islamic principles but was deceived by al-Shabab and their murderous ways."[119]

In December 2008, Major Nidal Malik Hasan, a US Army officer and psychiatrist, killed thirteen and wounded over thirty others, during a mass shooting attack at Fort Hood, Texas. Hasan communicated with and was influenced by Anwar al-Awlaki. Hasan justified his attack by claiming the US military was at war with Islam. In August 2013, Hasan was convicted on murder and attempted murder charges arising from the attack. Later that month, Major Hasan was sentenced to death. The day after the attack, Hasan's family, through his cousin Nader, condemned the attack, stating, "We are mortified and there is no justification, whatsoever, for what happened...We cannot explain, nor do we excuse or understand, what happened."[120]

In June 2009, James von Brunn, a Holocaust denier with neo-Nazi and Christian Identity ties, shot and killed a security guard, Stephen Johns, at the Holocaust Museum in Washington, DC. Von Brunn, who ran the racist website the Holy Western Empire, had served some eight years for trying to kidnap Federal Reserve Board members in 1981.

Von Brunn's son Erik condemned his father's attack and was remorseful about the death of Mr. Johns. After the shooting, Erik indicated his father "should not be remembered as a brave man or a hero, but a coward unable to come to grips with the fact he threw his and his families lives away for an ideology that fostered sadness and anguish."[121] In a March 2012 interview, Erik lamented that his father's actions had caused Erik to lose his fiancée and work prospects.

In February 2010, Joe Stack committed suicide by crashing his single-engine plane into an office building in Austin, Texas. Stack targeted the edifice because it housed some two hundred Internal Revenue Service employees. The incident resulted in the loss of IRS manager Vernon Hunter and thirteen injuries. Stack, who espoused virulent anti-IRS precepts, published a manifesto online before his attack. After the incident, Stack's wife, Sheryl, released a statement stating, "Words cannot adequately express my sorrow or the sympathy I feel for everyone affected by this unimaginable tragedy."[122] Hunter's wife, Valerie, sued Sheryl, alleging that Stack's wife was negligent. More specifically, Hunter's widow claimed Sheryl should have known her husband was a threat to others. The night before Stack's attack, Sheryl had taken her daughter to a hotel as she was troubled by her husband's behavior.

In March 2017, Khalid Masood killed five and injured fifty others while driving over pedestrians at Westminster Bridge in London. Afterward, Masood stabbed to death a policeman near the Houses of Parliament. Masood was shot and killed at the scene.

A week before his attack, Masood phoned a family member that there would be news of his death. This development, Masood claimed, would be a happy occasion as he would be in paradise. Masood's mother, Janet Ajao, said of her son's onslaught, "I do not condone his actions or support the beliefs he held that led him to committing this atrocity."[123] Masood's attacks appear to have been prompted by his support of jihad. British authorities had investigated his association with a British jihadi cell several years earlier.

Some parents are unaware of the radicalization their children are experiencing. For instance, Katharina Wenzel, whose sixteen-year-old daughter Linda left Pulsnitz, Germany, to marry a jihadi fighter in Syria, noted in July 2016, "I am devastated by the fact that she was apparently completely brainwashed and persuaded to leave the country by someone and that she managed to hide it from me."[124] In July 2017, Linda was apprehended with some two dozen ISIS female members in Mosul, Iraq. In September 2017, Iraqi prosecutors initiated criminal charges against Linda. She faces the death penalty for her collaboration with ISIS.

Family Members Killing Other Kin in Support of Terror

In October 2014, Lisa Borch, a fifteen-year-old, and her Iraqi-immigrant boyfriend, Bakhtiar Mohammed Abdulla, a twenty-nine-year-old, stabbed to death her mother, Tina Römer Holtegaard, in Kvissel, Denmark. The night before the multiple stabbing, Borch and Abdulla watched hours of ISIS beheading videos. Borch and Abdulla were convicted of the murder and sentenced to nine and thirteen years in prison, respectively. The pair had planned to travel to Syria and join ISIS. Through an earlier relationship with a married Swedish man, Borch had become engrossed in radical Islam. In court testimony, Borch's stepfather, Jens Holtegaard, said Borch often spoke glowingly of ISIS and its brutality.

In January 2016, an ISIS fighter, Ali Saqr al-Qasem, shot and killed his mother, Lena al-Qasem, in a public execution in Raqqa, Syria. Ali carried out his mother's punishment—death—for the crime of apostasy. Ali informed ISIS superiors that Lena planned to leave Raqqa and asked Ali to join her.

In June 2016, twenty-year-old twin brothers, Khaled and Saleh al-Oraini stabbed their father, mother, and twenty-two-year-old brother in Riyadh, Saudi Arabia. Their mother died of her injuries. She had objected to the twins' plans to travel to Syria and fight on behalf of the Islamic State. Saudi authorities captured the twin brothers as they tried to escape along the Saudi-Yemeni border.

Punishing Families

A policy of destroying the family home of a terrorist who conducts an attack has been implemented as a deterrent. This approach was used in Israel in some circumstances until 2005.[125] Subsequently, this tool was used sparingly, although as recently as 2014, on the home of a terrorist who killed five people at a synagogue in Jerusalem was destroyed.[126] In some cases, the family is well aware of their kin's participation in terrorism, while at other times, there is scant or no knowledge of such involvement. It is not clear whether this response encourages terrorism or deters it.[127]

Two types of home demolitions took place. According to one study, precautionary demolitions, occurring prior to an attack, were shown to increase potential terrorist acts by almost 49 percent. In contrast, punitive demolitions were shown to be an effective deterrent. They reduced overall terrorist acts by up to 15 percent.[128]

In some cases, the Israeli Supreme Court denied the government's request to conduct a home demolition, noting that a family could not have had knowledge of their kin's terrorist plans as he had not lived in the family home for a long period.[129] House demolitions "date back to a 1945 British Mandate emergency regulation in pre-state Palestine that allowed the British military to confiscate and destroy any home used to discharge a weapon or any home used by a person who violated military law."[130]

Analogously, in the past, Israel expelled the families of some terrorists from Israel, including the West Bank, to Gaza. This, too, was undertaken with the goal of undermining the attractiveness of participating in terrorism.[131]

In a December 2015 interview, then-presidential candidate Donald Trump said, "The other thing with the terrorists is you have to take out their families, when you get these terrorists, you have to take out their families. They care about their lives, don't kid yourself. When they say they don't care about their lives, you have to take out their families."[132]

Conclusion

This chapter presented instances of family terror networks as well as baseline principles relevant to this form of extremism. Additionally, this section dealt with family terror networks exhibited in: patriarchs, couples, those searching for love, the role of overseas travel, terror-organized crime nexus, investigations, prosecution of kin, nonprofits, expanding the network, and financial benefits to family members of terrorists.

Other subjects shared included: kin killing extremists, concerns about a child's behavior, family members' knowledge of kin's terrorist activities, family preventing terrorist activities, attempting to prevent the death of a terrorist, family supporting and condemning activities of kin, and family members killing other kin to support terror. This chapter demonstrates that family affiliated terrorism comprises many types of behaviors and activities that affect the frequency and scope of this breed of terrorism.

CHAPTER 3

Case Studies Involving Family Terror Networks

Introduction

There are many examples of family affiliated extremism, ranging from participation in extremist groups and encouraging radicalism to providing support to advance a particular ideology to undertaking or calling for terror attacks or hate crimes. The case studies covered in this chapter comprise variants of family terror networks, encompassing parents and their children, spouses, siblings, cousins, and multiple other family members. By presenting these cases, the reader will better appreciate the range of such instances in the United States and abroad.

Fathers and Sons

The cases presented here include Hamid and Umer Hayat and the former's participation in a terror training camp in Pakistan. Next, Adnan el Shukrijumah's role in al Qaeda overseas is covered with a notation of his father's (Gulshair) links to convicted jihadists in the United States. Subsequently, Ku Klux Klan leader Raymond Foster's murder of a recruit and his son's assistance after that incident are covered. Later, the activities and deaths of the sovereign citizen tandem Jerry (father) and Joseph (son) Kane following a shootout with police are addressed. Afterward, the roles of sovereign citizen and militia extremists Bruce (father) and Joshua (son) Turnidge are related. A similarly ideologically inclined pairing Wade (father) and Christopher (son) Lay show the involvement of this family network in conducting a crime that was envisioned to fund future violent attacks.

These cases all illustrate the different influences and roles that fathers and sons can play in family affiliated terrorism: from funding and supporting terror abroad to disseminating extremism at home that pushes a child to ultimately embrace terrorism, including kinetic attacks against police, to supporting and participation in other ideologically linked crimes.

Hayat

Hamid Hayat emigrated from Pakistan with his father, Umer. Hamid left California to obtain terror training abroad. Between October 2003 and November 2004, Hamid attended a Jaish-e-Mohammed (JeM) jihadist training camp in the Balakot area of Pakistan. Umer funded Hamid's travel and gave him other monies while his son was abroad. In May 2005, Hamid told US law enforcement the training facility he attended offered paramilitary training (weapons, explosives, hand-to-hand combat) and classroom instruction (ideological rhetoric detailing opposition to the United States). Hamid advised his interrogators that he asked to come to the United States to carry out a jihadi mission. He was arrested the following month.

In July 2006, Hamid was found guilty of providing material support or resources to terrorists and giving untruthful statements to the FBI in matters related to international/domestic terrorism. Hamid provided himself as "material support" by attending a jihadi training camp in Pakistan. He intended to return to the United States and conduct jihad. Hamid was sentenced to twenty-four years in prison. Umer pleaded guilty to lying to federal agents and served about one year. But for the father's financial support, perhaps his son would have never received terror training or would have done so at a later date.

Shukrijumah[133]

Adnan el Shukrijumah, a Saudi-born naturalized US citizen and senior al Qaeda operative, was killed in Pakistan in 2014. He was suspected of being involved in several al Qaeda plots in the United States, Panama, Norway, and the United Kingdom. In the late 1990s, Adnan allegedly received terror training in Afghanistan.

Adnan's father, Gulshair, was at one point a translator for Sheikh Abdel Rahman, the inspirational leader of the 1993 World Trade Center attack. In 1996, Rahman was convicted of terror plots in New York, including the 1993 incident. Gulshair was a character witness for Clement Rodney Hampton-El. Hampton was convicted with Rahman in relation to New York City (NYC) terror plots. Hampton also served as a mujahedin in Afghanistan.

Although he was not accused of terror activity, Gulshair's links with Rahman and Hampton-El raised concerns of his knowledge of terror plots. Gulshair had received religious instruction in Egypt and Saudi Arabia before becoming a missionary for the Saudi government in the Caribbean. Later, Gulshair moved to the United States. Given Gulshair's closeness to well-known terrorists, it is reasonable to presume that Adnan was exposed to jihadist ideologies at home.

Foster

In November 2008, Cynthia Lynch came across Raymond Foster's small faction of the Ku Klux Klan in Louisiana (Bogalusa Sons of Dixie Knights) online. She interacted with Foster regarding her interest in traveling from Oklahoma to join his group. After taking part in an initiation, Lynch had a change of heart and chose to leave the group. Not taking it well, Foster shot and killed Lynch in Sun, Louisiana. In 2010, Raymond Foster pleaded guilty to the second-degree murder of Cynthia Lynch. Foster was sentenced to life in prison.

Foster's son Shane, who was present during Lynch's murder, pleaded guilty to obstruction of justice. Shane burned evidence and hid Lynch's body. Shane was sentenced to three years in prison. Two other persons present at the killing pleaded guilty to charges ranging from providing false information to obstruction of justice. Raymond's influence over his son was clear as Shane participated in various Klan functions organized by his father. Additionally, Raymond's wife complained that her husband forced her kids to attend Klan events, including initiations of new members.

Kane

Jerry Kane and his son, Joseph, were enticed by sovereign citizen ideology. Jerry Kane had a multiyear history of questioning governmental authority, including verbal threats to judges and law enforcement. Based in Forest, Ohio, for several years, Jerry Kane received over two dozen citations from police there, including citations for having junk cars and high grass at his home. According to Forest Police Chief Howard Rickabaugh, Jerry Kane threatened him: "The next time you come on my property, you're a dead man."[134] Kane called a judge who sentenced him to community service "a treasonous piece of garbage."[135] In an April 2003 court filing, Jerry Kane declared himself a sovereign man, claiming immunity from government authority.

The following year, Kane was sentenced to community service for not wearing a seat belt and not having a license plate. He demanded from the judge who sentenced him $100,000 per day in gold or silver for each day of the community service. From 2006 until their deaths, Jerry and his son traveled across the United States giving workshops on how to remove mortgage obligations using sovereign citizen tactics.

In April 2010, the Kanes were stopped at a checkpoint in Carrizozo, New Mexico. Jerry Kane was arrested for driving with a suspended/revoked license and concealing his identity. Jerry spent three days in jail before posting bond. One month later, Jerry wrote a letter to the arresting officer, requesting $80,000 for use of his name in the arrest report.

In May 2010, Joseph Kane shot and killed West Memphis, Arkansas, policemen Sergeant Brandon Paudert and Officer Bill

Evans during a traffic stop. The Kanes were killed later that day when confronted by police in a Walmart parking lot. Incidentally, the minivan the Kanes used in the West Memphis incident was traced back to the Ohio-based House of God's Prayer, where Jerry Kane claimed he was the pastor. The church's former pastor, Harold Ray Redfeairn, was an Aryan Nation leader who tried to kill a law enforcement officer in 1993.

According to Jerry's friends and family, Joseph was isolated from children his age and others, as he was homeschooled and "was exposed to nothing but Jerry. [Joseph]...has been exposed to a lifetime of invective and rants and pseudo-legal stuff."[136] Joseph's grandmother, Dianne Reustle, remarked her grandson would have met a different fate had he been away from his father's influence.

Here again, the father greatly influenced his son to support extremist ideology and participate in a kinetic attack aligned in support of the tenets. The fact that Joseph was a teenager when he killed the two police officers underscores the sway that a parent can have over a child's support of political violence.

Turnridge

Bruce Turnidge and his son Joshua had a complex and turbulent relationship, with disagreements over business and personal issues while sharing common perspectives and working together. Bruce exposed Joshua to an adoration of guns and a strong animus toward the federal government and police. Bruce was quoted as saying Timothy McVeigh, the mastermind of the 1995 Oklahoma City terrorist attack, was his hero, while both supported the attack. Prosecutors also alleged that the Turnidges held racist beliefs and fantasied about "building bombs, robbing banks, and starting a militia."[137] The pair held anti-government and militia views.

In December 2008, Woodburn, Oregon, Police Department Captain Tom Tennant and Oregon State Trooper Bill Hakim were killed trying to dismantle a bomb that was left at the West Coast Bank in Woodburn. Law enforcement investigators quickly tied the bombing to the Turnidges. The father-son team had placed the bomb at a bank in a botched extortion plot. Joshua's prepaid cell phone was found at the scene. Police deduced Joshua's involvement as the purchase of the phone had been caught on a Walmart surveillance tape. The Turnidges sought to use the proceeds to buttress a failing biodiesel business they owned. Several years before, Bruce's onion farm in Nevada had been foreclosed. These two business failings spurred the extortion plan.

In December 2010, a jury found the Turnidges guilty on eighteen counts, including aggravated murder, attempted aggravated murder, and assault. Additionally, the jury recommended the imposition of the death penalty for the aggravated murder conviction. The following month, Judge Tom Hart sentenced them to death and two consecutive ten-year terms in relation to the attempted murder charges, as two individuals were hurt in the blast. In May 2016, the Oregon Supreme Court upheld the convictions and death sentences of the Turnidges.

Lay

In May 2004, Wade Lay, then forty-four-years-old, and his son Christopher, twenty-years-old at the time, tried to rob the MidFirst Bank in Tulsa, Oklahoma. During the foiled incident, they shot and killed a bank security guard, Kenneth Anderson, who wounded the assailants. In 2005, a jury found them guilty of first-degree murder and attempted bank robbery. Wade was sentenced to death for the murder, while his son received a life sentence without parole. Both were also sentenced to twenty-five years in prison for the attempted bank robbery. Christopher's life sentence was upheld in 2006. Wade's death sentence was affirmed in 2008.

In planning the bank robbery, the Lays envisioned garnering funds to purchase weapons, which they would use to "avenge the United States government's attacks on Ruby Ridge and the Branch Davidians. The Lays believed that the United States government had become tyrannical and that they had to start a patriotic revolution as was done by America's founding fathers."[138] Wade said that he "wanted to spark a revolution. That is the truth. I've stood in the face of tyranny. I will continue to do so."[139] Moreover, Wade characterized the need for "strong convictions of the necessity to engage in defensive measures to protect himself and his family from tyranny."[140]

Husbands and Wives

The examples of spouses involved in terrorism shared here include a spectrum of extremist ideologies from jihadism to sovereign citizen and militia perspectives. The participants include a couple arrested at an airport on their way to the Islamic State (Jaelyn Young and Muhammad Dakhlalla). Next, a couple (Michael Wolfe and Jordan Furr) with their young children who had similar intentions is covered. Afterward, the case of jihadist spouses Paul and Nadia Rockwood, convicted of lying in relation to a terror investigation, is presented.

Later, the case of Zachary Chesser and Proscovia Nzabanita, who were involved in jihadist travel plans among other crimes, is addressed. Subsequently, the roles of jihadist Keonna Thomas and her husband, Shawn Parson, are highlighted, including her conviction in trying to provide material support to ISIS and Parson's death in Syria.

Lonnie and Karen Vernon mark a militia and sovereign citizen pair who planned the assassinations of government officials in Alaska. Then, the case of common-law sovereign citizen spouses George Sibley, Jr. and Lynda Lyon-Block is shared.

Young/Dakhlalla

Jaelyn Young and Muhammad Dakhlalla had grand plans for their new life in the so-called Islamic State. Young resolved to aid injured ISIS fighters. Jaelyn also informed an undercover agent she was good in chemistry and math, which might aid the group. Young, too, hoped to raise Islamic State cubs (children). Dakhlalla, with competency in computers and media, expected to serve as a warrior or in media relations for the group.

The couple met while students at Mississippi State University and married in an Islamic ceremony in Mississippi in June 2015. Jaelyn was a convert to Islam while Muhammad had been raised as one. Both were US citizens. Jaelyn's father was a policeman and Navy veteran. Muhammad's father was a local Muslim cleric.

The FBI took notice of Jaelyn's social media presence supportive of ISIS in May 2015. In a disturbing post, Jaelyn's expressed her joy and support for Muhammad Youssef Abdulazeez's 2015 jihadist shootings in Chattanooga, which killed five military personnel. Later, FBI undercover operatives, purported to be ISIS recruiters, connected with Jaelyn and Muhammad. These government officials facilitated the couple's plans to live in Dawlah (ISIS-controlled territory).

The couple was arrested in August 2015 at a Columbus, Mississippi, airport. From Columbus, they had planned a trip designed to get them to Syria. By March 2016, the couple had pleaded guilty to conspiracy to provide material support to ISIS. Muhammad was sentenced to eight years. Jaelyn received four additional years, as she was perceived as being more fervent than her husband.

In an interview after his sentencing, Muhammad argued that he was blinded by love: "And, you know, that love can ultimately...blind out your intelligence, your reasoning. I believe that. I mean, without that love there, I don't believe I would be here today, with my charge and talking to you today...I wouldn't have even considered it at all."[141] Both individuals appeared remorseful regarding their intentions to join ISIS. Jaelyn said she was ashamed of her actions. Muhammad condemned the group and its activities. Still, they had planned to join the group and assist it in military activities as fighters or supporters.

Wolfe/Furr

In July 2013, Michael Wolfe concluded he wanted his family to live in Syria under ISIS control. His wife, Jordan Furr, was apprehensive about such a move, especially since the couple had two young children. During an August 2013 meeting with an undercover FBI employee, Furr said her husband "just wants to hop into Syria. He's just ready to die for his deen [religion]. He's ready to die for someone; for something."[142]

In January 2014, Wolfe told two undercover FBI employees and his wife that the family did not seek travel to Syria for "a better work environment or cheaper rent."[143] In the ensuing month, Wolfe watched videos on foreign fighters with his wife and an undercover FBI employee. In April 2014, Wolfe told undercover employees he was doing "physical preparations for jihad to include martial arts, running, and Cross-Fit."[144] This training would prepare him for when he contributed to "the concert."[145] (That term signified taking part in the Syrian jihad.)

Furr's premonitions about her husband's plans were justified. In June 2014, Wolfe and his family entered Houston's George Bush International Airport to take a flight to Toronto. From there, the family intended to travel to Iceland and then Denmark. In Denmark, Wolfe proposed to meet a man tasked with assisting the family with travel to Turkey and then Syria. Authorities arrested Wolfe as he tried to board a plane for the first leg of the trip. In June 2015, Wolfe pleaded guilty to seeking to give material support to ISIS. Later that month, he was sentenced to nearly seven years in prison.

After Wolfe pleaded guilty, Furr insisted that the undercover employees—a pair portraying themselves as husband and wife—had pushed her husband into the plot. "My husband never came to him with any idea on how to do anything. It was like this guy, you know, everything was his plan, everything was his idea, everything was his...master plan. And my husband was just a pawn."[146] Neither Furr nor her children face any criminal charges.

Rockwood

Paul Rockwood Jr. served in the US Navy. In December 2001, Paul converted to Islam and attended a Falls Church, Virginia, mosque, Dar al-Arqam. At the mosque, Rockwood was exposed to the radical teachings of Ali al-Timimi. Al-Timimi was sentenced to life in prison for inspiring others to fight in Afghanistan on behalf of the Taliban. Also, Paul was exposed to the perspectives of Anwar al-Awlaki.

In 2006, Paul and his wife, Nadia, moved to Alaska. There, Paul continued his interest in jihad. He visited websites that discussed making explosives and detonating bombs. In late 2009, Paul discussed using mail bombs and possibly killing targets by shooting them in the head. He also presented recommendations about where to place explosives to kill people in simultaneous attacks. The attacks were anticipated to occur in 2011.

The FBI received a tip about Paul's suspicious activities. Paul interacted with an undercover Alaska state trooper and discussed assassinations to avenge the deaths of Muslims at the hands of the US government. The two discussed setting up a list of people in Alaska and elsewhere whom they intended to murder. Paul's wife carried a list of fifteen persons who should be assassinated. The intended victims were all based outside Alaska. Around this period, Paul and his wife discussed leaving Alaska for the United Kingdom.

In April 2010, the Rockwoods admitted misrepresenting facts to federal agents in relation to a terrorism investigation. Paul was sentenced to eight years in prison. Nadia received five years' probation.

Chesser/Nzabanita

In October 2010, American Zachary Chesser pleaded guilty to charges of communicating threats against the writers of the *South Park* TV show, soliciting jihadists to squander police resources by placing suspicious packages in public places, and attempting to provide material support to al-Shabaab. Chesser admitted that he twice tried to travel to Somalia for the purpose of joining al-Shabaab and engaging in jihad as a foreign fighter. During his second such try, Chesser brought along his infant son as a cover to avoid possible suspicion.

Chesser also promoted an online "Open Source Jihad," whereby he provided operational tips to would-be jihadists and links to the screening manuals of the Transportation Security Administration (TSA), among other documents. In February 2011, Chesser received twenty-five years in prison.

Chesser's wife, Proscovia Nzabanita, was the daughter of a Ugandan diplomat in the United States. Nzabanita also supported jihadi tenets. In November 2010, she pleaded guilty to lying to a federal agent who was investigating her husband on terrorism-related activities. Nzabanita was required to return to Uganda. Nzabanita had joined Chesser in his first failed try to join al-Shabaab. She could not take part in the second try as her mother hid her passport.

Ultimately, Chesser's mother, Barbara, sought custody of his son, whose mother is Nzabanita. This development occurred after the FBI revealed the boy could not be brought to Jordan to be with his mother. Barbara was granted custody when a judge deemed the father and mother to be unfit parents.

Thomas/Parson

Keona Thomas, a thirty-year-old mother of two daughters from Philadelphia, Pennsylvania, referred to herself as "Young Lioness," and "Fatayat Al Khilafah," meaning "girl of the caliphate."[147] Thomas was very active on Twitter. She often disseminated pro-ISIS and jihadi messages. She tweeted, "When you're a mujahid [martyr], your death becomes a wedding."[148] Additionally, she communicated with jihadi fighters in Somalia and Syria as well as a Jamaica-based jihadi cleric.

Thomas sought to travel to Syria. Once there, she hoped to become a martyr for ISIS. In March 2015 she purchased a flight from Philadelphia to Barcelona, Spain. From Spain, Thomas intended to fly to Turkey. From Turkey, Thomas planned to take a bus to Syria.

Thomas developed an online romance with a Syria-based fighter, Shawn Joel Parson. Parson was a Trinidadian who had once lived in the United States. The pair later married in an online ceremony via Skype. Parson was killed in a coalition-led drone attack in Syria in September 2015.

In April 2015, Thomas was charged with attempting to give material support to ISIS. She pleaded guilty to the aforementioned charges a year later. In September 2017, Thomas was sentenced to eight years in prison. Here again, we witness the leverage of an already radicalized spouse.

Vernon

In January 2013, Lonnie Vernon, a member of the militia group Alaska Peacemakers Militia (APM), was sentenced to nearly twenty-six years in prison after pleading guilty to conspiracy to murder federal officials and several federal firearms crimes. In June 2012, Vernon was found guilty of these charges in an investigation that included APM's founder Francis Cox and APM member Coleman Barney. An informant recorded the three conspiring to kill government officials. The impetus for the plan was to avenge the prospective arrest of Cox.

In August 2012, Lonnie and his wife, Karen, admitted their guilt in a February 2011 conspiracy to kill Chief US District Court Judge Ralph Beistline and an internal revenue agent. The Vernons, who were over $165,000 behind on their taxes, supported sovereign doctrine. They felt the government could not force them to pay taxes. They obtained the addresses of Judge Beistline's family and provided directions to an informant. The Vernons were arrested after they bought two hand grenades and a pistol with a silencer from the informant. The Vernons planned on using those items to kill Judge Beistline and the internal revenue agent.

Thinking they might be killed during a confrontation with police, the couple left friends and family a letter showing their defiance to the government: "We will not freely give our home, land, and personal property to this tyrant, nor will we die cowards, licking their jackboots."[149] Likewise, the following description of the couple's home is illustrative of their anti-government mindset: at "the Vernons' home, loaded weapons were found at nearly every entrance and window, hostile signs hung nailed to tree trunks and on stakes at the entrance of their graded driveway. The signs warned that trespassers would be shot before any questions were asked. Long rants against the government and the IRS were part of some of those signs."[150]

Karen was sentenced to twelve years in prison. Karen's lawyer claimed her husband was the instigator of the plot. Whatever the truth, the couple planned the murderous plots and suffered the consequences.

Sibley and Lyon Block

George Sibley Jr. and his common-law wife, Lynda Lyon Block, shared anti-government tenets with others through a newsletter and other avenues. The newsletter was funded by a $20,000 inheritance Sibley had received. Their radicalism was manifested in the destruction of their birth certificates, driver's licenses, and car registrations, as they claimed federal and state law did not require such intrusions. Such activities are now characterized as core sovereign citizen actions.

Following a confrontation with Lyon Block's ex-husband in August 1993, the couple was convicted of felony assault charges. Following allegations police were going to arrest them for failing to attend a sentencing hearing, the two took her children and drove to a Georgia-based safe house run by the patriot movement. In October 1993, the family was traveling to Mobile, Alabama, where they stopped at the Walmart so Lyon Black could make a call at a pay phone.

Officer Motley approached Sibley's car after a customer saw Lyon Block's boy in the car mouthing the words "Help me." Motley asked Sibley for his driver's license but was rebuffed; Sibley said he had no connections with the state. Likewise, Sibley refused Motley's request that he move away from the car. Sibley then shot Motley. Shortly afterward, Lyon Block shot Motley. After killing Motley, the two were stopped at a roadblock, where they surrendered. Their car contained three handguns, two semiautomatic rifles, an M-14 rifle, and more than 1,500 rounds of ammunition.

As there was a question as to who fired the fatal shot, both were prosecuted for murder, and both were convicted. Subsequently, their death sentences were carried out. At their trials, they claimed to be acting in self-defense against an illegal arrest since Sergeant Motley did not have the authority and was in his position illegally. Sibley said that Motley's interaction was a "false arrest. And I just don't buy that whatsoever. That is a clear trespass against me."[151] Lyon Block claimed, "I acted instinctively. I defended my husband."[152]

These instances of family affiliated tied to multiple ideologies encompassing distinct plots are merely snapshots of how such extremism is exhibited in some marriages. The natural bond and commonality of purpose ingrained in marital relations are accentuated when the pair ultimately becomes zealous followers of radical doctrines.

Siblings

Next, examples of siblings participating in terror activities are shared. The frequency of sibling-linked terror occurs due to the intrinsic bonds and influences that a sibling relationship can foster. First, the international terror plot of four Khayat brothers is shared. Second, the collaboration of convicted jihadist terrorists Raees and Sheheryar Alam Qazi is examined. Third, the terror plans of brothers Muhammad Ibrahim and Ahmed Ibrahim Bilal as well as their coconspirators are explained. Fourth, the al Qaeda in the Arabian Peninsula–linked terror network involving brothers Yahya Farooq and Ibrahim Zubair Mohammad as well as others is recounted. Fifth, the case of two sets of brothers in a Minnesota-based ISIS-aligned cell is revealed.

Sixth, the roles of jihadi-inspired Boston Marathon bombers and brothers Tamerlan and Dzhokhar Tsarnaev are covered. Seventh, instances of brothers conducting terror attacks in unison or at different targets (e.g., Mohamed and Omar Maha in Morocco) are presented. Eighth, Karim and Foued Mohamed-Aggad, along with Hammad and Hassan Munshi, mark iterations of siblings traveling abroad for terror training or plans for terrorist activities at home. Ninth, the case of teenage Moroccan twin sisters Imane and Sanae al Ghariss who intended to conduct suicide bombings along with a friend is described.

Brothers

Khayats[153]

In July 2017, several Australian brothers of Lebanese descent planned to rupture an Etihad flight from Sydney, Australia, to the United Arab Emirates (UAE) with over four hundred persons onboard. The three jihadist Khayat brothers—Amer, Mahmoud, and Khaled—and their Raqqa, Syria–based ISIS commander brother, Tarek, hatched an elaborate plan. They decided Amer would conduct a suicide attack by detonating luggage containing an explosives-packed Barbie doll and meat mincer. The reason for designating the Etihad flight was to punish Australia and the United Arab Emirates for its presence in the anti-ISIS military coalition.

The Khayats' plans failed when Amer tried to check in the explosives. Airline personnel told Amer his baggage was fifteen pounds overweight. Rather than electing to remove other items, Amer left the explosives with one of his brothers. He boarded the flight, which landed in the United Arab Emirates. Afterward, Amer took a connecting flight to Lebanon. Once there, Amer raised the suspicions of Lebanese authorities. Amer insisted he was traveling to Beirut for his wedding. However, Amer had given the same reason for travel on earlier trips. Ultimately, Lebanese authorities learned from Amer that his brother Tarek had devised the terror plot. With that admission, Amer was arrested and held at Roumieh prison in Beirut.

After Lebanese officials informed Australian authorities of the airplane plot (British and American intelligence had also informed Australian officials about the plot), Mahmoud and Khaled were detained in Australia for preparing or planning a terrorist strike. The brothers had also designed a hydrogen sulfide–laden improvised explosive device to detonate in a public place in Australia. ISIS operatives had shipped military-grade explosives by cargo freight from Turkey to Australia. These items were to be used in the failed airport bombing and theoretical gas attack.

Besides the arrest of the Australia-based Khayats, another familial group was taken into police custody in relation to the airplane plot. Khaled Merhi and his son Abdul were originally held as coconspirators in the plot. Afterward, Khaled was charged with possessing a prohibited weapon (a homemade Taser). A pre-existing terror nexus existed with the Merhis. Their relative Ahmed Merhi was an Australian who joined ISIS in Syria in 2014.

Qazi

Jihadist brothers Raees and Sheheryar Alam Qazi, who were naturalized US citizens from Pakistan, had different responsibilities in their terror plot in the United States. Raees intended to undertake an attack in New York City to avenge the deaths of Afghans killed during US drone strikes and obtained terror training in Pakistan. He considered a suicide attack or the use of a remote-control device.

Sheheryar, who was aware of his younger brother's plans, had explosives-related materials at his home and provided Raees with money and housing. US government authorities knew of Raees's radicalization since his anti-US comments in 2010 to a security guard on his departure from the United States to Pakistan. In March 2015, the brothers pleaded guilty to conspiring to give material support to terrorists, among other charges. In June 2015, Raees and Sheheryar were sentenced to twenty and thirty years in prison, respectively.

Bilal

Brothers Muhammad Ibrahim and Ahmed Ibrahim Bilal were part of the seven-member Oregon-based terror cabal that called itself Katibat Al-Mawt ("The Squad of Death"). During summer 2001, they undertook martial arts training and firearms practice so they could carry out jihadi attacks in Afghanistan or elsewhere. At the request of one of their coconspirators, Habis al Saoub, the brothers planned to travel to Afghanistan. In October 2001, the brothers traveled to China, seeking to enter Pakistan, and then Afghanistan.

Before moving to Oregon as teenagers, the Bilals lived in Sudan and Saudi Arabia. In Oregon, the Bilals lived with their aunt, while their parents lived in Saudi Arabia. The brothers had several dead-end jobs and failed marriages. In September 2003, the Bilals pleaded guilty to conspiracy to aid the Taliban and to a weapons offense. Ahmed, the elder brother, received a ten-year prison sentence. Muhammad was sentenced to eight years.

Also implicated in the plot with the Bilals was Jeffrey Battle, another member in the Bilal's cabal. In November 2003, Battle pleaded guilty to conspiracy to levy war against the United States. The following month, Battle was sentenced to eighteen years in prison. In September 2003, Battle's ex-wife, Martinique Lewis, pleaded guilty to money laundering in connection with Battle's travel plans to Afghanistan. In December 2003, she was sentenced to three years in prison.

Mohammad

Yahya Farooq Mohammad, his brother Ibrahim Zubair, and two coconspirators colluded to raise funds and provide other items to terrorists. More specifically, they provided equipment to the leader of al Qaeda in the Arabian Peninsula, Anwar al-Awlaki in Yemen. In July 2009, Yahya traveled to Yemen and gave an aide to al-Awlaki some $22,000. Moreover, Yahya admitted to soliciting the kidnapping and murder of a judge, Jack Zouhary, who was assigned to his terror case.

In April 2017, Yahya pleaded guilty to conspiracy to furnish and conceal material support to terrorism. Also, Yahya acknowledged soliciting a crime of violence in Ohio. In November 2017, Yahya was sentenced to twenty-seven and a half years in prison. The brothers, originally from India, had both obtained university degrees in the

United States. Ibrahim and the remaining coconspirators (brothers Asif Ahmed Salim and Sultane Room Salim) are awaiting trial. In summary, this cabal was composed of two sets of brothers.

Farah and Omar

In June 2016, Minnesota-based Mohamed Farah was convicted of conspiracy to murder in Syria on behalf of ISIS, providing material support to the group, and perjury. Five months later, he was sentenced to thirty years in prison for the offenses. That same month, Mohamed's brother, Adnan, was sentenced to ten years in prison for conspiracy to offer tangible aid to ISIS.

The brothers were part of a nine-member Minnesota-based group of acquaintances of Somali descent who were adjudicated for conspiracy to provide material support to ISIS. One of the codefendants, Guled Omar, served as the emir (leader) of the group. Omar was sentenced to thirty-five years in prison. In 2007, Guled's brother, Ahmed Ali Omar, left Minnesota and traveled to Somalia. Ahmed is believed to have joined al-Shabaab. Guled sought to follow in his brother's footsteps, although with intent to aid ISIS rather than al-Shabaab.

Tsarnaev

Jihadi-inspired brothers Tamerlan and Dzhokhar Tsarnaev detonated two pressure-cooker bombs at the finish line of the Boston Marathon in April 2013, killing three and injuring over 260 others. Tamerlan, the elder of the two, strongly influenced his brother to participate in the plot. At other junctures in his life, Dzhokhar looked up to and sought to emulate his brother.

Tamerlan was killed during a police pursuit of the coconspirators in the days following the attack. In April 2015, Dzhokhar was found guilty of thirty criminal counts, including using a weapon of mass destruction resulting in a death. A month later, Dzhokhar was sentenced to death.

Maha

In April 2007, two brothers, Mohamed and Omar Maha, conducted a suicide bombing near the US consulate in Casablanca, Morocco. While both brothers perished in the attack, only one other person was injured. Three other people, including an individual wearing a suicide belt, were arrested near the attack. Omar, the younger brother, was suspected of involvement in previous attacks in Casablanca. A group claiming to be al Qaeda in the Islamic North Africa (formerly the Salafist Group for Call and Combat) took responsibility for the strike.

Mohamed-Aggad

Brothers Karim and Foued Mohamed-Aggad traveled with several other men from France to Syria in 2013. There, they received terror training from Islamic State members. Upon Foued's return to France, he took part in the Islamic State–directed attacks in Paris in November 2015. Foued was one of several gunmen who killed over eighty persons at the Bataclan concert venue. Earlier, he had been denied positions with the French military and law enforcement services. Foued believed this was because his parents were born in North Africa.

Following Karim's return to France, he was arrested. Karim was later convicted of receiving support from the Islamic State and of being part of the jihadi recruitment network. While the two brothers did not participate in the same attack—one was captured beforehand—they were part of the same group.

Munshi

In 2008, an eighteen-year-old, Hammad Munshi, was the youngest UK citizen to be convicted of terrorism. In 2015, it was reported that Hammad's seventeen-year-old brother, Hassan, had traveled to Syria with a classmate to join the Islamic State. It is noteworthy that Hammad was enticed into extremism through the internet by UK-based Aabid Khan. In 2008, Aabid, along with his cousin Sultan Muhammad, was convicted of possessing materials for terrorism purposes. Aabid and Sultan were imprisoned for twelve and ten years, respectively.

Sisters

Ghariss

In religiously inspired terrorism, some prospective terrorists inquire about the legitimacy of political violence under religious law. Teenage Moroccan twin sisters Imane and Sanae al Ghariss contemplated committing a suicide bombing. They sought counsel on its validity under Islamic law from a cleric at a Rabat mosque. The moderate cleric said such an assault would be illegitimate.

Several Moroccan Muslim fundamentalist groups (including Ahl Assounna wal Jamaa and Fakir wal-Hijra) supported such actions and provided documentation on violent jihad. The two sisters and their teenage female friend, Hakima Rijlane, intended to conduct a suicide bombing at a Rabat supermarket but were discovered by authorities. The three teenagers were sentenced to five years in prison for forming a criminal organization to undertake a terror incident. Five adult conspirators were taken into custody as well.

Uncle-Nephew

In May 2016, a British court convicted Junead Khan and his uncle, Shazib Khan, for planning to travel to Syria to join the Islamic State. Junead was also found guilty of planning to attack a US Air Force base, Lakenheath, in the United Kingdom. The following month Junead and Shazib were sentenced to life and eight years, respectively. While contemplating their plot, Junead exchanged encrypted messages with British-born, Syria-based ISIS operative Junaid Hussain. Hussain encouraged the attack and provided Junead with information on how to make explosives. In August 2015, a US coalition–led drone attack killed Hussain.

Cousins

Arbabsiar

Between spring 2011 and October 2011, cousins Manssor Arbabsiar, a naturalized US citizen from Iran, and Gholam Shakuri, an Iran-based member of the Qods Force, as well as other Iran-based coconspirators, plotted to bomb a Washington, DC, restaurant. At the dining establishment, they envisioned someone assassinating the Saudi ambassador to the United States. Arbabsiar traveled to Mexico several times where he met with a Drug Enforcement Agency confidential source (CS). The CS had posed as an associate of the Mexican drug trafficking organization Los Zetas.

Arbabsiar hired the CS and purported accomplices to undertake the assassination. With Shakuri's approval, Arbabsiar wired about $100,000 to a bank account in the United States as a down payment for the expected killing of the ambassador. In July 2011, the CS told Arbabsiar he would use four men for the attack. Also, the CS said the hit would cost $1.5 million. The CS said there might be innocent bystanders. Arbabsiar told the CS, "They want that guy [the ambassador] done [killed]. If the hundred go with him, f--k 'em."[154]

The CS said half the $1.5 million should be provided before the attack or Arbabsiar should travel to Mexico as collateral. Arbabsiar did the latter, the Mexican government put him on a plane back to the United States, and he was arrested at JFK Airport in New York. In October 2011, the cousins were charged with conspiracy to kill a foreign official, conspiracy to engage in foreign travel and use of interstate and foreign commerce facilities in the commission of murder for hire, conspiracy to use a weapon of mass destruction (explosives), and conspiracy to commit an act of international terrorism transcending national boundaries. Furthermore, Arbabsiar was charged with a count of foreign travel and use of interstate and foreign commerce facilities in carrying out a murder for hire.

In October 2012, Arbabsiar pleaded guilty to conspiracy to commit murder across borders and two counts of murder for hire. In May 2013, he was imprisoned for twenty-five years. Shakuri is believed to be in Iran.

Ahmed

Zubair Ahmed is a graduate of the University of Illinois at Champaign-Urbana and studied medicine in Chicago. Khaleel Ahmed worked as a cashier at a warehouse store. In May 2004, these American cousins traveled to Egypt. After their return from Egypt in July 2004, they discussed, sought, and received instruction on firearms from another individual in Cleveland (Marwan el-Hindi, a former Chicago resident). Also, the cousins discussed training in countersurveillance techniques and sniper rifles with el Hindi. In January 2009, the cousins pleaded guilty to conspiracy to provide material support to terrorists who intended to murder US military forces abroad. In July 2010, Zubair and Khaleel were sentenced to ten and eight years in prison, respectively, for those crimes.

Multiple Family Member Involvement

Next, a number of instances in which there are several family members involved in various facets of terrorist activities or concealment thereof are shared. First, the participation of the jihadi-linked Zazi clan is enumerated. Second, the cabal of brothers Dritan and Shain Duka; a brother-in-law, Mohamad Ibrahim Shnewer; and others in a terror plot are described. Third, the family terror network comprising Daniel Boyd and his sons, Zakariya and Dylan, along with the larger jihadi cabal they formed, is described. Fourth, the terror network comprised of Rasel Raihan; his sister, Zakia Nasrin; and her husband, Jaffrey Khan, is presented. Fifth, the case of jihadist sisters Salma and Zahra Halane, their brother, and cousin in support of jihadism is discussed. Sixth, the ISIS-linked Maute Group in the Philippines and Dawood clan in the United Kingdom are covered. Seventh, the sovereign citizen–aligned Smith and Bixby families, both involved in the murder of police officers, are presented. These cases illustrate the capacity of family members to influence others to such an extent that they will plot, travel, and kill in the name of an extremist ideology.

Zazi[155]

In August 2008, Najibullah Zazi, a legal US resident from Afghanistan, and high school friends Zarein Ahmedzay (also a legal US resident from Afghanistan) and Adis Medunjanin (naturalized US citizen from Bosnia), agreed to travel to Afghanistan with plans to join the Taliban to fight coalition forces. Upon arrival in Peshawar, Pakistan, they attempted to enter Afghanistan but were turned back at the border. In Peshawar, the trio used an introduction from Najibullah's cousin, Amanullah Zazi, an Afghan who was in Pakistan at the time. Amanullah's contact was a Pakistan-based imam. The imam introduced Najibullah to an al Qaeda facilitator. The al Qaeda operative then put them in contact with Saleh al-Somali and Rashid Rauf (key al Qaeda operatives, both killed in US drone attacks in Pakistan) and later Adnan Shukrijumah, another al Qaeda senior leader. The al Qaeda leaders explained that it would be more suitable for the Americans to undertake strikes in NYC than in Pakistan.

The trio accepted al Qaeda's proposal. In Pakistan, al Qaeda operatives got weapons training for Zazi, Ahmedzay, and Medunjanin. Zazi received additional explosives training and emailed notes on that topic for later access. In January 2009, Zazi went back to Denver, Colorado. The others returned to NYC.

In June 2009, the three met and agreed to conduct suicide bombings in NYC during the month of Ramadan. They agreed that Zazi and Ahmedzay would assemble the devices, and all three would carry out suicide attacks on NYC subway lines. In July and August 2009, Zazi purchased the components to make TATP, a highly unstable explosive, in Colorado.

On September 8, 2009, Zazi rented a car and drove from Denver to NYC. He took with him explosives and other materials necessary to build the bombs. Zazi arrived in NYC on September 10, intending that he and Ahmedzay would construct the bombs prior to the three conspirators undertaking attacks on September 14, 15, or 16. That day, Zazi was pulled over in a traffic stop by the NYC Port Authority at the request of the FBI and released. His rental car was towed and then searched by law enforcement.

New York City cleric Ahmad Afzali, an informant, told Zazi that he was under law enforcement observation. Zazi and Ahmedzay discarded the explosives and bomb-making materials. Zazi was arrested in Denver in September 2009. In February 2010, he pleaded guilty to conspiracy to use explosives in the United States, conspiracy to murder abroad, and providing material support to al Qaeda. Surprisingly, as of September 2018, Zazi has not been sentenced.

In February 2010, Medunjanin was charged with conspiracy to use a weapon of mass destruction (explosive bombs) against people or property in the United States, conspiracy to commit murder in a foreign country, providing material support to a foreign terrorist organization (al Qaeda), and obtaining military-type training from an FTO (al Qaeda). Medunjanin pleaded not guilty, but in May 2012, he was found guilty of the charges. In November 2012, he was sentenced to life in prison.

In April 2010, Ahmedzay pleaded guilty to conspiracy to use a weapon of mass destruction (explosive bombs) against persons or property in the United States, conspiracy to commit murder in a foreign country, and giving tangible aid to al Qaeda. He received a sentence of life in prison.

In July 2011, Mohammed Wali Zazi, Najibullah's father, was found guilty of "destroying bomb-making materials and conspiring to obstruct"[156] the investigation into the plot of his son and associates. Before being interviewed by US authorities about his son, Mohammed received a tip from a New York–based imam that Najibullah was under investigation. Mohammed lied about not knowing Najibullah's cousin, who introduced his son to a Pakistan-based imam, who introduced Najibullah to al Qaeda agents. In addition, Mohammed failed to disclose that he requested that his family members destroy Najibullah's bomb-making materials. Mohammed was sentenced to four and a half years in prison.

In January 2010, Najibullah's cousin Amanullah Zazi pleaded guilty to obstructing justice by destroying chemicals and other bomb-making materials that Najibullah prepared. Amanullah also pleaded guilty to giving material support to the cabal to receive al Qaeda training. In December 2012, Amanullah was sentenced to forty months in prison. In January 2010, Najibullah's uncle by marriage Naqib Jaji pled guilty to obstructing justice in relation to the destruction of bomb-making materials. In August 2013, Jaji was sentenced to three years' probation after the judge took into consideration his cooperation in the investigation of Najibullah.

Duka and Shnewer

In December 2008, brothers Dritan and Shain Duka were convicted of "conspiracy to murder members of the US military, possession of machine guns, possession and attempted possession of machine guns in furtherance of a crime of violence, and two counts of possession of firearms by an illegal alien."[157] Another brother, Eljvir, was convicted of "conspiracy to murder members of the US military and possession of firearms by illegal aliens."[158] Eljvir's brother-in-law, Mohamad Ibrahim Shnewer, instigator of the seven-man jihadi cabal that planned to attack US military installations, including Fort Dix, New Jersey, was similarly adjudicated. The Duka brothers and Shnewer were sentenced to life in prison.

Boyd[159]

After converting to Islam in high school, Daniel Boyd moved to Pakistan in 1989 under the sponsorship of a Muslim relief group. Between 1989 and 1992, Daniel received instruction at terrorist training camps in Pakistan and Afghanistan. He engaged with the mujahedeen against the Soviets in Afghanistan. In 1991, Daniel and his brother Charles robbed a bank in Peshawar, Pakistan. They were convicted of the theft and sentenced to have their right hands and feet amputated. The sentence was never carried out. The brothers were members of Hezb-e-Islami, a militant Afghan group.

After leaving Pakistan, Daniel proceeded to the United States, settled in North Carolina, and raised a family. After years of attending moderate mosques in North Carolina, Daniel held Friday prayers at his home. Around this point, he acquired many firearms and conducted military training. In July 2009, law enforcement arrested seven men from a jihadist group led by Daniel. The cabal members were US citizens. The group (including two of Boyd's sons) planned terrorist attacks against overseas sites such as in Kosovo, Jordan, and the Gaza Strip. The terror cell also considered attacking the US marine base in Quantico, Virginia.

In February 2011, Daniel pleaded guilty to conspiring to give material support to terrorists (CMST) and conspiring to murder abroad. In August 2012, he was sentenced to eighteen years in prison. Daniel was thirty-nine at the time of his arrest. His nickname was Saifullah, or "Sword of God."

In December 2011, Daniel's sons, Zakariya and Dylan, pleaded guilty to CMST and received prison sentences of nine and eight years, respectively. In June 2013, they had their punishments reduced by about one year each due to "changed circumstances." Zakariya and Dylan were twenty and twenty-two, respectively, at the time of their arrest.

Nasrin, Khan, and Raihan

Zakia Nasrin and Jaffary Khan met on an online dating site. Nasrin was a student at Ohio State University and lived in Columbus. Her brother, Rasel Raihan, lived with the couple before the trio left to join ISIS in Syria in May 2014. They reached their destination two months later. Apparently, Nasrin exposed Raihan to radical Islam. Khan supposedly embraced jihadi tenets before meeting Nasrin.

In Syria, Raihan joined ISIS as a fighter. He was killed in a coalition air strike in Syria. Nasrin and Khan reportedly worked at a hospital in Raqqa. The pair has a young daughter, who was purportedly born in Syria.

Halane

Salma and Zahra Halane were sixteen-year-old twin sisters, daughters of Somali refugees in the United Kingdom. The girls grew up in Chorlton, Manchester, in the United Kingdom. They were outstanding students who planned on becoming doctors. The pair was radicalized over the internet and left their home in June 2014. They are thought to have married jihadis. Their prospective husbands likely funded their travel. Salma and Zahra are believed to be in Raqqa.

Also, their brother traveled to Somalia, where he linked up with al Shabaab. The girls were also affected by his dedication to jihad. The Halane sisters are cousins of UK-based Abdullahi Ahmed Jama Farah, twenty. In August 2016, Farah received seven years in prison for assisting his friend, Nur Hassan, with traveling to Syria to join ISIS.

Maute

The Maute (Family) Group, based in Mindanao, Philippines, was formed in 2012. In 2014, the Maute Group established an

ISIS-associated organization, the Islamic State of Lanao.[160] In December 2015, the group formed the Islamic State Province in East Asia (ISPEA), which served as an umbrella entity for Filipino groups that swore allegiance to ISIS.[161] Brothers Abdullah and Omarkayam Maute served as vice chairman of military operations and political affairs, respectively, of ISPEA. Other clan members play leadership roles in ISPEA, including Mohammad Khayam, who heads operations and intelligence; parents Cayamora (father) and Farhana (mother), who oversee finance and logistics; and several brothers (Abdulrahman, Abdul Azis, and Hamza).[162]

Dawood

During May–June 2015, British sisters Sugra (thirty-four), Zohra (thirty-three), and Khadija (thirty) Dawood took their nine children (ages three to fifteen) to Saudi Arabia. From there, the group traveled to Turkey and Syria. The sisters traveled without their spouses as they desired to live in the Islamic State with their children. The siblings followed in the footsteps of their brother, Ahmed, twenty-one. Prior to June 2014, Ahmed had traveled to Syria to fight for ISIS.

Smith

In August 2012, two Saint John Parish, Louisiana, sheriff's deputies, Brandon Nielsen and Jeremy Triche, were shot and killed by Brian Smith and Kyle Joekel. The ambush of the deputies occurred at a trailer park in LaPlace, Louisiana, where the Smiths lived. Smith and Joekel were charged with the first-degree murder of the deputies. As of January 2018, they are awaiting trial.

The murderers were part of a family affiliated sovereign citizen group, led by Brian's father, Terry. Terry was charged with attempted first-degree murder. He is awaiting trial in 2018. In 2016, Terry was sentenced to life in prison for sexually abusing his stepdaughter.

Derrick Smith, Brandon's brother and Terry's son, pleaded guilty in May 2013 to "accessory after the fact to attempted first-degree murder and possession of a firearm by a convicted felon."[163] Derrick was sentenced to twelve years for the firearm offense and five years for the accessory charge, to be served concurrently. Derrick was released in April 2017, after serving less than half his sentence.[164] Two others, Terry Smith wife's, Chanel Skains, and Britney Keith, pleaded to accessory after the fact charges in November 2012 and April 2013, respectively.

Bixby

Spouses Rita and Arthur Bixby had a long history of anti-government and sovereign citizen tactics (e.g., baseless lawsuits, tax protests, armed threats). These activities occurred in New Hampshire, where the Bixbys' home was foreclosed because of nonpayment of property taxes. The pair subsequently moved to Abbeville, South Carolina, to be close to their son, Steven, who lived there. Steven worked in construction and vending sectors in Abbeville. He was influenced by his parents' aggressive anti-government rhetoric, affinity for guns, and the New Hampshire state motto, "Live Free or Die."

In December 2003, Steven shot and killed Abbeville County Sheriff's Deputy Danny Wilson and South Carolina Magistrate's Constable Donnie Ouzts at the home of his parents. Deputy Wilson was shot and killed through the front door as he approached the residence. Steven shot and killed Constable Ouzts when he arrived to follow up on Wilson. Following a fourteen-hour gunfight at the home, Steven and Arthur were taken into custody. Rita surrendered to authorities at Steven's apartment.

The murders arose as a result of a long dispute between the Bixbys and the South Carolina Department of Transportation (SCDOT), which was planning to expand a roadway near the Bixbys' home, which was adjacent to the South Carolina Highway 72. In December 2003, the Bixbys threatened SCDOT employees trying to enter their property, promising "there would be hell to pay" and "threatening to kill us for trespassing."[165] The Bixbys continued with their threats during a subsequent visit to the property by SCDOT employees. Rita explained that they wanted this moment, the sheriff's department had no authority over them, and they would fight till their last breath.[166]

As with other so-called sovereign citizens, Steven and Rita claimed that Steven acted in self-defense when he shot and killed the two law enforcement officers who, the Bixbys claimed, had trespassed on their property. In February 2007, Steven was convicted of both murders and other charges, including kidnapping and conspiracy. The South Carolina Supreme Court and US Supreme Court affirmed Steven's conviction and death sentence. Arthur was deemed incompetent to stand trial for murder because of dementia. He was involuntarily institutionalized and died in September 2011. In October 2007, Rita was convicted of accessory before the fact and criminal conspiracy in the murders. She was imprisoned for life for the former conviction and five years for the latter. Rita died in prison in September 2011.

Conclusion

There are different types of family affiliated extremism, ranging from participation in extremist groups and encouraging radicalism to providing support to advance a particular ideology to undertaking or calling for undertaking terror attacks or hate crimes. The examples presented in this chapter include distinct family affiliated terrorism, encompassing parents and their children, spouses, siblings, nephews-uncles, cousins, and multiple family members. The family members discussed here planned and periodically carried out diverse plots, provided material support to kin or others, and tried to travel abroad to take part in terrorist activities, among other actions. These examples illustrate the expansive nature and scope of family terror networks in the United States and overseas.

The frequency and lethality of kin connected terrorism demonstrate that this type of violence merits a distinct framework by which to assess it. The family terror networks model described in the next chapter seeks to categorize and better comprehend this form of terrorism.

CHAPTER 4

Predicting Family Terror Networks

Introduction

This chapter presents a model for predicting family terror networks. Analysis of selected case studies in accordance with the model is then presented. Afterward, lessons learned from over one hundred case studies involving terror family networks are shared. Next, limitations of the model and shortcomings in the breadth of case studies are delineated.

Model for Predicting Family Terror Networks

The purpose of forging a model to predict family terror networks is to aid the government, private sector, nonprofits, nongovernmental organizations, and the public to anticipate and understand possible kin-linked extremism. The model posits that family networks and relationships are highly impactful on terrorist participation. By understanding the influences of families in the creation of terrorists, anticipating the likelihood of participation in terrorism is enhanced. Such an appreciation can contribute to incapacitating future terrorists.

This schematic was crafted after assessing 118 families affiliated with terrorism involving 138 instances of kin relationships (e.g., brothers, husbands/wives, and fathers/sons). These case studies encompassed terror cells of divergent ideological leanings (e.g., jihadism, sovereign citizens, militias, and hate aligned). Moreover, the model addresses circumstances when household members' efforts to radicalize kin are ineffective. Therefore, the design does not argue that having a radical in the family would automatically cause a family member to support extremism.

The path of family terror networks follows six stages. At Stage 1, a family member (F1) is exposed to a radical ideology and supports a movement associated with this extremist tenet. The reasons for an individual joining the movement or group include:

- Belief that the ideology is correct and merits support

- Revenge for real or perceived victimization

- Socioeconomic marginalization and alienation

- Political marginalization and alienation

- Protection against perceived oppressors

- Acceptance, respect, or status

- Pressure from family, friends, and community

- Expunging dishonor due to moral indiscretion

- Seeking purpose or excitement in life

- Mental disability

- Alternative to failures or setbacks

Depending on who or how F1 is radicalized, F1 may join or collaborate with other like-minded extremists: either in a cabal or formal group. In turn, F1 may support the group by raising money, gathering supplies, getting paramilitary training, conducting surveillance, testing security of a target, recruiting others, or undertaking an attack. Alternatively, F1 may become self-radicalized and not cooperate with another person.

During Stage 2, the family member (F1) approaches another family member (F2) or multiple family members (F3-4) about the possibility of following the extremist ideology. At Stage 3, a family member (F2) or multiple family members (F3-4) accept, accept with reservations, or reject the extremist tenets of their family member.

In Stage 4, Several options are conceivable. F1 takes part in a terrorist act or otherwise supports the movement. F1 and F2 carry out a terrorist attack or support the movement. Alternatively, F1 and F2 may leave extremism. Another path affords either F1 or F2 to remain enthralled by radicalism while the other's support ends. F3/F4 may follow any of the paths of F1/F2.

At Stage 5, assuming F2 has left radicalism (or never accepted it initially), F2 may try to directly influence F1 to leave radicalism or indirectly do so by reaching out for aid from others (e.g., law enforcement, religious and civic communities, friends, etc.). Alternatively, assuming F1 has left radicalism, F1 may pursue efforts to dislodge F2 from extremism along the same path mentioned in this stage.

During Stage 6, F1 may decide to: leave radicalism, protest F2's efforts, leave the premises (assuming they live together), cease communications with F2, attack F2, or pursue other actions. Alternatively, F2 may decide to follow the same path mentioned in this stage.

A diagram detailing the model follows:

Model Predicting Family Terror Networks (Alexander, 2019)

STAGE 1 - F1 (family member) is exposed to and embraces an extremist ideology.

STAGE 6 - F1 may decide to: leave radicalism, protest F2's efforts, leave the premises (assuming they live together), cease communications with F2, attack F2, or pursue other actions. Alternatively, F2 may decide to follow the same path mentioned in this stage.

STAGE 2 - F1 approaches another family member (F2) or multiple family members (F3-4).

STAGE 5- Assuming F2 has left radicalism (or never accepted it initially), F2 may try to directly influence F1 to leave radicalism or indirectly do so by reaching out for aid from others (e.g., law enforcement, religious and civic communities, friends, etc.). In contrast, assuming F1 has left radicalism, F1 may pursue efforts to dislodge F2 from extremism along the same path mentioned in this stage.

STAGE 3 - F2 or multiple family members (F3-4) accept, accept with reservations, or reject the extremist tenets.

STAGE 4 - Several options are conceivable. F1 takes part in a terrorist act or otherwise supports the movement. F1 and F2 carry out a terrorist attack or support the cause. Alternatively, F1 and F2 may leave extremism. Another path affords either F1 or F2 to remain enthralled by radicalism while the other's support ends. F3/F4 may follow any of the paths of F1/F2.

Application of Case Studies to the Model

Brothers

Jihadi-inspired brothers Tamerlan and Dzhokhar Tsarnaev detonated two pressure-cooker bombs at the finish line of the Boston Marathon in April 2013, killing three and injuring over 260 others. Tamerlan, the elder of the two, influenced his brother to take part in the plot. Dzhokhar mistakenly ran over and killed Tamerlan while police pursued the pair in the days following the attack. In April 2015, a jury found Dzhokhar guilty on thirty criminal counts, including using a weapon of mass destruction that resulted in death. A month later, Dzhokhar was sentenced to death.

Applying the model to the Tsarnaev brothers, Tamerlan is viewed as F1, who radicalizes his brother, Dzhokhar, F2. The two (F1 and F2) conducted the Boston Marathon bombings and subsequent mayhem in the Boston area. There is reporting that their parents at some point held anti-American perspectives. Inquiry into Tamerlan's wife's possible involvement in the Boston Marathon attacks did not lead to any criminal prosecution.

In this case, Stages 1 and 2 were followed as described. At Stage 3, F2 accepted the jihadi tenets presented by F1. At Stage 4, F1 and F2 conducted the attacks. Stages 5 and 6 were not reached as the brothers carried out the bombings at Stage 4.

Fathers and Sons

North Carolina–based Daniel Boyd (F1) infused his sons, Zakariya (F2) and Dylan (F3), with jihadi ideology. In 2012, F1 was sentenced to eighteen years in prison for conspiring to provide material support to terrorists (CMST) and conspiring to murder abroad. His sons, F2 and F3, pleaded guilty to CMST. They received prison sentences of eight and seven years, respectively. Besides F2 and F3, F1's jihadi cabal included other individuals outside the family.

In the Boyd case, Stages 1 and 2 were followed as depicted. At Stage 3, F2 and F3 accepted the jihadi ideals offered by F1. At Stage 4, the trio, in concert with others, conspired to provide aid to extremists. Stages 5 and 6 were not reached as the father and sons were involved in the conspiracy at Stage 4.

Jerry Kane, the father (F1), traveled across the United States with his teenage son Joseph (F2) preaching facets of sovereign citizen ideology, such as paying mortgages with fictitious financial instruments. F1 indoctrinated F2 with sovereign citizen ideals, particularly having a strong animosity against police. During a 2010 traffic stop in Arkansas, F2 shot and killed two police officers with an assault rifle. The pair was subsequently shot and killed by police.

In the Kane case, Stages 1 and 2 were followed as portrayed. At Stage 3, F2 accepted the extremist tenets presented by F1. At Stage 4, F2 murdered the police officers, most likely at the behest of F1. Stages 5 and 6 were not reached as an attack was carried out at Stage 4.

Oregon-based Bruce Turnidge (F1) held strong anti-government and militia perspectives. F1 influenced his son Joshua (F2) with those ideals. In 2010, they were convicted of the murder of two policemen who had attempted to dismantle a bomb at a bank in Oregon as well as two counts of attempted murder. In 2011, the father and son received death sentences.

In this case, Stages 1 and 2 were followed as shared. At Stage 3, F2 accepted the radical themes presented by F1. At Stage 4, F1 and F2 plotted the bombing. Stages 5 and 6 were not reached as the father and son conducted an attack at Stage 4.

Husbands and Wives

Jaelyn Young (F1) and Muhammad Dakhlalla (F2) fell in love and married. F1 became enamored with ISIS propaganda. According to F2, she convinced him that the pair should try to travel to Syria to live in the Islamic State. The pair was arrested at the airport on their first leg to travel to Turkey and, ultimately, Syria. They pleaded guilty to conspiracy to provide material support to an FTO, ISIS. F2 was sentenced to eight years. F1 received four additional years, as she was perceived as being a more fervent extremist than her husband.

In this instance, Stages 1 and 2 were followed as described. At Stage 3, F2 accepted the extremist tenets presented by F1. At Stage 4, F1 and F2 tried to travel to Syria to join a terrorist organization. Stages 5 and 6 were not reached as the couple attempted to travel abroad at Stage 4.

Michael Wolfe (F1) embraced an extremist ideology, jihadism. Later, he approached his wife, Jordan Furr (F2), about the possibility of following that ideology. She reluctantly agreed to try to take their minor children (F3/F4) to Syria and join the Islamic State. Ultimately, F1 was arrested while trying to board a flight overseas with his family. He pleaded guilty to attempting to provide material support to ISIS. Subsequently, F1 was sentenced to nearly seven years in prison. None of the other family members were prosecuted; F3/F4 were minors, and F2 was not deemed adequately culpable.

In this case, Stages 1 and 2 were followed as represented. At Stage 3, F2 accepted the extremist tenets presented by F1. At Stage

4, F1 and F2 tried to go to Syria to join ISIS. Stages 5 and 6 were not prompted as the couple sought to travel abroad at Stage 4.

After the December 2015 San Bernardino attack, authorities investigated familial and other links to the married-couple shooters Syed Rizwan Farook (F1) and Tashfeen Malik (F2). It appears that both held jihadist perspectives prior to meeting online and getting married. Their extremism coalesced during marriage—so much so that the pair carried out a terror incident involving gunfire and improvised explosive devices (the latter malfunctioned). The pair killed fourteen and injured twenty-one others during the incident. Police killed the perpetrators during a subsequent car chase and shootout.

In this circumstance, at Stage 1 both F1 and F2 were radicalized prior to meeting. At Stage 2, the pair discovered that they both held jihadist beliefs. Rather than attempting to dissuade the other from such a perspective, the couple's zeal for jihad was enhanced at Stage 3. At Stage 4, F1 and F2 carried out an attack. Stages 5 and 6 were not reached as the couple conducted an attack at Stage 4.

Jerad Miller (F1) became a fervent admirer of militia, conspiratorial, and other extremist ideologies. He exposed these sentiments to his wife, Amanda (F2). In 2014, F1 and F2 assassinated two police officers at a Las Vegas, Nevada, restaurant. Subsequently, the couple made their way to a Walmart, where F2 killed a Good Samaritan who had confronted F1. Police killed F1 in an ensuing shootout at the store. F2 was killed by a self-inflicted gunshot.

In this example, Stages 1 and 2 were followed as defined. At Stage 3, F2 accepted the extremist tenets presented by F1. At Stage 4, F1 and F2 carried out their deadly plot. Stages 5 and 6 were not triggered as the couple undertook an attack at Stage 4.

Cousins

Hasan Edmonds (F1) and his cousin Jonas Edmonds (F2) appear to have been equally committed to traveling abroad to join ISIS. If both could not make the trip, then F2 would stay and conduct a terror attack in Illinois. While F1 made initial communications with an FBI undercover employee discussing his and his cousin's interest in traveling to Syria to join the Islamic State (and possibly carry out an attack in the United States), F2 frequently interacted with additional FBI undercover employees. The cousins ultimately met in person with another undercover FBI employee. The pair was convicted of ISIS-related activities, among others. F1 and F2 received thirty years and twenty-one years in prison, respectively.

In this case, Stages 1 and 2 were followed as described. At Stage 3, F1 and F2 both shared jihadi ideologies. At Stage 4, F1 planned to travel to Syria and join ISIS, while F2 intended to carry out an attack in the United States. Stages 5 and 6 were not initiated as the cousins sought to put their plans into place at Stage 4.

Lessons Learned from Case Studies

This book covered 118 case studies of family participation in terrorism. These 118 families encompassed 138 occurrences of kin relationships (e.g., husband and wives, brothers, and fathers and sons) involved with terrorism. After all, a family may have more than two persons involved terror-related activities. In aggregate, these many instances of family relationships involved in terrorism were exhibited along the following spectrum:

- Husbands/Wives (43/138 cases or 31.16%)

- Brothers (36/138 cases or 26.09%)

- Fathers/Sons (15/138 cases or 10.87%)

- Cousins (11/138 cases or 7.97%)

- Siblings (other than sister-sister, brother-brother) (9/138 cases or 6.52%)

- Uncles/Nephews (4/138 cases or 2.90%)

- Parents/Children (3/138 cases or 2.17%)

- Prospective Husbands/Wives (3/138 cases or 2.17%)

- Sisters (3/138 cases or 2.17%)

- Mother/Son (3/138 cases or 2.17%)

- Stepfather/Stepchildren (3/138 cases or 2.17%)

- Father/Sons-Daughters (1/138 cases or .72%)

- Uncle/Niece (1/138 cases or .72%)

- Brother-in-Law (1/138 cases or .72%)

- Cousin-in-Law (1/138 cases or .72%)

- Ex-Husband/Ex-Wife (1/138 cases or .72%)

Particularly noteworthy, the results above show that 57% of the 138 family ties comprised from cases involving fairly equal amounts of husbands/wives (43/138 or 31%) and brothers (36/138 or 26%). As such, these case studies suggest that family affiliated terrorism occurs most readily in husbands/wives and brothers. These results are attributable to the bonds that coalesce during courtship and marriage. The frequency of brothers in this study underscores the potency of sibling relationships as well as the higher frequency of male participation in terrorism over females.

Three other sources of family terror connections contributed about 25% or so of such instances, namely: fathers/sons (15/138 cases or 10.87%), cousins (11/138 cases or 7.97%), and siblings (other than sister-sister, brother-brother) (9/138 cases or 6.52%). In contrast, five other manifestations of family terror networks ranged between 2% to 3%, such as: uncles/nephews (4/138 cases or 2.90%), parents/children (3/138 cases or 2.17%), prospective husbands/ wives (3/138 cases or 2.17%), sisters (3/138 cases or 2.17%), mother/ son (3/138 cases or 2.17%), and stepfather/stepchildren (3/138 cases or 2.17%). The five remaining paradigms of kin connected extremism—father/sons- daughters, uncle/niece, brother-in-law, cousin-in-law, and ex-husband/ex-wife—occurred only once each among the 138 instances of kin relationships or .75%, for a total of 3.6%.

The case studies chosen for the book did not arise from a systematic methodology (e.g., using a set of prosecutions during a period or another data set). Instead, I initially came across instances of family connected terrorism through media reports, and then specifically sought out such occurrences. As such, the conclusions drawn from these instances may overemphasize the prevalence of some types of family ties and underestimate others. Still, the significant occurrence of husbands/wives and brothers in these findings suggest that these family forms are prevalent in family terror networks.

The instances of extremist ideals associated with family-linked terrorism in this data set were:

- Jihadism (100/118 or 84.75%);

- Sovereign Citizens (5/118 or 4.24%)

- White Supremacy (5/118 or 4.24%)

- Militia and Sovereign Citizen (2/118 or 1.69%)

- White Supremacy, Sovereign Citizen, and Militia (2/118 or 1.69%)

- Hezbollah (2/118 or 1.69%)

- State-sponsored (Iran) (1/118 or .85%)

- Christian Identity/Anti-abortion/Anti-LGBTQ (1/118 or .85%)

Overwhelmingly, jihadism was the ideology connected to the 118 instances of families affiliated with terrorism that were reviewed. This type of extremism was found in 85% of the cases with other precepts occurring comparatively fairly rarely (15%). Among the non-jihadists associated with kin terrorism, they were affiliated with mostly right-wing extremism (e.g., sovereign citizens, militia, and white supremacy).

The preponderance of cases connected to jihadism occurred due to several factors. First, according to the U.S. State Department, the majority of terrorism occurring globally both in terms of incidents and affiliated groups is associated with jihadism, principally Sunni-connected groups such as ISIS or al-Qaeda. Second, the cases chosen in the study came from media reports that tend to cover jihadi-linked terrorism more frequently than non-jihadi instances of extremism. Third, while many cases involved individuals in the United States, significant instances of family terrorism based overseas were covered as well. The latter cases, too, were nearly exclusively linked to jihadism.

Limitations of the Model and Case Studies

The model for predicting family terror networks is prone to some limitations. While 118 cases of families involved in terrorism were reviewed in crafting the model, the data set does not cover all circumstances of kin-connected influences. Consequently, the conclusions reached do not include insights that could arise from a larger data set. Also, there is sometimes incomplete information regarding how an individual was radicalized. In other instances, individuals might not be influenced exclusively by a family member but rather simultaneously affected by other forces.

The model was constructed without the benefit of field research, which would have yielded greater insights than those available from secondary resources. Still, field research in some of these cases would be impossible (as operatives are dead), challenging (as operatives are in prison and possibly uncooperative), or inaccessible (in conflict zones). Also, field interviews and follow-up would have been very costly and lengthy to undertake without significant funding and a team of researchers.

The impetus for a person to become a terrorist can be multidimensional. As such, to characterize family links over other factors may overstate the potency of the former over other variables that attract someone to radicalism. Still, the model does not argue that the family is the sole factor affecting radicalization and possible participation in terrorism. Rather, it tries to establish a typology for this phenomenon of terrorism and a framework by which to understand this threat.

Future research focusing on right-wing, left-wing family, secular, and single-issue aligned terror networks would aid in gaining a better appreciation of kin connected extremism associated with those ideologies. Also, more case studies could address similarities and differences within family associated terrorism that follows distinct extremist doctrines. Furthermore, examining which family relationships correlate more readily to the execution of terror attacks versus those that do not would be beneficial.

CHAPTER 5

Law Enforcement Responses to Family Terror Networks

Introduction

This chapter covers law enforcement responses to terrorism and its relation to combating kin connected terrorism. Among the topics covered are police interactions with terrorists, including: responding to kinetic incidents, conducting investigations and surveillance, receiving tips about suspicious people and activities, and interacting with community organizations and persons. Additional themes communicated in this chapter are the means to find terrorists, missed signs in discovering terrorists, the role of traffic stops, the role of community policing, the participation of the public, improved communications, leveraging technology, preventing the next attack, responding to a terrorist strike, terrorists targeting police and responses, and international cooperation. These many law enforcement methodologies in fighting terrorism can be implemented with vigor against the challenges emanating from family affiliated terror.

Finding Terrorists

Terrorists, whether inside or external to a family network, do not operate in a void. Nor are terrorists invisible. They have jobs, family, friends, neighbors, coworkers, classmates, and other individuals in their lives. Terrorist operatives shop, use banks and credit cards, rent storage units, acquire components for explosives, and buy weapons. These contacts might be aware of the radicalization and extremist activities of others in their social network.

Operatives may enroll at educational institutions, take part in activities at recreation centers, attend religious services, and contribute to civic institutions. Participation in such institutions may mask malevolent activities such as terrorism. Some extremists leave electronic footprints (online, landline/mobile phones), which contribute to the prospects of detention. Also, radicals use encrypted technologies making identification more difficult.

Terrorists can be discovered at locations where radicalization and recruitment transpire, such as religious, educational, and recreational institutions; workplaces, and prisons. One can also find radicals at meetings and demonstrations aligned with an extremist group's ideology. Also, terrorists are sometimes recognizable through indicators such as vehicle/residential identifiers (bumper stickers and no trespassing signs) and physical/verbal identifiers (tattoos and extremist-infused rants). Even lone wolves rarely live in complete isolation, often articulating their animus online and interacting with others through that medium, and, occasionally, in person.

Law enforcement can come across individual extremists while investigating traditional criminal acts. These crimes might be precursor crimes so the terrorist can gain funds or materials to use in a prospective terror attack. These crimes may involve counterfeiting or identity theft. False documents and misuse of identification could hide illicit activities. After the 2016 Berlin truck attack, law enforcement found the perpetrator's (fake) identity papers and fingerprints in the truck used in the massacre. The terrorist met his demise in Italy after police asked him to show identification at a train station.

Additionally, a person may conduct a breach or an attempted intrusion of a secure location. Proprietary documents or materials may be stolen or diverted for future use to gain access to a site. Other actions indicative of mobilization toward terrorism—a state in which one concludes using violence is justified and necessary— here or abroad include referencing an interest in a martyrdom operation, expressing plans to travel to a war zone or elsewhere overseas to join a terror group, seeking guidance for justifying violent acts, and recruiting others to join a cabal.[167]

Other opportunities to find individuals involved in terrorism include routine police duties, such as conducting traffic stops, responding to calls for service, seeking witnesses to crimes, and investigating activities. Tips alleging suspicious behavior may arise from an individual's employees, coworkers, friends, neighbors, and strangers. Alternatively, individuals can be involved in suspicious travel domestically or internationally.

At some stage, radicals may articulate their extremist perspectives to others. They may vocalize their calls for violence online, offline, or both. Those active online may follow extremist websites, social media networks, blogs, and online forums. Additionally, they may get guidance online on multiple terror tools, such as communications, radicalization, recruitment, fundraising, explosives, tactics, targeting, and financing their operations.

Radicalization processes can occur quickly, so the time between radicalization and a kinetic incident may not prove particularly attenuated.[168] In other circumstances, an otherwise marginalized person may also have mental issues. Such a condition could be observable by family and acquaintances.

Police come across radicals in other venues and circumstances. For instance, police may see an individual dealing with a known criminal or terrorism suspect. Likewise, police may follow up on a person who previously participated in terrorism or other crimes. Law enforcement interacts with suspects through referrals from informants, businesses, nonprofits, nongovernmental organizations, and the public.

Police may interact with a terror suspect online or offline undercover activities. Police get unsolicited tips from family members about their kin's prospective plot. At times, an officer receives a direct threat from a perpetrator, either in person and online.

Behaviors associated with the eight signs of terrorism include individuals conducting surveillance, gathering information, testing security, acquiring funds and supplies, acting suspiciously, impersonating police or security personnel, undertaking dry runs, and getting into position to undertake an attack. These indicators of terrorism can arise at various stages of the terror cycle, depending on the operative(s) and their sophistication.[169]

Moreover, suspicious activities can be distinguished by whether they are readily observable, observable, or hidden. Similarly, these worrying actions can be differentiated among immediate, medium-term, and long-term concerns. Depending on the classification, police will need to respond to these behaviors with varying levels of urgency. Other points to weigh are whether these troubling activities are dangerous on their own accord (independent factors) or only with others (dependent factors).[170]

Using encrypted technologies and digital currencies such as Bitcoin impedes the discovery of terrorists and their networks. Extremists directly associated with a formal group tend to have good terror tradecraft, including communications, targeting, making explosives, and performing the attack. In contrast, lone wolves or cabals are less adept at evading detection owing to absence of training.

Police challenges exist even when authorities suspect that an individual is involved with extremism. For instance, constant surveillance is time consuming and costly financially and in terms of manpower. The likelihood of catching terrorist fugitives depends on many factors, including the skillfulness of the terror operative, their support network, whether they make their way to a safe zone or ungovernable area, the capabilities of intelligence and law enforcement communities, and the public's contribution in ferreting out the operation.

Terror incidents may take place in areas where the perpetrators live. Alternatively, an attack may happen many miles away from their homes, including overseas. Analogously, both before and after an attack, individuals can be involved in hiding or moving across country.

By appreciating the characteristics of terror financing, law enforcement and others can gain insight into whether an individual might be involved in terrorism. Terrorists source their funds from licit and illicit means. The sources of such legally obtained funds include personal accounts, family, friends, corporate donations, loans, legal donations, litigation settlements, government entitlements, and crowdfunding. Illicit funding sources for terrorists include drugs, weapons, human trafficking, human smuggling, extortion, fraud, robbery, theft, pickpocketing, cigarette or commodity smuggling, traditional commerce, charities, and state sponsorship.[171]

Foreign fighters[172] have financed their travels by using their savings, funds from jobs, student loans, funds from family for university, stolen checks, and proceeds from litigation settlements. Funds designated for terrorist conduct may be moved through the following modes: cash, traveler's checks, checks, wire transfers, money service business (licensed/unlicensed), hawalas, new payment systems (internet, mobile, digital currencies, preloadable cards), and casinos, among others.

Missed Signs[173]

In September 2017, FBI Director Christopher Wray announced that his agency had a thousand open domestic terrorism cases and a corresponding number of homegrown violent extremist investigations, such as individuals connected with ISIS. After high-profile terror attacks, media reports abound that police may have had prior contact with the perpetrators.

FBI terror investigations have three different layers of inquiry: an assessment, a preliminary investigation, and a full investigation. What the FBI may do during these variant processes with reference to terror suspects broadens as greater concerns about the individual take hold. The FBI is the lead agency in investigating federal terrorism cases, but state, local, and tribal law enforcement can contribute to such investigations.[174] In fact, traditional policemen often contact terror suspects during calls for service, at traffic stops, and from tips from community members.

Well-known cases of alleged missed signs of terrorism include:

- Esteban Santiago (killed five in Fort Lauderdale in January 2017)

- Ahmad Rahimi (detonated explosives in New York and New Jersey in September 2016)

- Omar Mateen (killed forty-nine in Orlando in June 2016)

- Tamerlan Tsarnaev (along with his brother, Dzhokhar, killed three and injured hundreds at the Boston Marathon in April 2013)

- Major Nidal Hasan (killed thirteen and injured dozens at Fort Hood in Texas in November 2009).

There are differences in the degrees of suspicious terrorist behavior among the aforementioned operatives. Yet the commonality is the perception that the individuals did not commit a crime prior to their strikes. Thereby, the would-be perpetrators were not arrested.

In retrospect, things may appear as missed signs, but in reality, police investigated the matter, but the case did not justify an arrest. For instance, there might have been contradictory or incomplete information about the suspect's threat posture. The individual may have lacked indicators of mobilization. Also, the police are often forced to respond to many criminal and other challenges simultaneously (e.g., organized crime, cybercrime) while having limited resources (e.g., time, budget, manpower, technology). Other considerations may also arise, causing police to lack focus on potential terror suspects. Analogously, there are too many extremists for police to monitor concurrently, so some are not monitored—or are not monitored closely.

To be sure, in the past, police were informed of possible terror-ist plots through referrals or tips from the suspect's family, friends, acquaintances, informants, and the general public. Additionally, the government may obtain a tip from an overseas partner or another source. Also, law enforcement may notice a suspect when they come across him or her online, such as on an extremist forum.

The police can pursue these tactics following receipt of a tip:

- Investigate and determine that the individual does not merit further attention

- Assess whether the suspect merits additional inquiry due to terror or non-terror concerns

- Fail to investigate in a timely manner

- Monitor for a period

- Undertake a sting operation with an informant and/ or undercover agent

- Respond to a terror incident

Law enforcement may not be able to prevent a terrorist event if the suspect becomes more radicalized than when initially inves-tigated or moves toward violence rapidly and hides it well. Failure may arise because police inadequately assessed the risk or did not proceed because of political correctness.

Admittedly, police actions may merit some criticism if they fail to take seriously an individual who exhibits multiple indicators of extremism. Also, police may monitor an individual at one point but be unaware that he or she traveled or returned from abroad.

Likewise, there are instances of inadequate sharing of information, wherein local police do not contact the fusion center or FBI Joint Terrorism Task Force. Also, mental health challenges facing a suspect may complicate the determination of whether an individual is a true threat.

Another contributor to missed signs is a police department's culture. Some police departments, especially small agencies, do not view terrorism as a likely risk in their communities. Rather, the focus of their duties is on traffic offenses and common crimes. In turn, this sentiment is largely exhibited in the actions of officers in those agencies. Also, if department leadership is unsupportive of counterterrorism training, individual officers do not enroll in such courses. Failure to receive such training will undermine an officer's ability to recognize conduct that may have a nexus with terrorism.

When there is adequate evidence that individuals are involved in terrorist activities, law enforcement often succeeds in monitoring such persons and arresting them as circumstances permit. The capabilities of law enforcement to uncover suspected terrorists are manifold, but they cannot find every terrorist before they strike. Civil society, too, plays a contributing role in identifying persons who have been radicalized and mobilized as the next terror actors.

Traffic Stops[175]

Law enforcement has used traffic stops to detect criminal activity for decades. Its use in the terrorism context gained greater resonance since the 9/11 attacks. After the strikes, authorities discovered that three of the four pilot hijackers—Mohamed Atta, Ziad Jarrah, and Hani Hanjour—were involved in traffic stops while in the United States.

Pilot ringleader Atta was stopped twice in Florida. In April 2001, he received a ticket for driving without a license. Subsequently, a bench warrant was issued due to his failure to appear in that traffic infraction. When Atta was ticketed for speeding in July 2001, the issuing officer was unaware of the bench warrant.

In addition, muscle hijacker Nawaf al-Hazmi was pulled over for speeding in Oklahoma in April 2001. September 11 pilot Hanjour is believed to have been in the car with al-Hazmi during the traffic stop. Three months later, police stopped Hani Hanjour for speeding in Virginia.[176] On September 9, 2001, Ziad Jarrah was pulled over for the same offense in Maryland. Within days, Jarrah piloted United Airlines flight 93, which crashed near Shanksville, Pennsylvania. Had only one of the four September 11 pilots been available that fateful day, clearly, world affairs during the past nearly two decades would have been different.

During a traffic stop, police officers should carefully examine the driver's license, vehicle registration, and insurance. There are red flags of possible criminal and/or terrorist activity that present themselves during traffic stops. Consequently, cops should inquire when the driver's license and vehicle registration are not from the same state, when an altered or forged license or title is suspected, when the driver's license photo does not match the driver, or when the vehicle title is in the name of someone other than the driver. Other items that might be deemed suspicious in light of these circumstances: surveillance equipment (binoculars, infrared cameras), maps, sketches, bomb-making components, incendiaries, police scanners, disguises, and containers.

Additionally, if a passport and international (or foreign) driver's license are given to the officer, careful review is warranted. After all, these may indicate illegal entry into the country. Terrorists may travel abroad, including to terrorist-supporting countries, where terror-training camps exist, or gateways to such nations. Possessing multiple identification instruments and different names is often a serious indicator of other wrongdoing.

During a traffic stop, officers should look for things that are inconsistent or incongruous. One such example might be a driver claiming to be on a long vacation or business trip but possessing no luggage. The number of vehicle occupants, their demeanor (e.g., vehicle activity indicative of reconnaissance at a government building or school), and the basis of the stop (e.g., speeding, driving erratically, driving without a license) are parts of the totality of circumstances that officers should weigh.

Officers should consider requesting consent searches when circumstances permit. A paradigm shift is necessary as searches can stymie terrorist and extremist activities. Presently, police officers ask for consent to search a car during traffic stops only infrequently. Obstacles to such inquiries include training that does not encourage such a request, fear that a search would not yield any sign of criminality, and fear of allegations of discrimination.

The occupants of the vehicle may also give off clues. Officers should look for dissonance such as inappropriate clothing. Terrorists may wear long sleeve shirts or coats in hot weather to conceal weapons, explosives (e.g., a suicide bomb belt), illegal drugs, documents, or cash. Terrorists may travel considerable distances from where they live to raise funds, recruit other members, or carry out terrorist attacks. Drivers and passengers who travel great distances may appear exhausted.

Najibullah Zazi, convicted of plans to commit a suicide bombing in New York City in 2009, drove from Colorado to New York with precursors of explosives in his vehicle. Similarly, terrorists might travel with others in their group, including in single or multiple cars or vans.

Other factors in adducing a potential terrorist during a stop include observation through plain view of weapons or components, unusual or large quantities of specific products such as disposable cell phones, fertilizers (without an agricultural nexus), or bumper stickers with violent, extremist messages. These signals may have officer safety benefits as they give notice of a potentially dangerous individual.

Globally, terrorists and extremists have targeted law enforcement for strategic, operational, and tactical reasons, including during traffic stops. Additionally, radicals have killed US law enforcement during traffic stops on various occasions. To enhance officer safety during traffic stops, law enforcement must stay alert and recognize that there is no routine traffic stop. In doing so, they must not let their guard down. Police officers must undertake a thorough search of the vehicle and recognize danger signs, such as rapid movements of hands. Police should also wait for backup should circumstances warrant.

Community Policing

The benefits of community policing are manifold. For example, it can aid in raising awareness of the role that police can play in reducing crime in communities. Also, such police efforts can assist in creating affinities, understanding, and cooperation with community members. Police involvement in community affairs can contribute to increasing public vigilance and resilience. Furthermore, neighborhood policing can help develop sources, gain insights on suspicious persons and activities, and appreciate where to possibly use informants and undercover agents in future sting operations. Additionally, high profile involvement in communities can deter crime in the area.

Vulnerable communities can take various steps to help reduce criminal activities, including terrorism. For instance, they may participate in training activities, such as citizen academies. Vulnerable communities can start or expand dialogue with police so that a better understanding of the needs and worries of the community is relayed. Neighborhood residents can cosponsor and attend police-community meetings and forums so links can be forged or strengthened. Once police solidify relationships with a neighborhood, they can develop bonds with individual families. In doing so, police can discover an existing family terror cabal, encourage activities within the family to expunge radicalism that may exist in a clan, or prevent infiltration of extremism within a home.

To ensure that police are mindful of the demands facing particular communities, neighborhood leaders should encourage and aid efforts to recruit police officers from their communities. The results of such efforts are improved community relations, fewer people becoming extremists, and less terrorism.

Role of the Public

The public's involvement in informing authorities about possible terrorist activities merits close attention. Since 9/11, the public has often recognized these signs of terrorism, informed law enforcement, and aided in preventing potential large-scale incidents. In particular, industry can facilitate identifying suspicious behavior that could have a nexus with terrorism. Many business sectors can keep an eye out for the suspicious appearance, peculiar transactions, and odd activities of their clients and employees.[177] More specifically, the US Department of Justice created flyers for sectors (e.g., hotels/motels, financial institutions, firearms shops and ranges) to increase their participation in observing behavior that are possibly indicative of terrorism.[178]

The burden of safeguarding society against acts of terrorism does not rest solely with government. It is everyone's responsibility.

Improving Communications

There is a need for improved communications and information dissemination among intelligence, law enforcement, and corrections professionals nationally, regionally, and internationally. While authorities have made great efforts worldwide in combating terrorism, occasionally mistakes occur regarding investigation, surveillance, detention (e.g., a suspect in custody commits suicide), or release of a terrorist.

Such counterterrorism mishaps came to light after several large-scale attacks in Europe (Paris in 2015 as well as Berlin, Brussels, and Nice in 2016). Unfortunately, such debacles will be replicated although, hopefully, with less regularity and dire consequences. Heightened awareness about terror threats, elicitation of tips, and responses to requests for information about suspects from private security employees and the public have proved helpful and should continue to be encouraged.

Individuals can provide tips to authorities about suspected terrorists. This came to the forefront in October 2016, when two Syrian refugees contacted German authorities upon recognizing a suspected terrorist who sought refuge at their apartment. German authorities published through social media and in multiple languages (including Arabic) the identity of that wanted man.

Leveraging Technology

Law enforcement exploits the capacities of technology to undermine extremists. The police monitor open-source websites, blogs, and social media using commercial and proprietary software. Law enforcement also engages in crafting sting operations, occasionally initiated online. More specifically, police find an extremist online while monitoring a forum or through a tip from the public. Additionally, technology companies and social media firms remove the extremist content of their customers with varying degrees of success.

Law enforcement can observe and access data from an extremist's online and telephonic activities through search warrants relating to physical and electronic matters. State and federal courts, including the Foreign Intelligence Surveillance Act (FISA) Court, issue such search warrants. Furthermore, the FBI can get limited insights on a terror suspect's internet, telephonic, and financial profile from issuing national security letters to third parties.

Police leverage many types of technology products and services in combating terrorism. Among the technologies in use are computer hardware, software, and peripherals; license plate readers; StingRays (machines that simulate cell towers); infrared cameras; GPS devices; and trace detectors.

There is an extensive public-private counterterror partnership in the technological realm. But tensions exist when police seek cooperation from companies to access the technology equipment of their clients. For example, after the San Bernardino shootings by the husband and wife team, police requested Apple's aid to enter the perpetrators' phones. Apple declined to assist in that circumstance, leading the FBI to use other sources to penetrate the phones. That instance became a renewed focal point on how much assistance is to be extended. Ultimately, the US government spent $900,000 to purchase a tool from a third-party provider to hack the phone.[179]

Additionally, police have used a Grayshift LLC iPhone-hacking (unlocking) box called GrayKey, which works only on Apple products. The device allows police forensic investigators to unlock passwords and download nearly all the data available on the device. At a cost of $15,000, GrayKey can resolve some of the issues that law enforcement faced in unlocking the devices of the San Bernardino terrorist attackers.[180]

A principal challenge for law enforcement in leveraging technology to combat terrorism is shifting through an enormous amount of multilingual electronic communications and other activities on the internet, such as electronic fund transfers via PayPal, Bitcoin, and other electronic payment systems and cryptocurrencies. Impeding the capacity to review all these actions are inadequate staffing levels, limited funding, emerging technologies, and new funding modalities.

Another frustration is terrorists' use of encrypted communications, including instant messaging apps, and new technologies not easily monitored (e.g., PlayStation). Other impediments to success have included the occasional lack of cooperation from companies (e.g., Twitter, Facebook, Apple) in removing extremist content or aiding in accessing a suspect's products and services.

However, in light of complaints, such firms have increased their efforts to remove extremist content from their websites and instrumentalities. For instance, in June 2017, Facebook, Microsoft, Twitter, and YouTube created the Global Internet Forum for Counter Terrorism, whose goal is to undermine terrorists' capacity to use of the Internet to promote and glorify terrorism, extremism, and violence. Additionally, Jigsaw, an incubator within the firm Alphabet (Google), focuses on leveraging technology to combat violent extremism on the Internet, among other activities.

Preventing the Next Attack

It is crucial to undertake risk and vulnerability assessments so that an attack is unlikely. Such security assessments consider assets needing protection and their vulnerability and criticality. It is critical for jurisdictions to make a list of the most likely government, private sector, nonprofit, and nongovernmental organization targets.

Various steps come into play when trying to harden prospective terror targets. Security and technology products and services can be integrated into fortifying existing targets. Specific items will be adopted depending on the threats and the resources available. It is crucial to use security layering. Such redundancies ensure a single breach will still face other obstacles.

Collaboration between government and industry in the security realm—sharing best security practices and intelligence about current and emerging threats—is important. Raising security awareness among employees and customers can aid in deterring or mitigating a threat.

Large-scale, high-profile attacks can have significant political implications both domestically and internationally. For example, terror incidents refocus public attention to finding solutions attenuated with border controls, asylum law, integration of immigrants, designation of the threat (e.g., Salafist, Jihadist, Takfirism) and its source, privacy and security debates, and the shift toward nativism over globalism.

Security efforts at respective targets may be insufficient due to the element of surprise, weaponry of the assailant(s), and the impossibility of 100 percent vigilance every second in all locations, whether in one city or beyond. Fortunately, in the case of the Berlin attack, the carnage was limited due to triggering of the automatic braking system that resulted in the truck being brought to a stop after about 250 feet. In contrast, the truck used in the Nice attack in July 2016 did not have this feature.[181]

Responding to an Attack

Several variables are relevant in combating a terror attack. It is crucial to determine what form of attack police are facing: a bombing, an active shooter, a vehicle attack, a cyberattack, or a biological-chemical-radiological attack. Upon discerning the type of attack, police must detain or otherwise neutralize the attacker.

Terror incidents may not prove static as an active shooter situation can evolve into a hostage scenario—the converse. Sometimes, a terror attack may involve multiple attackers at several locations, occurring simultaneously. There may arise secondary explosives at a particular location as well, combined with a second wave of attackers.

Other problems police face in responding to an attack are imperfect information and highly fluid scenarios. Also, with the goal of incapacitating an active shooter as quickly as possible, police may forgo immediately tending to the wounded. When police do respond to an incident, several departments may arrive on the scene, triggering incident command issues. Upon detainment of the terrorist perpetrator, the public safety exception to giving a Miranda warning is used.

Police also use traffic stops and calls for service to undermine terrorists. There has been extensive use of informants and undercover agents in conducting sting operations, resulting in terrorism convictions. Using informants and undercover agents in vulnerable communities has resulted in some pushback by those who believe these operations stigmatize such populations. Some have raised concerns that the amount of time and effort surrounding sting cases undercuts police focus on "actual" plots.

Terrorists Targeting Police and Responses[182]

Police should raise awareness of safety risks arising from domestic and international terrorists. They should undertake risk and vulnerability assessments on law enforcement assets, adopt physical and information security upgrades, and modify operational practices. However, such measures are often not adopted because of their perceived costs in terms of finances, time, and manpower and the false impression—particularly in the United States—that the threats against police are largely a challenge in other countries.

Sadly, spontaneous vehicle or knife attacks against police are difficult to overcome. Such types of incidents appear to be occurring more frequently worldwide.

Overview

In 2016, terrorists embracing a myriad of ideologies attacked police worldwide 1,760 times in dozens of countries, the US State Department reported. That year, police were the second most frequent target of terrorists, after private citizens and their property (4,734).

Globally, terrorists have targeted police using a variety of tactics, including bombs, grenades, land mines, guns, fire, vehicles, and knives. The settings of terror strikes against police included police stations, vehicles, housing and training facilities, checkpoints, and in other locations (while providing security, at home, while commuting). Other occasions when terrorists and non-terrorists attacked police include ambush and arrest situations, during the investigation of suspicious persons/circumstances, traffic stops, protests, and tactical situations (responding to a barricaded offender, during a hostage taking, while capturing a high-risk offender).

Terrorists view police as an instrumentality of the oppressor state. As such, police are regarded as a legitimate target. After all, police can aid in undermining terror group activities, from radicalization and recruitment to financing and kinetic activities. Indeed, police have inflicted damage to terror groups' goals. Police have arrested or killed key leadership and operatives, including in the aftermath of an attack.

When terrorists target law enforcement, the government's credibility is undermined. The populace loses faith in the government's role to protect itself and its citizens. Public resolve is weakened when police are viewed as unable to defend themselves. Terror groups are emboldened by tarnishing the police's capabilities.

Police accelerate the likelihood of their victimization due to a heightened posture against terrorist goals. More specifically, police have become increasingly active in combating terror through their use of undercover agents, the leveraging of traffic stops and calls for service, intelligence gathering and sharing, and community outreach to vulnerable communities and beyond.

Attacks Against Police Overseas

Terrorists may carry weapons (guns or knives) while traveling. They have no reticence about using weapons against police during traditional interactions. Four days after the Berlin incident, two police officers approached a suspicious-looking person at a train station near Milan, Italy, at around 3:00 a.m. By sheer luck, it was Tunisian-born Anis Amri. Amri refused to produce identity documents when asked and reached for a gun in his backpack. After shooting one officer and wounding him, Amri fled. He hid himself behind a car before he was shot and killed by another officer. At that point, Italian police were unaware that Amri was in Italy—as were German authorities, for that matter.

In 2015, Iraqi refugee Rafik Mohamad Yousef was shot and killed by a German police officer after stabbing a policewoman with a three-inch knife in Berlin. German police came across Yousef in response to a call of a suspicious person. Yousef had been imprisoned for planning the assassination of former Iraqi Prime Minister Ayad Allawi during his visit to Germany in 2004. Yousef was sentenced to eight years in prison for participation in that plot and belonging to a terrorist organization. Yousef was under watch upon his return to Berlin in 2013 but removed an electronic ankle-monitoring device on the day of the stabbing.

Attacks Against US Law Enforcement

In the United States, a variety of ideologically aligned terrorists and extremists threaten police: sovereign citizens, militia members, those aligned with hate groups and ethno-racists, single-issue operatives, foreign terrorist organization (FTO) members, those inspired by FTOs, and others. According to the FBI, forty-six US policemen were killed during felonious incidents in 2017, although most of these occurred in non-terror incidents. While these figures may not appear high, the challenges of extremists and terrorists against American law enforcement do exist as elaborated below.

Extremists and terrorists have targeted US police for over a century. Likewise, police have been killed or injured during other attacks aimed at civilians at large. During the Haymarket Square attack in Chicago in May 1886, an anarchist threw an explosive and killed seven police and four civilians. The April 1995 Oklahoma City bombing, perpetrated by a sovereign citizen–militia cabal of Timothy McVeigh and Terry Nichols, resulted in 168 people killed, including 19 children and 8 federal law enforcement members. Using civilian airlines as missiles, on September 11, 2001, violent jihadists killed nearly 3,000 people, among them 72 law enforcement members.

Since then, extremists and terrorists have targeted US police in multiple preplanned attacks. In June 2014, Jerad and Amanda Miller shot and killed two Las Vegas police officers at a pizza restaurant. The Millers supported an array of extremist ideologies, including white nationalist, sovereign citizen, and militia themes. Gavin Long, a black separatist with sovereign citizen views, killed two Baton Rouge, Louisiana, policemen and a county deputy sheriff in July 2016.

Five months later, in an apparent ISIS-inspired attack, Edward Archer shot Philadelphia Police Department Officer Jesse Hartnett multiple times, severely injuring him. Miraculously, Harnett returned fire and wounded Archer. Later, the authorities captured the assailant. In October 2014, Zale Thompson swung a hatchet at two New York Police Department (NYPD) officers, injuring one officer in the head and another in the arm. The jihadist and black separatist–aligned perpetrator was shot and killed by other police at the scene.

In November 2013, Paul Ciancia shot and killed TSA officer Gerardo Hernandez at Los Angeles International Airport (LAX). Ciancia shot and injured two other TSA agents and a passenger during the incident. Ciancia was shot by responding LAX police and taken into custody. In September 2016, Ciancia pleaded guilty to the murder and related charges. Two months later, he was sentenced to life in prison. Ciancia was enraptured by a variety of anti-government ideologies.

Attacked While Responding to and Investigating Terror Incidents

Likewise, police have been injured while reacting to other terror attacks in the United States. In August 2012, white supremacist Wade Page shot and murdered six people and injured three others during an attack at a Sikh temple in Oak Creek, Wisconsin. Page also shot and severely injured a police officer who arrived at the incident. Although initial indications were that police killed Page, it was later determined that he took his own life.

In July 2015, Muhammad Youssef Abdulazeez attacked two military locations in Chattanooga, Tennessee, killing five persons and injuring two others, including a police officer. Police killed Abdulazeez during a shootout. He was inspired by a foreign terrorist organization.

Six months later, Syed Rizwan Farook and his wife Tashfeen Malik attacked a meeting and holiday party organized by his employer in San Bernardino, California. The couple killed fourteen and wounded twenty-two. Two police officers were injured during a shootout with the assailants that occurred several hours after the attack. The pair claimed to have undertaken the attack on behalf of ISIS.

In June 2016, Omar Mateen killed forty-nine persons and injured fifty-three others at Pulse, a gay nightclub in Orlando, Florida. Following several gunfire exchanges and hostage negotiations with Mateen, police shot and killed him. Mateen pledged allegiance to ISIS during a 911 call and referenced additional jihadist figures.

In September 2016, Jason Falconer, an off-duty Avon, Minnesota, police officer, shot and killed a jihadist-inspired terrorist, Dahir Adan, at the Crossroad Center Mall in Saint Cloud, Minnesota. Adan had lunged at Falconer several times with steak knives. Falconer identified himself as a police officer and told Adan to drop the knives. After Adan did not follow the orders, Falconer shot and killed him. Before that interaction, Adan had stabbed ten shoppers and a mall employee—all of whom survived.

Campus police in the United States have been on the front line in combating terrorism, as exemplified by two recent events. In a November 2015 ISIS-inspired attack, University of California at Merced student Faisal Mohammad used a hunting knife to stab four individuals on campus. Two responding campus police officers shot and killed Mohammad as he was fleeing from the scene.

In November 2016, an Ohio State University (OSU) student, Abdul Razak Ali Artan, drove a car onto the sidewalk and tried to run over pedestrians. After exiting the car, Artan stabbed passersby with a butcher knife. He injured eleven persons, some with the vehicle and others with the knife. Shortly thereafter, OSU policeman Alan Horujko shot and killed Artan. The perpetrator appeared to have been radicalized by jihadist propaganda, including that of ISIS and al Qaeda in the Arabian Peninsula.

In September 2014, Alton Nolen beheaded a female coworker and tried to behead another woman at a Vaughan food plant in Moore, Oklahoma. Mark Vaughan, the company's chief executive officer and an Oklahoma County reserve deputy, shot and wounded Nolen. Responding police officers took Nolen into custody. Nolen's Facebook profile had photos and commentary supportive of jihadi beheadings. In September 2017, Nolen was found guilty of first-degree murder and assault charges. Afterward, Nolen was sentenced to death for the murder plus 130 years for the assaults.

Other Threats Against Police

Police are at risk in other venues, such as while conducting searches of individuals and their homes and following up on suspicious persons. Also, a terrorist may seek retribution against an officer involved in undermining his terror plans.

While FBI agents were executing a search warrant at his New York home in June 2015, ISIS supporter Fareed Mumuni repeatedly stabbed an FBI agent with a large knife. Fortunately, the agent suffered only minor injuries as his body armor bore the brunt of the attack. Mumuni, who was part of an ISIS cabal that planned attacks in New York City and travel to the Middle East, was subsequently taken into custody. He later admitted plans to conduct a suicide attack using a pressure-cooker bomb against law enforcement. In February 2017, he pleaded guilty to conspiring and trying to provide material support to ISIS, attempted murder of federal officers, and assaulting/conspiring to assault federal officers.

In September 2016, Ahmad Khan Rahami shot and injured a Linden, New Jersey, police officer who was investigating a tip about a terror suspect involved in pressure-cooker bombings in New York and New Jersey. The officer survived being shot in the abdomen thanks to his bulletproof vest. Other officers chased Rahami and exchanged fire with the suspect, injuring him. He was then taken into custody.

Rahami was charged on multiple state and federal terrorism and attempted murder charges. In February 2018, Rahami was sentenced to two life terms in prison following convictions in October 2017 on federal charges regarding the New York bombing and attempted bombing. Rahami was inspired by variant jihadist ideologies, including ISIS.

In September 2012, Adel Daoud, a self-radicalized jihadist, was arrested in a sting operation while planning to detonate what he believed was a vehicle-borne explosive outside a Chicago bar. Later, Daoud was indicted for soliciting the murder of an undercover FBI agent whom he had met in the planned attack. As of April 2018, criminal proceedings against Daoud are ongoing.

In May 2013, Hysen Sherifi was sentenced to life in prison for conspiring to hire a hit man to behead three FBI agents and three witnesses who testified in his earlier terror trial. In that case, Sherifi was convicted of a terror conspiracy involving other jihadist operatives. Sherifi had recruited his brother Shkumbin and a woman, Nevine Aly Elshiekh, to arrange the murder-for-hire plot. In May 2013, Shkumbin and Elshiekh were sentenced to three years and forty-six months in prison, respectively, for the pair's conspiracy to commit the murder for hire.

Terror Suspects Surrender

Sometimes, terrorists have given up voluntarily following police responding to a terror incident. For instance, Naveed Haq killed one person and injured five during an attack with two semi-automatic pistols at the Seattle Jewish Federation office in July 2006. After negotiating with police, Haq surrendered. He was convicted on several charges arising from the attack and was given a life sentence. Haq has been characterized as a lone wolf, triggered by anti-Israeli and anti-Semitic perspectives.

In June 2009, Carlos Bledsoe carried out a drive-by shooting at a military recruiting station in Little Rock, Arkansas. The attack resulted in the death of one US soldier and the injury of another. After the incident, Bledsoe intended to drive to Memphis, Tennessee, and change vehicles. However, he was stopped by police and exited his car without incident. Bledsoe, who claimed affiliation with al Qaeda in the Arabian Peninsula, was sentenced to life in prison.

Tamerlan and Dzhokhar Tsarnaev detonated two improvised explosive devices at the April 2013 Boston Marathon, killing 3 and injuring over 260. In the days after the attack, Tamerlan shot and killed Sean Collier, a Massachusetts Institute of Technology (MIT) police officer, while one Boston Police Department officer, Dennis Simmonds, died in 2014 from injuries resulting after the brothers released homemade bombs from their car during a police chase.

Dzhokhar ran over and killed his brother Tamerlan while evading police. Dzhokhar ultimately surrendered after being shot by police while hiding in a boat in a driveway in Watertown, Massachusetts. (The homeowner had discovered Dzhokhar in his boat.) Dzhokhar was found guilty of perpetrating the attacks and sentenced to death. Jihadist perspectives influenced this cabal.

In January 2017, Esteban Santiago shot and killed five persons and wounded six others at Fort Lauderdale International Airport. After emptying two ammunition magazines, Santiago dropped his pistol, lay on the ground, and waited for police to arrest him. Later that month, Santiago was indicted on twenty-two federal charges stemming from the incident, including the use of firearms at an international airport and causing deaths there. Santiago had a history of mental illness. Among other things, he claimed being monitored by the government and simultaneously forced him to watch ISIS videos.

International Cooperation

International cooperation in combating terrorism is critical. Terrorists and their associated groups are mobile, transverse borders—with their radicalization, recruitment, financing, and operations—and are capable of striking globally. Consequently, national, regional, and internationally oriented law enforcement, intelligence, and military organizations must collaborate and leverage capabilities against transnational terror actors: homegrown individuals aligned with foreign terrorist groups and international groups sending operatives to transcend borders.

The United Nations Counter-Terrorism Centre (UNCCT) was created "to assist in meeting capacity-building needs of Member States, while strengthening United Nations' counter-terrorism expertise."[183] The United Nations Counter-Terrorism Implementation Task Force (CTITF) strengthens "coordination and coherence of counter-terrorism efforts of the United Nations system." The CTITF is composed "of 38 international entities which by virtue of their work have a stake in multilateral counter-terrorism efforts."[184] Other international efforts in combating terrorism include Interpol's Counter-Terrorism Fusion Centre, which "investigates the organizational hierarchies, training, financing, methods, and motives of terrorist groups."[185]

Likewise, regional efforts in combating terrorism are doing important work. For instance, Europol's European Counter Terrorism Centre is "an operations centre and hub of expertise that reflects the growing need for the EU [European Union] to strengthen its response to terror."[186] Additionally, the Southeast Asia Regional Centre for Counter-Terrorism was forged "to be a regional centre of excellence in training and research on counter-terrorism."[187] Furthermore, law enforcement agencies across the globe tend to cooperate in combating terrorism by sharing intelligence, capturing suspected terrorists, preventing attacks, and responding to incidents.

Conclusion

This chapter discussed law enforcement responses to terrorism that likewise have applicability in undermining kin connected extremism. The issues addressed in this chapter included the means to find terrorists, missed signs in discovering terrorists, the role of traffic stops, community policing, the contribution of the public, improving communications, leveraging technology, preventing the next attack, responding to a terrorist attack, terrorists targeting police and responses, and international cooperation. Law enforcement's capacity to combat terrorism in general and family affiliated terrorism in particular is challenging. Yet, it is critical to prevent the expansion of terrorism in the United States and abroad.

To reiterate, law enforcement must utilize the methodologies addressed in this chapter to forge expanded efforts in combating family terror networks. As such, it is imperative that police investigate possible family connections with extremism when encountering every terror suspect. After all, radicalization of an individual does not occur in a vacuum. Rather—as demonstrated in the over one hundred case studies presented in this book—it can arise from a family setting. Therefore, familial links that contribute to terrorism should not be ignored.

EPILOGUE

Family terror networks are likely to remain prevalent for various reasons. Belief systems advocating political violence exist in some family units. It is natural to share enthusiasm about newly found ideology, including extremist tenets, with easily swayed family members. The ability of family members to pressure others to support extremism remains strong. The leverage is that much stronger when exerted by a parent or sibling. The enticement of following in the footsteps of a family member will likely continue in earnest.

The ability to attract multiple family members to terrorism will cause terror groups to continue to exploit this subset of group membership. Best practices of terrorism are easily passed to other members of a family. Ideas percolating within a family rubric are deemed more legitimate than outside concepts. These conditions make it difficult to dislodge kin from radicalism. External and competing ideas often have a hard time penetrating a family setting.

A family member is largely unlikely to inform authorities of their kin's radicalism. So, this avenue for discovery is often not available. Detecting radical activity remains difficult for law enforcement. Challenges exist in countering violent extremism among nonprofits, nongovernmental organizations, industry, and the public at large. Easily accessible and inexpensive technologies and transportation enable people, ideas, and monies to move rapidly and inexpensively. These circumstances enhance the movement of extremists, their ideas, and monies.

There is declining apprehension about openly supporting extremism. For instance, there is less reticence about participating in extremism-linked rallies. These circumstances allow for confirmation of radicalism that has developed within a family, among other sources. Additionally, offline and online radicalization nodes enable family terror networks to expand existing terror cells.

In sum, families can serve as incubators for radicalism. This segment of social networks will feature prominently and perilously in domestic and international terrorism environs for the foreseeable future. This book provided an analysis of the varied and complex themes related to the challenging and disturbing topic of family terror networks. Going forward, further inquiry into other facets of family affiliated terrorism and their ramifications is needed.

APPENDIX

Family Terror Network Cases Referenced in the Book

Name	Family Relationship	Ideology
1. Denis Cuspert Daniela Greene	Husband Wife	Jihadism
2. Jerad Miller Amanda Miller	Husband Wife	White Supremacy, Sovereign Citizen, and Militia
3. Hasan and Jonas Edmonds	Cousins	Jihadism
4. Muhammad Oda Dakhlalla Jaelyn Delshaun Young	Husband Wife	Jihadism
5. Michael Wolfe Jordan Furr	Husband Wife	Jihadism
6. Mohammed Khan Unidentified male minor Unidentified female minor	Brother Brother Sister	Jihadism
7. Alaa and Nader Saadeh	Brothers	Jihadism
8. Unidentified Sister 1 Farah Unidentified Sister 2 Farah	Sisters	Jihadism
9. Tamerlan and Dzhokhar Tsarnaev	Brothers	Jihadism
10. Ahmed and Hamza al-Ghamdi Ahmed al-Haznawi	Cousins	Jihadism
11. Wail and Waleed al-Shehri	Brothers	Jihadism
12. Nawaf and Salem al-Hamzi	Brothers	Jihadism
13. Ali Fauzi, Ali Ghufron, Ali Imron, and Amrozi Nurhasyim	Brothers	Jihadism
14. Brahim and Salah Abdeslam	Brothers	Jihadism
15. Abdelhamid and Younes Abaaoud Hasna Aitboulahcen	Brothers, Cousins Cousin	Jihadism

16. Khalid Sheikh Muhammad Ramzi Yousef	Uncle Nephew	Jihadism
17. Don Black Derek Black	Father Son	White Supremacy
18. Siddhartha Dhar Aisha Dhar	Husband Wife	Jihadism
19. Parents of Safia S. Safia S. Unidentified Male	Parents Child (Daughter)/ Sister Child (Son)/Brother	Jihadism
20. Imane and Sahne al Ghariss	Sisters	Jihadism
21. Habib Saleh Ghani Samantha Lewthwaite	Husband Wife	Jihadism
22. Cherif and Said Kouachi	Brothers	Jihadism
23. Junaid Hussain Sally Jones Jo Jo Jones	Husband/Stepfather Wife/Mother Son	Jihadism
24. Hysen and Shkumbin Sherifi	Brothers	Jihadism
25. Pat Rudolph Eric Rudolph	Mother Son	Christian Identity/ Anti-abortion/ Anti-LGBTQ
26. Khalid and Ibrahim el Bakraoui	Brothers	Jihadism
27. Unidentified Male Shannon Conley	Prospective husband Prospective wife	Jihadism
28. Unidentified Male 1 Aisha Kadad	Husband 1 Wife	Jihadism
29. Unidentified Male 2 Aisha Kadad	Husband 2 Wife	Jihadism
30. Unidentified Male Aqsa Mahmood	Husband Wife	Jihadism
31. Unidentified Male Luiza Gazuyeva	Husband Wife	Jihadism
32. Unidentified Male Aminat Kurbanova	Husband Wife	Jihadism

33. Magomed Illyasov Aminat Kurbanova	Husband Wife	Jihadism
34. Umalat Magomedev Dzhennet Abdurakhmanova	Husband Wife	Jihadism
35. Unidentified Male Khava Barayeva	Uncle Niece	Jihadism
36. Fadi Jaradat Hanadi Jaradat Salah Jaradat	Brother, Cousin Sister, Cousin Cousin	Jihadism
37. Larossi Abballa Sarah H.	Prospective Husband Prospective Wife	Jihadism
38. Adel Kermiche Sarah H.	Prospective Husband Prospective Wife	Jihadism
39. Hamsa and Hersi Kariye Mahad Kersi Hanad Abdullahi Mohallim Abdullahi Ahmed Abdullahi	Brothers/Cousins Cousin Cousin Cousin	Jihadism
40. Munir Abdulkader Unidentified male	Cousins	Jihadism
41. Abdullah and Ibrahim al-Asiri	Brothers	Jihadism
42. Abdulrahman and Ibrahim Saleh Muhammad al-Imir	Brothers	Jihadism
43. Ali Hussein Ali al-Shmari Sajida Mubarak Atrous al-Rishawi Two Unidentified Males	Husband Wife/Sister Brothers	Jihadism
44. Hebatullah Akhundzada Khalid	Father Son	Jihadism
45. Ahmed and Ezzit Raad	Brothers	Jihadism
46. Mustafa Cheikho Khaled Cheikho	Uncle Nephew	Jihadism
47. Lonnie Vernon Karen Vernon	Husband Wife	Militia, Sovereign Citizen
48. Osama bin Laden Saad, Khalid, and Hamza bin Laden	Father Sons, Brothers	Jihadism

49. Hamza bin Laden Unidentified Woman (Atta)	Husband Wife	Jihadism
50. Ahmed Said Khadr Abdul Karim Abdullah Abdurahman Omar	Father Son, Brother Son, Brother Son, Brother Son, Brother	Jihadism
51. Tom Metzger John Metzger	Father Son	White Supremacy
52. Ian Davison Nicky Davison	Father Son	White Supremacy
53. Syed Rizwan Farook Tafsheen Malik	Husband Wife	Jihadism
54. Omar Mateen Noor Salman	Husband Wife	Jihadism
55. Ramiz Zijad Hodzic Sedina Unkic Hodzic	Husband Wife	Jihadism
56. Roderick Moore Amber Catrece Moore	Husband Wife	Sovereign Citizen
57. Mohammed Sajid Khan Shasta Khan	Husband Wife	Jihadism
58. Issam Goris Muriel Degauque	Husband Wife	Jihadism
59. Moez Garsallaoui Malika el Aroud	Husband Wife	Jihadism
60. Abdessatar Dahmane Malia el Aroud	Husband Wife	Jihadism
61. Suhan Abdul Rahman Hoda Muthana	Husband Wife	Jihadism
62. Unidentified Male Samra Kesinovic	Husband Wife	Jihadism
63. Unidentified male Sabina Selimovic	Husband Wife	Jihadism
64. Abdul Ghameed Abbas Grace Khadija Dare Isa Abbas	Husband/Stepfather Wife/Mother Son	Jihadism

65. Unidentified Male Linda Wenzel	Husband Wife	Jihadism
66. Ali and Jarallah al Marri	Brothers	Jihadism
67. Mahmoud and Haider Kourani	Brothers	Hezbollah
68. Tuhin Shahensha Mustakim and Ifthekar Jaman	Brothers	Jihadism
69. Omar Deghayes Jaffar, Abdullah, and Amer Deghayes	Uncle Brothers/Nephews	Jihadism
70. Mohamad and Chawki Hammoud	Brothers	Hezbollah
71. Youssef Abdulazeez Muhammad Youssef Abdulazeez	Father Son	Jihadism
72. Abu Sayyaf al-Iraqi Umm Sayyaf	Husband Wife	Jihadism
73. Abu Bakr al-Baghdadi Saja al-Dulaimi	Husband Wife	Jihadism
74. Falah Ismail al-Jasim Saja al-Dulaimi	Husband Wife	Jihadism
75. Hamid al-Dulaimi Omar al-Dulaimi Saja al-Dulaimi	Father Son/Brother Daughter/Sister	Jihadism
76. Ghassan Elashi Mousa Abu Marzook	Cousins-in-Law	Jihadism
77. Mohamed bin Laden Unidentified Woman -Atef	Husband Wife	Jihadism
78. Frank Acona Malissa Ann Acona	Husband Wife	White Supremacy
79. Three Unidentified Males Wafa Idris	Brothers Sister	Jihadism
80. Sabri Essid Mohamed and Abdelkader Merah Souad Merah	Stepfather Stepsons/Brothers Stepdaughter/Sister	Jihadism
81. Amedy Coulibaly Hayat Boumeddiene	Husband Wife	Jihadism
82. Ibrahim and Musa al-Akari	Brothers	Jihadism

83. Khaled and Saleh al-Oraini	Brothers	Jihadism
84. Umer Hayat Hamid Hayat	Father Son	Jihadism
85. Gulshair el Shukrijumah Adnan el Shukrijumah	Father Son	Jihadism
86. Raymond Foster Shane Foster	Father Son	White Supremacy
87. Jerry Kane Joseph Kane	Father Son	Sovereign Citizen
88. Bruce Turnridge Joshua Turnridge	Father Son	White Supremacy, Sovereign Citizen, and Militia
89. Wade Lay Christopher Lay	Father Son	Militia and Sovereign Citizen
90. Paul Rockwood Nadia Rockwood	Husband Wife	Jihadism
91. Zachary Chesser Proscovia Nzabantia	Husband Wife	Jihadism
92. Shawn Joel Parson Keonna Thomas	Husband Wife	Jihadism
93. George Sibley Lynda Lyon-Block	Husband Wife	Sovereign Citizen
94. Amer, Mahmoud, Khaled, and Tarek Khayat	Brothers	Jihadism
95. Raees Alan Qazi Sheheryar Alan Qazi	Brothers	Jihadism
96. Muhammad Ibrahim Bilal Ahmed Ibrahim Bilal	Brothers	Jihadism
97. Jeffrey Battle Martinique Battle	Ex-Husband Ex-Wife	Jihadism
98. Yahya Farooq Mohammad Ibrahim Zubair Mohammad	Brothers	Jihadism
99. Asif Ahmed Salim Sultane Room Salim	Brothers	Jihadism
100. Mohamed Farah Adnan Farah	Brothers	Jihadism

101. Guled Omar Ahmed Ali Omar	Brothers	Jihadism
102. Mohamed and Omar Maha	Brothers	Jihadism
103. Karim and Foued Mohamed-Aggad	Brothers	Jihadism
104. Hammad and Hassan Munshi	Brothers	Jihadism
105. Aabid Khan Sultan Muhammad	Cousins	Jihadism
106. Imane and Sane al Ghariss	Sisters	Jihadism
107. Jazib Khan Junead Khan	Uncle Nephew	Jihadism
108. Mansoor Arbabsiar Gholam Shukri	Cousins	State-sponsor (Iran)
109. Khaleed and Zubair Ahmed	Cousins	Jihadism
110. Mohammed Zazi Najibullah Zazi Amanullah Zazi	Father Son/Cousin Cousin	Jihadism
111. Dritan, Shain, and Eljrir Duka Mohamad Ibrahim Shnewer	Brothers Brother-in-law	Jihadism
112. Daniel Boyd Dylan and Zakirya Boyd	Father Sons, Brothers	Jihadism
113. Rasel Raihan Zakia Nasrin Jaffrey Khan	Brother Sister, Wife Husband	Jihadism
114. Unidentified Male Farah Salma and Zahra Halane Abdullah Ahmed Jama Farah	Brother/Cousin Sisters/Cousin Cousin	Jihadism
115. Abdullah, Omarkayan, Abdul Rahman, Abdul Azis, and Hamza Maute Cayamora Maute Farhana Maute	Brothers, Sons Father, Husband Mother, Wife	Jihadism
116. Ahmed Dawood Khadija, Sugra, Zohra Dawood	Brother Sisters	Jihadism

117. Terry Smith Chanel Skains Brian and Derrick Smith	Father, Husband Wife Sons, Brothers	Sovereign Citizen
118. Arthur Bixby Rita Bixby Steven Bixby	Father, Husband Mother, Wife Son	Sovereign Citizen
Total number of families: 118	**Distribution of Family Relationships – 138:** (One family may have two or more types of relationships involving terror-aligned individuals) Husbands/Wives (43/138 cases or 31.16%); Brothers (36/138 cases or 26.09%); Fathers/Sons (15/138 cases or 10.87%); Cousins (11/138 cases or 7.97%); Siblings (other than sister-	**Types of ideologies:** Jihadism (100/118 or 84.75%); Sovereign Citizens (5/118 or 4.24%); White Supremacy (5/118 or 4.24%); Militia and Sovereign Citizen (2/118 or 1.69%); White Supremacy, Sovereign Citizen, and Militia (2/118 or 1.69%); Hezbollah (2/118 or .85%); State-Sponsor (Iran) (1/118 or .85%); Christian Identity/Anti-abortion/Anti-LGBTQ (1/118 or .85%).
	sister, brother-brother) (9/138 cases or 6.52%); Uncles/Nephews (4/138 cases or 2.90%); Parents/Children (3/138 cases or 2.17%); Prospective Husbands/Wives (3/138 cases or 2.17%); Sisters (3/138 cases or 2.17%); Mother/Son (3/138 cases or 2.17%);	

	Stepfather/ Stepchildren (3/138 cases or 2.17%); Father/ Sons-Daughters (1/138 cases or .72%); Uncle/Niece (1/138 cases or .72%); Brother-in-Law (1/138 cases or .72%); Cousin-in-Law (1/138 cases or .72%); Ex-Husband/ Ex-Wife (1/138 cases or .72%)	

NOTES

Introduction

[1] Dean Alexander, "The Islamic State and Its Implications for Security," *Security Magazine*, September 8, 2015, https://www.securitymagazine. com/articles/86645-the-islamic-state-and-its-implications-for-security.

[2] Scott Glover, "The FBI Translator Who Went Rogue and Married an ISIS Terrorist," *CNN*, May 1, 2017, https://www.cnn.com/2017/ 05/01/politics/investigates-fbi-syria-greene/index.html; United States of America v. Daniela Greene, Motion to Unseal and Substitute Redacted Versions of Some Documents. US District Court for DC, April 17, 2015, https://extremism.gwu.edu/sites/g/ files/zaxdzs2191/f/Greene%2C%20Daniela%20-%20Motion%20 to%20Unseal.pdf.

[3] Jason Burke, "'Gangsta Jihadi' Denis Cuspert Killed Fighting in Syria," *Guardian*, January 19, 2018. https://www.theguardian.com/ world/2018/jan/19/gangsta-jihadi-denis-cuspert-killed-fighting-in-syria.

[4] Matthew Walberg and Michael Muskal, "Dad of Female Las Vegas Shooter Begged Her Not to Marry Jerad Miller," *Los Angeles Times*, June 9, 2014, http://www.latimes.com/nation/nationnow/la-na-amanda-jared-miller-father-las-vegas-shooting-20140609-story. html.

[5] Matt Pearce, John M. Glionna, and Matthew Walberg, "Las Vegas Shooters Saw Government as the Enemy," *Los Angeles Times*, June 9, 2014, http://www.latimes.com/nation/la-na-vegas-shooters-20140610-story.html.

[6] Howard Klopowitz, "Read Las Vegas Shooter Jerad Miller's Anti-Government Manifesto," *International Business Times*, June 9, 2014, http://www.ibtimes.com/read-las-vegas-shooter-jerad-millers-anti-government-manifesto-photo-1596345.

[7] Matthew Walberg and Michael Muskal, "Dad of Female Las Vegas Shooter Begged Her Not to Marry Jerad Miller," *Los Angeles Times*, June 9, 2014, http://www.latimes.com/nation/nationnow/la-na-amanda-jared-miller-father-las-vegas-shooting-20140609-story.html.

[8] Mark Berman, "Terror in the American Desert," *Washington Post*, June 14, 2014, https://www.washingtonpost.com/news/post-nation/wp/2014/06/14/terror-in-the-american-desert/?utm_term=.aaf51f99c442.

[9] "Vegas Killers Hoped Shooting Would Be 'Beginning of the Revolution,'" *Newsweek*, June 10, 2014, https://www.newsweek.com/vegas-killers-hoped-shooting-would-be-beginning-revolution-254268.

[10] "Vegas Killers Wanted to 'Columbine' the Police," *Police Magazine*, June 10, 2014, http://www.policemag.com/channel/patrol/news/2014/06/10/vegas-killers-wanted-to-columbine-the-police.aspx?force-desktop-view=1.

[11] "US Army National Guard Soldier Pleads Guilty to Attempting to Provide Material Support to ISIL," US Department of Justice, Office of Public Affairs, December 14, 2015. https://www.justice.gov/opa/pr/us-army-national-guard-soldier-pleads-guilty-attempting-provide-material-support-isil; "Aurora Cousins Sentenced to Lengthy Prison Terms for Conspiring to Provide Material Support to ISIL," US Department of Justice, US Attorney's Office, Northern District of Illinois, September 20, 2016. https://www.justice.gov/usao-ndil/pr/aurora-cousins-sentenced-lengthy-prison-terms-conspiring-provide-material-support-isil.

[12] *Oxford Living Dictionaries*, no date, s.v. "family," https://en.oxford-dictionaries.com/definition/family.

[13] Elizabeth Shown Mills, "The Kinship Maze: Navigating it with Professional Precision," *Association of Professional Genealogists Quarterly*, 20(2) (2005), pp. 61-66, https://historicpathways.com/download/navkinmaze.pdf.

[14] *Terrorist Organizational Models: A Military Guide to Terrorism in the Twenty-First Century* (Fort Leavenworth, KS: US Army Training and Doctrine Command, August 15, 2007), https://fas.org/irp/threat/terrorism/guide.pdf.

[15] James Chriss, "The Functions of the Social Bond," *Sociology Quarterly* 48, no. 4 (Fall 2007): 689–712, https://www.jstor.org/stable/40220048?seq=1#page_scan_tab_contents.

[16] Steve Ressler, "Social Network Analysis as an Approach to Combat Terrorism: Past, Present, and Future Research," *Homeland Security Affairs* (July 2006), https://www.hsaj.org/articles/171.

[17] Stuart Koschade, "A Social Network Analysis of Jemaah Islamiyah: The Applications to Counter-Terrorism and Intelligence," *Studies in Conflict and Terrorism* 29, no. 6 (2006): 559–75, http://eprints.qut.edu.au/6074/1/6074.pdf.

[18] Dean Alexander, "All in the Family," *Peoria Journal Star*, June 17, 2016, http://www.pjstar.com/opinion/20160617/op-ed-all-in-family?page=1.; Dean Alexander, "Family-Affiliated Terrorism: From Paris to San Bernardino and Beyond," *Security Magazine*, January 1, 2016, https://www.securitymagazine.com/articles/86844-family-affiliated-terrorism-from-paris-to-san-bernadino-and-beyond.; Dean Alexander, "Paris Attacks and ISIS in the Family," *State Journal-Registrar*, November 20, 2015, http://m.sj-r.com/article/20151120/OPINION/151129973/13312/OPINION.; Dean Alexander, "Terror in the Family," *Intersec*, January 2014, http://www.intersecmag.co.uk/terrorism-jan14/.

[19] Dean Alexander. "ISIS Attack in US May Only Be a Matter of Time," *Peoria Journal Star*, November 21, 2015, http://www.pjstar.com/article/20151121/OPINION/151129914/2011/OPINION.

[20] Forrest Wickman, "Are Terrorists Often Brothers?" *Slate*, April 19, 2013, http://www.slate.com/articles/news_and_politics/explainer/2013/04/boston_bombing_suspects_dzhokhar_and_tamerlan_tsarnaev_how_often_are_brothers.html.

[21] Samantha Hawley and Ake Prihantari, "Break the Cycle: From Bombmaker, Brother of Bali Terrorists Now Fighting Radicalization," *ABC News,* August 17, 2017, http://www.abc.net.au/news/2017-08-17/former-bomb-maker-brother-of-bali-terrorists-fighting-radicalism/8814346.

[22] Jonathan Watts, "'These Boys Were Raised among Us': Terror Cell Town Reels after Catalonia Attacks," *Guardian*, August 22, 2017, https://www.theguardian.com/world/2017/aug/22/spain-attacks-these-boys-were-raised-among-us-the-town-where-terror-cell-was-born.; Souad Mekhennet and William Booth, "How a Dozen Young Men from a Small Town Secretly Plotted the Deadliest Terrorist Attack in Spain in More Than a Decade," *Washington Post*, August 20, 2017, https://www.washingtonpost.com/world/europe/how-a-dozen-young-men-from-a-small-town-secretly-plotted-the-deadliest-terrorist-attack-in-spain-in-more-than-a-decade/2017/08/19/f3d775de-844a-11e7-9e7a-20fa8d7a0db6_story.html?noredirect=on&utm_term=.75013469e51c.; Alissa J. Rubin, Patrick Kingsley, and Palko Karasz, "Barcelona Attack Suspects Had Ties to Imam Linked to ISIS," *New York Times*, August 20, 201, https://www.nytimes.com/2017/08/20/world/europe/spain-barcelona-attack-suspects.html.

[23] "Manchester Attack: Who was Salman Abedi?" *BBC*, June 12, 2017, https://www.bbc.com/news/uk-40019135.

[24] Hannah Beech, "After an Indonesian Family's Suicide Attack: A Quest for Answers," *New York Times*, May 27, 2018, https://www.

nytimes.com/2018/05/27/insider/indonesian-family-suicide-bomb-ers.html.; "Surabaya Attacks: Family of Five Bomb Indonesia Police Headquarters," *BBC*, May 14, 2018, http://www.bbc.com/news/world-asia-44105279.

[25] Alexander, "All in the Family"; Alexander, "Family-Affiliated Terrorism: From Paris to San Bernardino and Beyond"; Alexander, "Paris Attacks and ISIS in the Family; Alexander, "Terror in the Family."

[26] Niyazi Ekici, *The Dynamics of Terrorist Recruitment: The Case of the Revolutionary People's Liberation Party/Front (DHKP/C) and the Turkish Hezbollah* (Verlag VDM: Saarbrücken, Germany, 2010). https://www.amazon.com/DYNAMICS-TERRORIST-RECRUITMENT-Revolutionary-Liberation/dp/363924544X.

[27] "Plane Terror Suspects Convicted on All Counts," *CNN*, September 5, 1996 http://www.cnn.com/US/9609/05/terror.plot/.

[28] Benjamin Weiser, "The Trade Center Verdict," *New York Times*, November 13, 1997, https://www.nytimes.com/1997/11/13/nyre-gion/trade-center-verdict-overview-mastermind-driver-found-guilty-1993-plot-blow-up.html.

[29] "Pilot Sentenced to Life Term for Plot to Blow Up US Planes," *Chicago Tribune*, May 16, 1998, http://articles.chicagotribune.com/1998-05-16/news/9805160123_1_abdul-hakim-murad-philip-pine-airlines-jet-ramzi-yousef.

Chapter 1

[30] Yonah Alexander and Dean Alexander, *Terrorism and Business: The Impact of September 11, 2001* (Ardsley, NY: Transnational Publishers, 2002), https://brill.com/view/title/13942.

[31] Dean Alexander, "Terrorism Challenges Facing the Trump Administration," *Security Magazine*, January 1, 2017, https://www.securitymagazine.com/articles/87681-terrorism-challenges-facing-the-trump-administration.

[32] Ibid.

[33] "National Consortium for the Study of Terrorism and Responses to Terrorism: Annex of Statistical Information: Country Reports on Terrorism 2016," US Department of State, 2017, https://www.state.gov/j/ct/rls/crt/2016/272241.htm.

[34] Alexander, "Terrorism Challenges Facing the Trump Administration."

[35] "2016 Hate Crime Statistics Released," Federal Bureau of Investigation, November 13, 2017, https://www.fbi.gov/news/stories/2016-hate-crime-statistics.

[36] Peter Beinart, "The Rise of the Violent Left," *Atlantic*, September 2017, https://www.theatlantic.com/magazine/archive/2017/09/the-rise-of-the-violent-left/534192/.

[37] Dean Alexander, "The Sovereign Citizens Movement: Threats and Responses," *Security Magazine*, June 1, 2016, https://www.securitymagazine.com/articles/87159-the-sovereign-citizen-movement-threats-and-responses.

[38] Audrey Kurth Cronin, "Terrorist Motivations for Chemical and Biological Weapons Use: Placing the Threat in Context," Congressional Research Service, March 28, 2003, https://fas.org/irp/crs/RL31831.pdf.

[39] Dean Alexander, "Offline and Online Radicalization and Recruitment of Extremists and Terrorists," *Journal of Homeland Security*, September 2010.

[40] Veronika Bondarenko, "White Supremacist Explains What it Took for him to Rethink his Beliefs," *Business Insider*, August 23,

2017, https://www.businessinsider.com/white-supremacist-explains-what-it-took-for-him-to-rethink-his-beliefs-2017-8.

[41] *Countering Violent Extremism: A Guide for Practitioners and Analysts*, National Counterterrorism Center (May 2014): 20–21, https://www.documentcloud.org/documents/1657824-cve-guide.html.

[42] Ibid., 22.

[43] Ibid, 19.

[44] Justin Huggler, "German Teenager Who Stabbed Police Officer 'Told British Friend of Her Plans,'" *Telegraph,* June 18, 2016, https://www.telegraph.co.uk/news/2016/06/18/german-teen-who-stabbed-police-officer-in-isil-attack-told-briti/.; "From Hanover to IS: The Case of Safia S.," *DW*, October 19, 2016, https://www.dw.com/en/from-hanover-to-is-the-case-of-safia-s/a-36094144.; Lizzie Dearden, "Teenage Girl Jailed for Stabbing Police Officer in Germany's First Isis-Commissioned Attack," *Independent*, January 27, 2017, https://www.independent.co.uk/news/world/europe/germany-terror-attack-isis-islamic-state-hanover-train-station-police-officer-safia-s-15-teenage-a7551116.html.

[45] "UK Jihadist Junaid Hussain Killed in Syria Drone Strike, Says US," *BBC News*, August 27, 2015, https://www.bbc.com/news/uk-34078900.; Aisling Moloney, "Who is the White Widow, Sally Jones and How Did She Get Involved With ISIS," *Metro*, October 12, 2017, https://metro.co.uk/2017/10/12/who-is-the-white-widow-sally-jones-and-how-did-she-get-involved-with-isis-6994454.; Harry Cockburn, "Sally Jones: Who was the 'White Widow'? What We Know About the ISIS Member Killed in a US Drone Strike," *Independent*, October 12, 2017, https://www.independent.co.uk/news/world/middle-east/white-widow-sally-jones-killed-isis-uk-jihadi-us-drone-strike-syria-who-was-she-explainer-a7996521.html.

[46] "Rudolph's Mother: Son Not a 'Monster,'" *CNN*, August 22, 2005, http://www.cnn.com/2005/LAW/08/22/rudolph.mother/.

[47] Dean Alexander and John Avelar. "Lessons Learned from the 2016 Berlin Truck Attack," *Homeland Security Today*, January 9, 2017, https://www.hstoday.us/channels/global/exclusive-lessons-learned-from-the-2016-berlin-truck-attack.

[48] Ibid.

[49] Ibid.

[50] "Guidance for Federal Law Enforcement Agencies Regarding the Use of Race, Ethnicity, Gender, National Origin, Religion, Sexual Orientation, or Gender Identity," U.S. Department of Justice, December 2014, https://www.justice.gov/sites/default/files/ag/pages/attachments/2014/12/08/use-of-race-policy.pdf.

[51] Dean Alexander and Robert Cresero, "Is the Woman Next Door a Terrorist?" *Security Magazine*, September 2013, http://digital.bnpmedia.com/publication/?i=173995&p=54#{"page":"54","issue_id":173995.

[52] Dean Alexander. "The Islamic State's Lure to Foreign Women," *Jerusalem Post*, December 20, 2015, https://www.jpost.com/Opinion/Islamic-States-lure-to-foreign-women-437896.

[53] Jenny Deam, "Colorado Woman's Quest for Jihad Baffles Neighbors," *Los Angeles Times*, July 25, 2014, http://www.latimes.com/nation/la-na-high-school-jihadi-20140726-story.html.

[54] Ibid.

[55] Alexander, "The Islamic State's Lure to Foreign Women."

[56] Borzou Daragahi, "We Spoke to Women Who Married into ISIS in Syria. These Are Their Regrets," *BuzzFeed*, July 20, 2017, https://www.buzzfeednews.com/article/borzoudaragahi/the-women-who-married-into-isis-are-now-filled-with-regret#.fnRnBB1bw.

[57] Scott Campbell, "The Orphans That ISIS Left Behind," *Daily Mail*, July 16, 2017, https://www.dailymail.co.uk/news/article-4702208/Orphans-ISIS-left-Mosul-pulled-rubble.html.

[58] "Inside the Life of a 20-Year-Old Scottish Woman Who Ran Away to Become a Hardline Supporter of ISIS," *National Post*, January 24, 2015, https://nationalpost.com/news/inside-the-life-of-a-20-year-old-scottish-woman-who-ran-away-become-a-hardline-supporter-of-isis.

[59] Hanna Kozlowska, "Meet the Female Terrorists Keeping Putin Up at Night," *Foreign Policy*, January 22, 2014, https://foreignpolicy.com/2014/01/22/meet-the-female-terrorists-keeping-putin-up-at-night/.

[60] Robert Pape, Lindsey O'Rourke, and Jenna McDermit, "What Makes Chechen Women So Dangerous?" *New York Times*, March 30, 2010, https://www.nytimes.com/2010/03/31/opinion/31pape.html.

[61] Dean Alexander, "Terror Financing and Factors Facilitating its Growth," *Security Magazine*, September 6, 2011, https://www.securitymagazine.com/articles/82316-terror-financing-and-factors-facilitating-its-growth.

[62] Ibid.

[63] Dean Alexander, *Business Confronts Terrorism: Risks and Responses* (Madison, WI: University of Wisconsin Press, 2004), https://uwpress.wisc.edu/books/2619.htm.

[64] "Chemical Facility Anti-Terrorism Standards," Department of Homeland Security, last revised June 29, 2018, https://www.dhs.gov/chemical-facility-anti-terrorism-standards.

[65] Alexander, *Business Confronts Terrorism*.

[66] Ibid.

[67] Dean Alexander and Alex Halpern, "Emergency and Medical Response Planning for Mass Casualty Terror Attacks," *Security Magazine*, July 1, 2017, https://www.securitymagazine.com/articles/88103-emergency-medical-response-planning-for-mass-casualty-terror-attacks.

[68] Dean Alexander and Alex Cluster, "The Bastille Day Attack and the Islamic State's Global Tentacles," *Security Magazine*, July 18, 2016, https://www.securitymagazine.com/blogs/14-security-blog/post/87268-the-bastille-day-attack-and-islamic-states-global-tentacles.

[69] Dean Alexander, "Brussels Attacks Indicative of Jihadist Threats Facing the United States," *Security Magazine*, March 24, 2016, http://www.securitymagazine.com/articles/87032-brussels-attacks-indicative-of-jihadist-threats-facing-the-united-states.

[70] Zachary Jason, "And Now," *Boston College Magazine*, no date, https://www.bc.edu/bc-web/bcnews/campus-community/alumni/andnow.html.

[71] Deborah Hastings, "Two Brothers Lose Legs in Boston Bombings, Were Standing Near 8-Year-Old Boy," *New York Daily News*, April 16, 2013, http://www.nydailynews.com/news/national/brothers-lose-legs-boston-bombings-article-1.1318128.

[72] "Nice Attacks: Who Were the Victims?" *BBC*, August 19, 20016, https://www.bbc.com/news/world-europe-36805164.

[73] Doug Bolton, "Paris Attack Victims," *Independent*, November 18, 2015, https://www.independent.co.uk/news/world/europe/paris-attack-victims-list-french-government-identifies-all-129-people-killed-in-paris-terrorist-a6739116.html.

[74] Harry Readhead, "Paris Attacks," *Metro*, November 18, 2015, https://metro.co.uk/2015/11/18/paris-attacks-mother-and-grandmother-died-shielding-son-5-from-bullets-at-bataclan-5510961/.; Nicola Clark, "A Rare Night Out in Paris Ends in Tragedy for Two

Close Cousins, *New York Times*, November 17, 2015, https://www. nytimes.com/live/paris-attacks-live-updates/a-rare-night-out-ends- in-tragedy-for-two-close-cousins.

[75] Yonah Alexander and Dean Alexander, *Terrorism and Business: The Impact of September 11, 2001* (Ardsley, NY: Transnational Publishers, 2002), https://brill.com/view/title/13942.

Chapter 2

[76] Andrea Huncar, "3 ISIS Recruits from Edmonton Believed Killed," *CBC*, January 15, 2015, https://www.cbc.ca/news/ canada/edmonton/3-isis-recruits-from-edmonton-believed- killed-1.2901146.; Andrea Huncar, "Man Accused of Edmonton Jewelry Heist to Fund ISIS Funders," CBC, May 23, 2018, https:// www.cbc.ca/news/canada/edmonton/edmonton-terrorist-u-s-ex- tradition-fort-mcmurray-san-diego-court-1.4674994.

[77] "Pennsylvania Man Indicted for Soliciting Jihadists to Kill Americans," US Department of Justice, July 14, 2011, https:// www.justice.gov/opa/pr/pennsylvania-man-indicted-solicit- ing-jihadists-kill-americans.; Leah Nelson, "Internet Messages Detail 'Nazi Jihadist's' Radicalization," Southern Poverty Law Center, July 19, 2011, https://www.splcenter.org/hate- watch/2011/07/19/internet-messages-detail-%E2%80%98nazi-ji- hadist%E2%80%99s%E2%80%99-radicalization.; "Pennsylvania Man Sentenced for Terrorist Solicitation and Firearms Offense," US Department of Justice, July 16, 2013, https://www.justice.gov/opa/ pr/pennsylvania-man-sentenced-terrorist-solicitation-and-fire- arms-offense.

[78] "Osama bin Laden's Son Vows to Avenge His Father's Death," *CBS News*, July 10, 2016, https://www.cbsnews.com/news/ osama-bin-laden-son-hamza-vows-to-avenge-fathers-death/.

79 Martin Chulov, "Hamza bin Laden has Married Daughter of Lead 9/11 Hijacker, Say Family," *Guardian*, August 5, 2018, https://www.theguardian.com/world/2018/aug/05/hamza-bin-laden-marries-daughter-of-911-hijacker-mohammed-atta.

80 "A Quick Sketch of the Omar Khadr Family," *National Post*, July 24, 2017, https://nationalpost.com/pmn/news-pmn/canada-news-pmn/a-quick-sketch-of-omar-khadrs-family.

81 Ibid.

82 Ibid.

83 "Omar Khadr: The Case, the Compensation, and the Media," *Al Jazeera*, August 6, 2017, https://www.aljazeera.com/programmes/listeningpost/2017/08/omar-khadr-case-compensation-media-170805131345055.html.

84 Maham Abedi, "Here's Why Omar Khadr is Getting $10M from the Canadian Government," *Global News*, July 4, 2017, https://globalnews.ca/news/3573619/omar-khadr-canada-compensation/.

85 "Chronology: A Timeline of the Khadr Family's Travels and Alleged Activities," *Frontline*, Undated. https://www.pbs.org/wgbh/pages/frontline/shows/khadr/family/cron.html.

86 Michelle Shepard, "Court Rejects Abdullah Khadr Extradition Request," *Toronto Star*, August 4, 2010, https://www.thestar.com/news/world/2010/08/04/court_rejects_abdullah_khadr_extradition_request.html.; "Abdullah Khadr extradition ruling upheld," CBC, May 6, 2011, https://www.cbc.ca/news/canada/abdullah-khadr-extradition-ruling-upheld-1.1101308.; "SCC Won't Hear Extradition Case of Abdullah Khadr," *CTV News*, November 3, 2011, https://www.ctvnews.ca/scc-won-t-hear-extradition-case-of-abdullah-khadr-1.720728.

87 Bryan Denson, "1998 Story: Legacy of a Hate Crime: Mulutega Seraw's Death a Decade Ago Avenged," *Oregon Live*, November

12, 2014, https://www.oregonlive.com/portland/index.
ssf/2014/11/1998_story_legacy_of_a_hate_cr.html.

[88] Martin Wainwright, "Neo-Nazi Ian Davison Jailed for 10 Years for Making Chemical Weapon," *Guardian*, May 14, 2010, https://www.theguardian.com/uk/2010/may/14/neo-nazi-ian-davison-jailed-chemical-weapon.

[89] Yonah Alexander and Dean Alexander, *The Islamic State: Combating the Caliphate Without Borders* (Lanham, MD: Lexington Books, 2015), https://rowman.com/ISBN/9781498525114/The-Islamic-State-Combating-The-Caliphate-Without-Borders.

[90] Lizzie Dearden, "James Foley Beheading: 'I Want to be the First UK Woman to Kill a Westerner,' Says British Jihadist in Syria," *Independent*, August 22, 2014, https://www.independent.co.uk/news/world/middle-east/james-foley-beheading-i-want-to-be-the-first-uk-woman-to-kill-a-westerner-says-british-jihadist-in-9684908.html.

[91] Sara Malm, "Has Jihadi Junior Been Smuggled 2,000 Miles to Sweden for an Operation?" *Daily Mail*, June 6, 2016, https://www.dailymail.co.uk/news/article-3627039/Has-Jihadi-Junior-smuggled-2-000-miles-SWEDEN-operation-Reports-claim-four-year-old-moved-Syria-bungling-ISIS-doctors-failed-treat-illness.html.

[92] Steve Swann, "Brother Campaigns for 'Enemy Combatant,'" *BBC*, January 24, 2009, http://news.bbc.co.uk/2/hi/americas/7848515.stm.; David Weinberg, "Analysis: Former al Qaeda Operative Freed, Sent Home to Qatar," *Long War Journal*, January 20, 2015, https://www.longwarjournal.org/archives/2015/01/former_al_qaeda_oper.php.

[93] United States of America v. Mahmoud Youssef Kourani, Indictment. Eastern District of Michigan, Southern Division, November 19, 2003, http://news.findlaw.com/cnn/docs/terrorism/uskourani111903ind.pdf.; "Hezbollah Fundraiser Sentenced to

Prison," *Los Angeles Times*, June 15, 2005, http://articles.latimes.com/2005/jun/15/nation/na-hezbollah15.

[94] Duncan Gardham, "Brothers of ISIS Poster Child Ifthekar Jaman Who Lived with Their Parents in Portsmouth While Helping to Sneak Terrorists to Syria Are Jailed for Six Years Each," *Daily Mail*, November 18, 2013, https://www.dailymail.co.uk/news/article-3324198/Brothers-ISIS-poster-boy-Ifthekar-Jaman-lived-parents-Portsmouth-helping-sneak-terrorists-Syria-jailed-six-years-each.html.

[95] Jason Meisner, "Boilingbrook Man Pleads Guilty to Terrorism Charge," *Chicago Tribune*, October 29, 2015, http://www.chicagotribune.com/news/local/breaking/ct-terror-case-bolingbrook-man-plea-20151029-story.html.; Jason Meisner, "Boilingbrook Man Given Almost 3½ Years to Join Islamic State," *Chicago Tribune*, November 18, 2016, http://www.chicagotribune.com/news/local/breaking/ct-islamic-state-terrorism-bolingbrook-man-met-20161118-story.html.

[96] Ashley Fantz, "Ex-Wife of ISIS Leader Abu Bakr al-Baghdadi: I Want a New Life in Europe," *CNN*, March 31, 2016, https://www.cnn.com/2016/03/31/europe/abu-bakr-al-baghdadi-isis-ex-wife-interview/index.html.; Kassem Hamade, "The Ex-Wife: My Escape from the Highest Leader of ISIS," *Expressen*, March 31, 2016, https://www.expressen.se/geo/kassem-hamade/the-ex-wife-my-escape-from-the-highest-leader-of-isis/.

[97] "No Cash for Terror: Convictions Returned in Holy Land Case," US Department of Justice, Federal Bureau of Investigation, November 25, 2008, https://archives.fbi.gov/archives/news/stories/2008/november/hlf112508.; "Federal Judge Hands Down Sentences in Holy Land Foundation Case," US Department of Justice, Office of Public Affairs, May 27, 2009, https://www.justice.gov/opa/pr/federal-judge-hands-downs-sentences-holy-land-foundation-case.

⁹⁸ Jason Burke, "Bin Laden and Son: The Grooming of a Dynasty," *Guardian*, September 23, 2001.https://www.theguardian.com/world/2001/sep/23/terrorism.afghanistan3.

⁹⁹ Marc Sageman, *Understanding Terror Networks* (University of Pennsylvania: Philadelphia, PA, 2004). http://www.upenn.edu/pennpress/book/14036.html.

¹⁰⁰ Naomi Zeveloff, "Does Aid to Palestinians Subsidize the Families of Terrorists?" *Forward*, August 23, 2016, https://forward.com/news/israel/348017/exclusive-does-aid-to-palestinians-subsidize-the-families-of-terrorists/.

¹⁰¹ Adam Rasgon, "Who Was the Perpetrator of the Jerusalem Terror Attack?" *Jerusalem Post*, January 8, 2017, https://www.jpost.com/Arab-Israeli-Conflict/Who-was-the-perpetrator-of-the-Jerusalem-terror-attack-477833.

¹⁰² Doyle Murphy, "KKK Wife Malissa Ancona Hoarded Cats, Popped Pills, and Police Say, Murdered the Local Imperial Wizard," *River Front Times*, March 8, 2017, https://www.riverfronttimes.com/stlouis/kkk-wife-malissa-ancona-hoarded-cats-popped-pills-and-police-say-murdered-the-local-imperial-wizard/Content?oid=3813315.

¹⁰³ Robert Patrick and Joel Currier, "Facing Charge of Murdering a Missouri KKK Leader, a Mother Turns on Her Son," *St. Louis Post-Dispatch*, October 28, 2017, https://www.stltoday.com/news/local/crime-and-courts/facing-charge-of-murdering-a-missouri-kkk-leader-a-mother/article_9f4e3630-6cb7-52e3-92b6-5d064b045697.html.

¹⁰⁴ "Lougher's Parents: No Words to Express Feelings," *CBS News*, January 11, 2011, https://www.cbsnews.com/news/loughner-parents-no-words-to-express-feelings/.

¹⁰⁵ James Bennet, "Arab Woman's Path to Unlikely 'Martyrdom,'" *New York Times*, January 31, 2002, https://www.nytimes.

com/2002/01/31/world/arab-woman-s-path-to-unlikely-martyr-dom.html?mcubz=1.

[106] "Lawyer for Widow of Marathon Bomber Says 'Patriot's Day' Portrays Her Unfairly," *WBUR*, December 23, 2016, http://www.wbur.org/morningedition/2016/12/23/katherine-russell-patriots-day.

[107] Holly Bailey, "The Unabomber's Not-So-Lonely Prison Life," Yahoo, January 28, 2016, https://www.yahoo.com/news/the-un-abomber-s-not-so-lonely-prison-life-210559693.html.

[108] "Only Hard Choices for Parents Whose Children Flirt With Terror," *New York Times*, April 6, 2016, https://www.nytimes.com/2016/04/10/us/parents-face-limited-options-to-keep-children-from-terrorism.html.; Jay Barmann, "Father of Fremont Terror Suspect Regrets Turning Him Into the FBI," *SFIST.com*, April 10, 2016, http://sfist.com/2016/04/10/father_of_fremont_terror_suspect_re.php.

[109] "Initiative to Address the Life Cycle of Radicalization to Violence, The Role of Families in Preventing and Countering Violent Extremism: Strategic Recommendations and Programming Options," Global Counterterrorism Forum, no date. https://www.thegctf.org/Portals/1/Documents/Toolkit-documents/English-The-Role-of-Familes-in-PCVE.pdf.

[110] Ibid.

[111] Ibid.

[112] Ibid.

[113] Glenn Greenwald, "The Killing of Awlaki's 16-Year-Old Son," *Salon*, October 20, 2011, https://www.salon.com/2011/10/20/the_killing_of_awlakis_16_year_old_son/. ; Glenn Greenwald, "Obama Killed a 16-Year-Old American. Trump Just Killed His 8-Year-Old Sister," *Intercept*, January 1, 2017, https://theintercept.

com/2017/01/30/obama-killed-a-16-year-old-american-in-yemen-trump-just-killed-his-8-year-old-sister/.

114 Greg Miller, "Legal Memo Backing Drone Strike That Killed American Anwar al-Awlaki Is Released," *Washington Post*, June 23, 2014, https://www.washingtonpost.com/world/national-security/legal-memo-backing-drone-strike-is-released/2014/06/23/1f48dd16-faec-11e3-8176-f2c941cf35f1_story.html?utm_term=.ba0dd1e5e50c.

115 John Litchfield, "How My Hate-Filled Family Spawned Merah the Monster," *Independent*, November 12, 2012, https://www.independent.co.uk/news/world/europe/how-my-hate-filled-family-spawned-merah-the-monster-8307341.html.

116 "Trial of Toulouse Shooter's Brother Reveals Chaotic Family of a French Jihadist," *Times of Israel*, October 19, 2017, https://www.timesofisrael.com/trial-of-toulouse-shooters-brother-reveals-chaotic-family-of-a-french-jihadist/.; Kim Willsher, "Toulouse Attack: Brother of Islamist Convicted of Links to Terror Group," *Guardian*, November 2, 2017, https://www.theguardian.com/world/2017/nov/02/toulouse-attack-brother-of-islamist-convicted-of-links-to-terror-group.

117 Melvin Bledsoe, Statement before Committee on Homeland Security, US House of Representatives, Washington, DC, March 10, 2011, https://homeland.house.gov/files/Testimony%20Bledsoe.pdf.

118 Gena Soma, "Parents Despair for Son Who Chose Life of Terror," *CNN*, June 7, 2013, http://www.cnn.com/2013/06/07/us/us-somalia-family-despair/index.html.

119 Greg Flakus, "Sadness at Home after Death in Somalia of US-Born Terrorist," *VOA News*, September 12, 2013, https://www.voanews.com/a/sadness-at-home-after-death-in-somalia-of-us-born-terrorist/1748838.html.

120 Matthew Stabley, "Inexplicable Shooting Mortified Suspect's Family: Cousin," *NBC Washington*, November 5, 2009, https://www.nbcwashington.com/news/local/Fort-Hood-Gunman-Recently-Worked-at-Walter-Reed-Reports-69328622.html.

121 Bill Turque, "Suspect's Son Says He Is Sorry It Was Holocaust Museum Guard, Not Dad, Who Died," *Washington Post*, June 13, 2009, http://www.washingtonpost.com/wp-dyn/content/article/2009/06/13/AR2009061302111.html.

122 "Iraq Vet Helped People Escape IRS Office," *CBS News*, April 16, 2017, https://www.cbsnews.com/news/iraq-vet-helped-people-escape-irs-office/.

123 Stephen Walter, "Westminster Terrorist Khalid Masood Told Family a Week before Attack," *Telegraph*, April 16, 2017, https://www.telegraph.co.uk/news/2017/04/16/westminster-terrorist-khalid-masood-told-family-member-week/.; "London Attack: Khalid Masood Mother 'Shocked and Saddened,'" *BBC*, March 27, 2017, https://www.bbc.com/news/uk-39411208.

124 Josie Ensor and Justin Huggler, "Teenage ISIL Bride from Germany Captured in Mosul," *Telegraph*, July 18, 2017, https://www.telegraph.co.uk/news/2017/07/18/teenage-german-isil-bride-captured-mosuls-old-city/.

125 Yishai Schwartz, "Israel's Home Demolition Policy Works," *New Republic*, December 8, 2014, https://newrepublic.com/article/120506/study-israels-home-demolitions-policy-works-it-moral.

126 Adam Chandler, "Can Israel Really Deter Attackers by Demolishing Their Homes?" *Atlantic*, November 19, 2014, https://www.theatlantic.com/international/archive/2014/11/can-israel-deter-attackers-by-demolishing-their-homes/382945/.

127 "Israel Will Not Demolish the Homes of Families Who Turn in Terrorists," *Times of Israel*, February 24, 2016, http://www.timesofisrael.com/

israel-wont-demolish-homes-of-families-who-turn-in-terrorists/.; Orlando Crowcroft, "Jerusalem Violence: Why Does Israel Bulldoze the Home of Terrorists?" *International Business Times*, October 6, 2015, https://www.ibtimes.co.uk/jerusalem-violence-why-does-israel-bulldoze-homes-terrorists-1522716.

128 Schwartz, "Israel's Home Demolition Policy Works."

129 "Israel's High Court Must Stop Collective Punishment of Terrorists' Families," *Haaretz*, April 4, 2016, https://www.haaretz.com/opinion/high-court-must-stop-demolitions-1.5427115.

130 Chandler, "Can Israel Really Deter Attackers by Demolishing Their Homes?"

131 Eyal Levy, "What Deters Terrorists Most Is the Thought of What Will Happen to Their Families," *Jerusalem Post*, March 16, 2016, https://www.jpost.com/Arab-Israeli-Conflict/What-deters-terrorists-most-is-the-thought-of-what-will-happen-to-their-families-448140.

132 Tom LoBianco, "Donald Trump on Terrorists: 'Take Out Their Families,'" *CNN*, December 2, 2015, https://www.cnn.com/2015/12/02/politics/donald-trump-terrorists-families/.

Chapter 3

133 "Al-Qaeda Chief Adnan el Shukrijumah 'Killed in Pakistan,'" *BBC News*, December 6, 2014, https://www.bbc.com/news/world-asia-30358538; "Former Broward Resident Who Became al-Qaeda Operative Killed in Pakistan: Reports," *Sun-Sentinel*, December 7, 2014, http://www.sun-sentinel.com/local/broward/fl-al-qaeda-adnan-el-shukrijumah-killed-20141207-story.html; Tom Hussain, "Florida al Qaida Commander was Betrayed by 'Mole': Pakistani Taliban," *McClatchy*, November 25, 2015, https://www.mcclatchydc.com/news/nation-world/world/article46463910.html.

[134] "Inside," *Commercial Appeal,* July 4, 2010, https://www.press-reader.com/usa/the-commercial-appeal/20100704/281487862613630.

[135] Ibid.

[136] Ibid.

[137] Barry Leibowitz, "Bruce and Joshua Turnidge, Father-Son Bank Bombers, Convicted of Murdering Two Oregon Cops," *CBS News,* December 8, 2010, https://www.cbsnews.com/news/bruce-and-joshua-turnidge-father-son-bank-bombers-convicted-of-murdering-two-ore-cops-in-08/.

[138] Lay v. Tramwell, United States District Court for the Northern District of Oklahoma, October 7, 2015, http://ok.findacase.com/research/wfrmDocViewer.aspx/xq/fac.20151007_0000407.NOK.htm/qx.

[139] "Guilty: Father and Son Convicted of Murder of Bank Security Guard," *SecurityInfoWatch,* September 27, 2005, http://www.securityinfowatch.com/news/10594789/guilty-father-and-son-convicted-of-murder-of-bank-security-guard.

[140] "Father, Son Convicted On Bank Robbery, Murder Charges," ADL, September 27, 2005, https://www.adl.org/news/article/father-son-convicted-on-bank-robbery-murder-charges.

[141] Scott Bronstein and Drew Griffin, "Young ISIS Recruit: I Was Blinded by Love," *CNN,* December 2, 2016, https://edition.cnn.com/2016/12/02/us/mississippi-isis-muhammad-dakhlalla-interview/index.html.

[142] United States of America v. Michael Todd Wolfe, Criminal Complaint, US District Court for the Western District of Texas, June 18, 2014, https://cchs.gwu.edu/sites/cchs.gwu.edu/files/downloads/Wolfe%20Criminal%20Complaint.pdf.

143 Ibid.

144 Ibid.

145 Ibid.

146 Dylan Baddour, "Wife: Undercover 'Friends' Pressured Man to Join ISIS," *Statesman*, October 22, 2014, http://www.mystatesman. com/news/local/wife-undercover-friends-pressured-austin-man-join-isis/rEHHcyfZi1sbM948oXiagL/.

147 Sam Wood, "Philly's 'Young Lioness' Indicted on Terrorism Counts," *Philadelphia Inquirer*, April 23, 2015, http://www.philly. com/philly/news/Feds_indict_Phillys_YoungLioness_on_terror-ism_charges.html.

148 "Timeline of Communications in Case of Philadelphia Woman Accused of Trying to Join ISIS," *Fox News*, April 3, 2015, http:// www.foxnews.com/us/2015/04/03/timeline-communica-tions-in-case-philadelphia-woman-accused-trying-to-join-is.html.

149 "Couple Admits to Planning Judge's Murder," *Alaska Republic*, August 27, 2012, http://www.alaskapublic.org/2012/08/27/couple-admits-to-planning-judges-murder/.

150 Jill Burke, "Foul-Mouthed Alaska Militia Member Gets Near-Life Sentence," *Anchorage Daily News*, September 26, 2016, https://www. adn.com/alaska-militias/article/foul-mouthed-alaska-militia-mem-ber-gets-near-life-sentence/2013/01/07/?page=0,1.

151 "Couple Appealing Death Sentence Claim Cop Killing Was Legal," *Los Angeles Times*, September 8, 1996, http://articles.latimes. com/1996-09-08/news/mn-41695_1_death-sentences.

152 Ibid.

153 Janet Fife-Yeomans, "Sydney Counterterror Raids: Police Charge Khaled Khayat, Mahmoud Khayat Over Alleged Plane Plot," *Daily Telegraph*, August 3, 2017. http://www.dailytelegraph.

com.au/news/nsw/sydney-counterterror-raids-police-charge-khaled-khayat-mahmoud-khaya-over-alleged-plane-plot/news-story/83b35dcc9f424196ebe9edb29b88bfe5; "Lebanon Monitored Australian Bomb Plot Suspects: Minister," *Reuters*, August 27, 2017, https://www.reuters.com/article/us-lebanon-security-emirates-australia-idUSKCN1B11A0; "Man Arrested in Sydney Counterterrorism Raids Charged With Weapons Offense and Released on Bail," *9News*, August 6, 2017, http://www.9news.com.au/national/2017/08/03/11/23/alleged-terror-plot-detainees-to-be-charged; Dean Alexander and Andrew Hyland, "Expecting the Unexpected in Aviation Terrorism," *Security Magazine*, June 27, 2016, http://www.securitymagazine.com/articles/87074-expecting-the-unexpected-in-aviation-terrorism.

[154] Alison Gendar, Scott Shifrel, and Larry McShane, "Iranian Plot to Kill Saudi Ambassador to the U.S. Foiled: Attorney General Eric Holder," *New York Daily News*, October 11, 2011, http://www.nydailynews.com/news/national/iranian-plot-kill-saudi-ambassador-u-s-foiled-u-s-attorney-general-eric-holder-article-1.962033.

[155] Dean Alexander, "Al Qaeda and al Qaeda in the Arabian Peninsula-Inspired, Homegrown Terrorism in the United States," *Defence Against Terrorism Review* 4(1), pp. 31-47, http://www.coe-dat.nato.int/publication/datr/volumes/datr7.pdf.

[156] "Father of Would-Be Suicide Bomber Convicted of Obstructing Terrorism Investigation," US Department of Justice, US Attorney's Office, Eastern District of New York, July 22, 2011, https://archives.fbi.gov/archives/newyork/press-releases/2011/father-of-would-be-suicide-bomber-convicted-of-obstructing-terrorism-investigation.

[157] "Three Brothers Sentenced to Life Terms for Conspiring to Kill US Soldiers," US Department of Justice, US Attorney's Office, District of New Jersey, April 28, 2009, https://archives.fbi.gov/archives/philadelphia/press-releases/2009/ph042809.htm.

158 Ibid.

159 Carrie Johnson and Spencer Hsu, "Terror Suspect Daniel Boyd Seemed to Have Typical Suburban Life," *Washington Post*, July 29, 2009, http://www.washingtonpost.com/wp-dyn/content/article/2009/07/28/AR2009072803193.html; Emery Dalesio, "Brothers Sentenced for Roles in Terror Plot," *San Diego Union-Tribune*, December 20, 2011. http://www.sandiegouniontribune.com/sdut-brothers-sentenced-for-roles-in-nc-terror-plot-2011dec20-story.html; "North Carolina Resident Found Guilty of Terrorism Violations," US Department of Justice, Office of Public Affairs, June 14, 2012, https://www.justice.gov/opa/pr/north-carolina-resident-found-guilty-terrorism-violations; "North Carolina Resident Daniel Patrick Boyd Sentenced for Terrorism Violations," US Department of Justice, US Attorney's Office, Eastern District of North Carolina, August 24, 2012. https://archives.fbi.gov/archives/charlotte/press-releases/2012/north-carolina-resident-daniel-patrick-boyd-sentenced-for-terrorism-violation.

160 "The Mautes of the Philippines: From Monied Family to the Islamic State," Reuters, June 22, 2017, https://www.reuters.com/article/us-philippines-militants-matriarch-idUSKBN19E0A9.; Jonathan Head, "Maute Rebel Group: A Rising Threat to Philippines," BBC News, May 31, 2017, http://www.bbc.com/news/world-asia-40103602.; Rommel Banlaoi, "The Maute Group and the Rise of Family Terrorism," *Rappler*, June 15, 2017, https://www.rappler.com/thought-leaders/173037-maute-group-rise-family-terrorism.

161 "Islamic State East Asia," Australian National Security, no date, https://www.nationalsecurity.gov.au/Listedterroristorganisations/Pages/Islamic-State-East-Asia.aspx.; Banlaoi, "The Maute Group and the Rise of Family Terrorism."

162 Banlaoi, "The Maute Group and the Rise of Family Terrorism."

[163] Juliet Linderman, "Derrick Smith, One of 7 Original Suspects Charged in St. John Parish Deputy Ambush, Pleads Guilty," *New Orleans Times-Picayune*, May 22, 2013, http://www.nola.com/crime/index.ssf/2013/05/derrick_smith_one_of_7_origina.html.

[164] Della Hasselle, "Inmate Convicted in Deaths of 2 La. Deputies Released on Parole," *Advocate*, April 6, 2017, https://www.police-one.com/officer-shootings/articles/324771006-Inmate-convicted-in-deaths-of-2-La-deputies-released-on-parole/.

[165] State v. Bixby, South Carolina Court of Appeals, December 17, 2010, http://law.justia.com/cases/south-carolina/court-of-appeals/2010/4768.html.

[166] Ibid.

Chapter 5

[167] "Homegrown Violent Extremist Mobilization Indicators for Public Safety Personnel," National Counterterrorism Center, 2017, https://publicintelligence.net/nctc-hve-indicators-2017/.

[168] "Preventing Radicalisation to Terrorism and Extremism," Radicalization Awareness Network, European Commission, 2018 https://ec.europa.eu/home-affairs/sites/home-affairs/files/what-we-do/networks/radicalisation_awareness_network/ran-best-practices/docs/ran_collection-approaches_and_practices_en.pdf.

[169] "8 Signs of Terrorism," Indiana Intelligence Fusion Center, no date, https://www.in.gov/iifc/2331.htm.

[170] "Homegrown Violent Extremist Mobilization Indicators for Public Safety Personnel," National Counterterrorism Center, 2017, https://publicintelligence.net/nctc-hve-indicators-2017/.

[171] Nicholas Ridley and, Dean Alexander, "Combating Terrorist Financing in the First Decade of the Twenty-First Century," *Journal of Money Laundering Control* 15(1), pp. 38-57 (2012), https://www.emeraldinsight.com/doi/abs/10.1108/13685201211194727.

[172] Dean Alexander, "Syria's Siren," *Intersec*, May 2014, http://www.intersecmag.co.uk/wp-content/uploads/2014/05/Syria-May14.pdf.; Dean Alexander, "International Fighters Flock to High Risk Battlegrounds," *Security Magazine*, September 1, 2014, http://www.securitymagazine.com/articles/85774-international-fighters-flock-to-high-risk-battlegrounds.

[173] Dean Alexander and Benjamin Arnold, "The Missed Signs of Terrorism," *Security Magazine*, January 5, 2018, https://www.securitymagazine.com/articles/88625-the-missed-signs-of-terrorism.

[174] Nora Ellingsen, "The Life Cycle of an FBI Terrorism Investigation," *Lawfare Blog*, June 20, 2016, https://www.lawfareblog.com/life-cycle-fbi-terrorism-investigation.

[175] Dean Alexander, "Terrorists: Stop!," *Intersec*, October 2013, http://www.intersecmag.co.uk/wp-content/uploads/2013/10/Trafficstop-Oct13.pdf.

[176] "Another Hijacker was Stopped for a Traffic Violation," *CNN*, January 9, 2002, http://edition.cnn.com/2002/US/01/09/inv.hijacker.traffic.stops/.

[177] "Suspicious Activity Reporting Indicators and Behaviors: Tools for Analysts and Investigators." Nationwide SAR Initiative, Feb. 2016 https://nsi.ncirc.gov/documents/SAR_Indicators_One-Pager.pdf.

[178] Communities Against Terrorism flyers, Ohio Homeland Security, no date, https://homelandsecurity.ohio.gov/printed_material.stm.

[179] "Senator Reveals that the FBI Paid $900,000 to Hack into San Bernardino Killer's iPhone," *CNBC*, May 5, 2017,

https://www.cnbc.com/2017/05/05/dianne-feinstein-reveals-fbi-paid-900000-to-hack-into-killers-iphone.html.

[180] Robert McMillan, "Meet Apple's Security Headache: The GrayKey, a Startup's iPhone-Hacking Box," *Wall Street Journal*, June 14, 2018, https://www.wsj.com/articles/the-hacking-box-that-led-to-a-golden-age-of-iphone-investigations-1528996893.

[181] Alexander and Avelar, "Lessons Learned from the 2016 Berlin Truck Attack."

[182] Dean Alexander. "Combating Terror Threats Against Police," *Homeland Security Today*, May 3, 2017, https://www.hstoday.us/channels/federal-state-local/exclusive-combating-terror-threats-against-police/.

[183] "About UNCCT," United Nations Office of Counter-Terrorism, United Nations Counter-Terrorism Center, no date, https://www.un.org/counterterrorism/ctitf/en/uncct/about.

[184] "About the Task Force," United Nations Office of Counter-Terrorism, Counter-Terrorism Implementation Task Force, no date, https://www.un.org/counterterrorism/ctitf/en/about-task-force.

[185] "Counter-Terrorism Fusion Centre," Interpol, no date, https://www.interpol.int/Crime-areas/Terrorism/Counter-Terrorism-Fusion-Centre.

[186] "European Counter Terrorism Centre—ECTC," Europol, no date, https://www.europol.europa.eu/about-europol/european-counter-terrorism-centre-ectc.

[187] Southeast Asia Regional Centre for Counter-Terrorism, no date, https://www.searcct.gov.my/about-searcct/introduction.

BIBLIOGRAPHY

Abedi, Maham. "Here's Why Omar Khadr is Getting $10M from the Canadian Government," *Global News*, July 4, 2017. https://globalnews.ca/news/3573619/omar-khadr-canada-compensation/.

Abir, Mahshid, and Christopher Nelson. "Saving Lives After Tragedy." *U.S. News & World Report.* December 14, 2015. https://www.usnews.com/opinion/blogs/policy-dose/articles/2015-12-14/what-san-bernardino-paris-and-boston-teach-us-about-crisis-response.

ADL. "Father, Son Convicted on Bank Robbery, Murder Charges." September 27, 2005. https://www.adl.org/news/article/father-son-convicted-on-bank-robbery-murder-charges.

Advisory Board Daily Briefing. "Terror in Brussels: How Belgium's Hospitals Are Treating Hundreds after Suicide Bombings." March 23, 2016. https://www.advisory.com/daily-briefing/2016/03/23/belgium-hospitals.

Alaska Republic. "Couple Admits to Planning Judge's Murder." August 27, 2012. http://www.alaskapublic.org/2012/08/27/couple-admits-to-planning-judges-murder/.

Alexander, Dean. "All in the Family." *Peoria Journal Star*, June 17, 2016. http://www.pjstar.com/opinion/20160617/op-ed-all-in-family?page=1.

Alexander, Dean. "Al Qaeda and al Qaeda in the Arabian Peninsula-Inspired, Homegrown Terrorism in the United

States," *Defence Against Terrorism Review* 4(1) (2012), pp. 31-47. http://www.coedat.nato.int/publication/datr/volumes/datr7.pdf.

Alexander, Dean. "Brussels Attacks Indicative of Jihadist Threats Facing the United States." *Security Magazine*, March 24, 2016. http://www.securitymagazine.com/articles/87032-brussels-at-tacks-indicative-of-jihadist-threats-facing-the-united-states.

Alexander, Dean. *Business Confronts Terrorism: Risks and Responses*. Madison, WI: University of Wisconsin Press, 2004. https://uwpress.wisc.edu/books/2619.htm.

Alexander, Dean. "Combating Terror Threats Against Police." *Homeland Security Today*, May 3, 2017. https://www.hstoday.us/channels/federal-state-local/exclusive-combating-terror-threats-against-police/.

Alexander, Dean. "Family-Affiliated Terrorism: From Paris to San Bernardino and Beyond." *Security Magazine*, January 1, 2016. https://www.securitymagazine.com/articles/86844-family-affili-ated-terrorism-from-paris-to-san-bernadino-and-beyond.

Alexander, Dean. "International Fighters Flock to High Risk Battlegrounds." *Security Magazine*, September 1, 2014. http://www.securitymagazine.com/articles/85774-international-fight-ers-flock-to-high-risk-battlegrounds.

Alexander, Dean. "ISIS Attack in US May Only Be a Matter of Time." *Peoria Journal Star*, November 21, 2015. http://www.pjstar.com/article/20151121/OPINION/151129914/2011/OPINION.

Alexander, Dean. "Offline and Online Radicalization and Recruitment of Extremists and Terrorists." *Journal of Homeland Security*, September 2010.

Alexander, Dean. "Paris Attacks and ISIS in the Family." *State Journal-Registrar*, November 20, 2015. http://m.sj-r.com/article/20151120/OPINION/151129973/13312/OPINION.

Alexander, Dean. "Syria's Siren." *Intersec*, May 2014. http://www.intersecmag.co.uk/wp-content/uploads/2014/05/Syria-May14.pdf.

Alexander, Dean. "Terror Financing and Factors Facilitating Its Growth." *Security Magazine*, September 6, 2011. https://www.securitymagazine.com/articles/82316-terror-financing-and-factors-facilitating-its-growth.

Alexander, Dean. "Terror in the Family." *Intersec*, January 2014. http://www.intersecmag.co.uk/terrorism-jan14/.

Alexander, Dean. "Terrorism Challenges Facing the Trump Administration." *Security Magazine*, January 1, 2017. http://www.securitymagazine.com/articles/87681-terrorism-challenges-facing-the-trump-administration.

Alexander, Dean. "Terrorists: Stop!" *Intersec*, October 2013. http://www.intersecmag.co.uk/wp-content/uploads/2013/10/Trafficstop-Oct13.pdf.

Alexander, Dean. "The Islamic State and Its Implications for Security." *Security Magazine*, September 8, 2015. http://www.securitymagazine.com/articles/86645-the-islamic-state-and-its-implications-for-security.

Alexander, Dean. "The Islamic State's Lure to Foreign Women." *Jerusalem Post*, December 20, 2015. http://www.jpost.com/Opinion/Islamic-States-lure-to-foreign-women-437896.

Alexander, Dean. "The Sovereign Citizens Movement: Threats and Responses." *Security Magazine*, June 1, 2016. https://www.

securitymagazine.com/articles/87159-the-sovereign-citi-zen-movement-threats-and-responses.

Alexander, Dean, and Alex Cluster. "The Bastille Day Attack and the Islamic State's Global Tentacles." *Security Magazine*, July 18, 2016. http://www.securitymagazine.com/blogs/14-security-blog/post/87268-the-bastille-day-attack-and-islamic-states-global-tentacles.

Alexander, Dean, and Alex Halpern. "Emergency and Medical Response Planning for Mass Casualty Terror Attacks." *Security Magazine*, July 1, 2017. https://www.securitymaga-zine.com/articles/88103-emergency-medical-response-plan-ning-for-mass-casualty-terror-attacks.

Alexander, Dean, and Andrew Hyland. "Expecting the Unexpected in Aviation Terrorism." *Security Magazine*, June 27, 2016. http://www.securitymagazine.com/articles/87074-expecting-the-unexpected-in-aviation-terrorism.

Alexander, Dean, and Benjamin Arnold. "The Missed Signs of Terrorism." *Security Magazine*, January 5, 2018. https://www.securitymagazine.com/articles/88625-the-missed-signs-of-terrorism.

Alexander, Dean, and John Avelar. "Lessons Learned from the 2016 Berlin Truck Attack." *Homeland Security Today*, January 9, 2017. https://www.hstoday.us/channels/global/exclusive-lessons-learned-from-the-2016-berlin-truck-attack/.

Alexander, Dean, and Robert Cresero. "Is the Woman Next Door a Terrorist?" *Security Magazine*, September 2013. http://digi-tal.bnpmedia.com/publication/?i=173995&p=54#{"page":"54","issue_id":173995.

Alexander, Yonah, and Dean Alexander. *The Islamic State: Combating the Caliphate Without Borders.* Lanham, MD: Lexington Books, 2015. https://rowman.com/ISBN/ 9781498525114/The-Islamic-State-Combating-The-Caliphate-Without-Borders.

Alexander, Yonah and Dean Alexander. *Terrorism and Business: The Impact of September 11, 2001.* Ardsley, NY: Transnational Publishers, 2002. https://brill.com/view/title/13942.

Al Jazeera. "Omar Khadr: The Case, the Compensation, and the Media," August 6, 2017. https://www.aljazeera.com/pro-grammes/listeningpost/2017/08/omar-khadr-case-compensa-tion-media-170805131345055.html.

Australian National Security. "Islamic State East Asia," no date. https://www.nationalsecurity.gov.au/ Listedterroristorganisations/Pages/Islamic-State-East-Asia.aspx.

Baddour, Dylan. "Wife: Undercover 'Friends' Pressured Man to Join ISIS." *Statesman,* October 22, 2014. http://www.mystatesman.com/news/local/wife-un-dercover-friends-pressured-austin-man-join-isis/ rEHHcyfZi1sbM948oXiagL/.

Bailey, Holly. "The Unabomber's Not-So-Lonely Prison Life." Yahoo, January 28, 2016. https://www.yahoo.com/news/the-un-abomber-s-not-so-lonely-prison-life-210559693.html.

Banlaoi, Rommel. "The Maute Group and the Rise of Family Terrorism." *Rappler,* June 15, 2017. https://www.rappler.com/ thought-leaders/173037-maute-group-rise-family-terrorism.

Barmann, Jay. "Father of Fremont Terror Suspect Regrets Turning Him Into the FBI," *SFIST.com*, April 10, 2016. http://sfist. com/2016/04/10/father_of_fremont_terror_suspect_re.php.

BBC. "Al-Qaeda Chief Adnan el Shukrijumah 'Killed in Pakistan,'" December 6, 2014. https://www.bbc.com/news/ world-asia-30358538.

BBC. "Brussels Explosions: What We Know about Airport and Metro Attacks." April 9, 2016. https://www.bbc.com/news/ world-europe-35869985.

BBC. "London Attack: Khalid Masood Mother 'Shocked and Saddened.'" March 27, 2017. http://www.bbc.com/news/ uk-39411208.

BBC. "London Attack: The Victims." April 7, 2017. https://www. bbc.com/news/uk-39363933.

BBC. "Manchester Attack: Who was Salman Abedi?" June 12, 2017. https://www.bbc.com/news/uk-40019135.

BBC. "Nice Attack: What We Know about the Bastille Day Killings." August 19, 2016. https://www.bbc.com/news/ world-europe-36801671.

BBC. "Nice Attacks: Who Were the Victims?" August 19, 20016. https://www.bbc.com/news/world-europe-36805164.

BBC. "Surabaya Attacks: Family of Five Bomb Indonesia Police Headquarters." May 14, 2018. http://www.bbc.com/news/ world-asia-44105279.

BBC. "UK Jihadist Junaid Hussain Killed in Syria Drone Strike, Says US," August 27, 2015. https://www.bbc.com/news/ uk-34078900.

Beckers Hospital Review. "How Paris Hospitals Responded to Last Weekend's Terrorist Attacks." November 17, 2015. https://www. beckershospitalreview.com/hospital-physician-relationships/ how-paris-hospitals-responded-to-last-weekend-s-terrorist-attacks.html.

Beckman, Milo. "Which Countries Terrorist Attacks Are Ignored by the US Media?" *FiveThirtyEight*, July 19, 2016. https:// fivethirtyeight.com/features/which-countries-terrorist-attacks-are-ignored-by-the-u-s-media/.

Beech, Hannah. "After an Indonesian Family's Suicide Attack: A Quest for Answers." *New York Times*, May 27, 2018. https:// www.nytimes.com/2018/05/27/insider/indonesian-family-suicide-bombers.html.

Beinart, Peter. "The Rise of the Violent Left," *Atlantic*, September 2017. https://www.theatlantic.com/magazine/archive/2017/09/ the-rise-of-the-violent-left/534192/.

Bennet, James. "Arab Woman's Path to Unlikely 'Martyrdom.'" *New York Times*, January 31, 2002. http://www.nytimes. com/2002/01/31/world/arab-woman-s-path-to-unlikely-martyrdom.html?mcubz=1.

Berman, Mark. "Orlando Hospitals Say They Won't Bill Pulse Shooting Survivors." *Washington Post*. August 24, 2016. https:// www.washingtonpost.com/news/post-nation/wp/2016/08/24/ orlando-hospital-says-it-wont-bill-pulse-shooting-survivors/?utm_term=.0f8f2cf89c6f.

Berman, Mark. "Terror in the American Desert." *Washington Post*, June 14, 2014. https://www.

washingtonpost.com/news/post-nation/wp/2014/06/14/
terror-in-the-american-desert/?utm_term=.67ba2ddf26a7.

Bledsoe, Melvin. Statement before Committee on Homeland
Security, US House of Representatives, Washington, DC, March
10, 2011. https://homeland.house.gov/files/Testimony%20
Bledsoe.pdf.

Bolton, Doug. "Paris Attack Victims." *Independent*, November 18,
2015. https://www.independent.co.uk/news/world/europe/
paris-attack-victims-list-french-government-identifies-all-129-
people-killed-in-paris-terrorist-a6739116.html.

Bondarenko, Veronika. "White Supremacist Explains What it Took
for him to Rethink his Beliefs," *Business Insider*, August 23,
2017, https://www.businessinsider.com/white-supremacist-ex-
plains-what-it-took-for-him-to-rethink-his-beliefs-2017-8.

Borger, Julian. "Chilling, Defiant: The Video Suicide Message of a
September 11Killer," *Guardian*, April 15, 2002. https://www.
theguardian.com/world/2002/apr/16/september11.usa2.

Bronstein, Scott, and Drew Griffin. "Young ISIS Recruit: I Was
Blinded by Love." CNN, December 2, 2016. https://edition.cnn.
com/2016/12/02/us/mississippi-isis-muhammad-dakhlalla-in-
terview/index.html.

Brooks, Dorothy. "Training, Drills Pivotal in Mounting Response
to Orlando Shooting." *AHC Media - Continuing Medical
Education Publishing*. August 1, 2016. https://www.reliasmedia.
com/articles/138237-training-drills-pivotal-in-mounting-re-
sponse-to-orlando-shooting.

Burke, Jason. "Bin Laden and Son: The Grooming of a Dynasty," *Guardian*, September 23, 2001. https://www.theguardian.com/world/2001/sep/23/terrorism.afghanistan3.

Burke, Jason. "'Gangsta Jihadi' Denis Cuspert Killed Fighting in Syria," *Guardian*, January 19, 2018. https://www.theguardian.com/world/2018/jan/19/gangsta-jihadi-denis-cuspert-killed-fighting-in-syria.

Burke, Jill. "Foul-Mouthed Alaska Militia Member Gets Near-Life Sentence." *Anchorage Daily News*, September 26, 2016. https://www.adn.com/alaska-militias/article/foul-mouthed-alaska-militia-member-gets-near-life-sentence/2013/01/07/?page=0,1.

Campbell, Scott. "The Orphans That ISIS Left Behind." *Daily Mail*, July 16, 2017. http://www.dailymail.co.uk/news/article-4702208/Orphans-ISIS-left-Mosul-pulled-rubble.html.

Carles, Michel, Jacques Francois Gonzalez, Francois Valli, and Loic Bornardon. "Mass Casualty Events and Health Organisation: Terrorist Attack in Nice." *Lancet*. November 12, 2016. https://www.thelancet.com/journals/lancet/article/PIIS0140-6736(16)32128-6/fulltext?rss=yes.

CBC. "Abdullah Khadr extradition ruling upheld," May 6, 2011. https://www.cbc.ca/news/canada/abdullah-khadr-extradition-ruling-upheld-1.1101308.

CBS News. "Iraq Vet Helped People Escape IRS Office." April 16, 2017. https://www.cbsnews.com/news/iraq-vet-helped-people-escape-irs-office/.

CBS News. "A Look Back at the Norway Massacre." February 18, 2013. https://www.cbsnews.com/news/a-look-back-at-the-norway-massacre/.

CBS News. "Lougher's Parents: No Words to Express Feelings." January 11, 2011. https://www.cbsnews.com/news/loughner-parents-no-words-to-express-feelings/.

CBS News. "Osama bin Laden's Son Vows to Avenge His Father's Death." July 10, 2016. https://www.cbsnews.com/news/osama-bin-laden-son-hamza-vows-to-avenge-fathers-death/.

Chalabi, Mona. "Terror Attacks by Muslims Receive 357% More Press Attention, Study Finds," *Guardian*, July 20, 2018. https://www.theguardian.com/us-news/2018/jul/20/muslim-terror-attacks-press-coverage-study.

Chandler, Adam. "Can Israel Really Deter Attackers by Demolishing Their Homes?" *Atlantic*, November 19, 2014. https://www.theatlantic.com/international/archive/2014/11/can-israel-deter-attackers-by-demolishing-their-homes/382945/.

Chicago Tribune. "Pilot Sentenced to Life Term for Plot to Blow Up US Planes." May 16, 1998. http://articles.chicagotribune.com/1998-05-16/news/9805160123_1_abdul-hakim-murad-philippine-airlines-jet-ramzi-yousef.

Chriss, James. "The Functions of the Social Bond." *Sociology Quarterly* 48, no. 4 (Fall 2007): 689–712. https://www.jstor.org/stable/40220048?seq=1#page_scan_tab_contents.

Chulov, Martin. "Hamza bin Laden has Married Daughter of Lead 9/11 Hijacker, Say Family," *Guardian*, August 5, 2018. https://www.theguardian.com/world/2018/aug/05/hamza-bin-laden-marries-daughter-of-911-hijacker-mohammed-atta.

CNBC. "Senator Reveals that the FBI Paid $900,000 to Hack into San Bernardino Killer's iPhone," May 5, 2017. https://www.cnbc.

com/2017/05/05/dianne-feinstein-reveals-fbi-paid-900000-to-hack-into-killers-iphone.html.

CNN. "Another Hijacker was Stopped for a Traffic Violation," January 9, 2002. http://edition.cnn.com/2002/US/01/09/inv. hijacker.traffic.stops/.

CNN. "Plane Terror Suspects Convicted on All Counts." September 5, 1996. http://www.cnn.com/US/9609/05/terror.plot/.

CNN. "Rudolph's Mother: Son Not a 'Monster.'" August 22, 2005. http://www.cnn.com/2005/LAW/08/22/rudolph.mother/.

CNN. "2015 Paris Terror Attacks Fast Facts." May 2, 2018. https://www-m.cnn.com/2015/12/08/europe/2015-paris-terror-attacks-fast-facts/.

Cockburn, Harry. "Sally Jones: Who was the 'White Widow'? What We Know About the ISIS Member Killed in a US Drone Strike," *Independent*, October 12, 2017. https://www.independent. co.uk/news/world/middle-east/white-widow-sally-jones-killed-isis-uk-jihadi-us-drone-strike-syria-who-was-she-explain-er-a7996521.html.

Commercial Appeal. "Inside." July 4, 2010. https://www.pressreader. com/usa/the-commercial-appeal/20100704/281487862613630.

Cronin, Audrey Kurth. "Terrorist Motivations for Chemical and Biological Weapons Use: Placing the Threat in Context." Congressional Research Service, March 28, 2003. https://fas. org/irp/crs/RL31831.pdf.

Crowcroft, Orlando. "Jerusalem Violence: Why Does Israel Bulldoze the Home of Terrorists?" *International Business Times*, October 6, 2015. https://www.ibtimes.co.uk/jerusalem-vio-lence-why-does-israel-bulldoze-homes-terrorists-1522716.

CTV News. "SCC Won't Hear Extradition Case of Abdullah Khadr," November 3, 2011. https://www.ctvnews.ca/scc-won-t-hear-extradition-case-of-abdullah-khadr-1.720728.

Dalesio, Emery. "Brothers Sentenced for Roles in Terror Plot," *San Diego Union-Tribune*, December 20, 2011. http://www.sandiegouniontribune.com/sdut-brothers-sentenced-for-roles-in-nc-terror-plot-2011dec20-story.html.

Daragahi, Borzou. "We Spoke to Women Who Married into ISIS in Syria. These Are Their Regrets." *BuzzFeed*, July 20, 2017. https://www.buzzfeed.com/borzoudaragahi/the-women-who-married-into-isis-are-now-filled-with-regret?utm_term=.cqO8vv2XY#.fnRnBB1bw.

Deam, Jenny. "Colorado Woman's Quest for Jihad Baffles Neighbors." *Los Angeles Times*, July 25, 2014. http://www.latimes.com/nation/la-na-high-school-jihadi-20140726-story.html.m.

Dearden, Lizzie. "James Foley Beheading: 'I Want to Be the First UK Woman to Kill a Westerner,' Says British Jihadist in Syria." *Independent*, August 22, 2014. http://www.independent.co.uk/news/world/middle-east/james-foley-beheading-i-want-to-be-the-first-uk-woman-to-kill-a-westerner-says-british-jihadist-in-9684908.html.

Dearden, Lizzie. "Teenage Girl Jailed for Stabbing Police Officer in Germany's First Isis-Commissioned Attack," *Independent*, January 27, 2017. https://www.independent.co.uk/news/world/europe/germany-terror-attack-isis-islamic-state-hanover-train-station-police-officer-safia-s-15-teenage-a7551116.html.

Denson, Bryan. "1998 Story: *Legacy of a Hate Crime: Mulutega Seraw's Death a Decade Ago Avenged,*" *Oregon Live*, November 12, 2014, https://www.oregonlive.com/portland/index. ssf/2014/11/1998_story_legacy_of_a_hate_cr.html.

DW. "From Hanover to IS: The Case of Safia S.," October 19, 2016. https://www.dw.com/en/ from-hanover-to-is-the-case-of-safia-s/a-36094144.

"8 Signs of Terrorism," Indiana Intelligence Fusion Center, no date. https://www.in.gov/iifc/2331.htm.

Ekici, Niyazi. *The Dynamics of Terrorist Recruitment: The Case of the Revolutionary People's Liberation Party/Front (DHKP/C) and the Turkish Hezbollah.* Saarbrücken, Germany: Verlag VDM, 2010. https://www.amazon.com/DYNAMICS-TERRORIST-RECRUITMENT-Revolutionary-Liberation/ dp/363924544X.

Ellingsen, Nora. "The Life Cycle of an FBI Terrorism Investigation," *Lawfare Blog*, June 20, 2016. https://www.lawfareblog.com/ life-cycle-fbi-terrorism-investigation.

Ensor, Josie, and Justin Huggler. "Teenage ISIL Bride from Germany Captured in Mosul." *Telegraph*, July 18, 2017. https://www.telegraph.co.uk/news/2017/07/18/ teenage-german-isil-bride-captured-mosuls-old-city/.

Europol. "European Counter Terrorism Centre—ECTC," no date. https://www.europol.europa.eu/about-europol/ european-counter-terrorism-centre-ectc.

Fantz, Ashley. "Ex-Wife of ISIS Leader Abu Bakr al-Baghdadi: 'I Want a New Life in Europe.'" *CNN*, March 31, 2016. http://

www.cnn.com/2016/03/31/europe/abu-bakr-al-baghdadi-isis-ex-wife-interview/index.html.

Federal Bureau of Investigation. "2016 Hate Crime Statistics Released." November 13, 2017. https://www.fbi.gov/news/stories/2016-hate-crime-statistics.

Fife-Yeomans, Janet. "Sydney Counterterror Raids: Police Charge Khaled Khayat, Mahmoud Khayat Over Alleged Plane Plot," *Daily Telegraph*, August 3, 2017. http://www.dailytelegraph.com.au/news/nsw/sydney-counterterror-raids-police-charge-khaled-khayat-mahmoud-khaya-over-alleged-plane-plot/news-story/83b35dcc9f424196ebe9edb29b88bfe5.

Flakus, Greg. "Sadness at Home After Death in Somalia of US-Born Terrorist." *VOA News*, September 12, 2013. https://www.voanews.com/a/sadness-at-home-after-death-in-somalia-of-us-born-terrorist/1748838.html.

Fox News. "Timeline of Communications in Case of Philadelphia Woman Accused of Trying to Join ISIS." April 3, 2015. http://www.foxnews.com/us/2015/04/03/timeline-communications-in-case-philadelphia-woman-accused-trying-to-join-is.html.

Frontline. "Chronology: A Timeline of the Khadr Family's Travels and Alleged Activities," Undated. https://www.pbs.org/wgbh/pages/frontline/shows/khadr/family/cron.html.

Gaarder, C., J. Jorgensen, K. M. Kolstadbraaten, K. S. Isaksen, J. Skattum, R. Rimstad, T. Gundem, A. Holtan, A. Walloe, J. Pillgram-Larsen, and P. A. Naess. "The Twin Terrorist Attacks in Norway on July 22, 2011: The Trauma Center Response."

Advances in Pediatrics. July 2012. https://www.ncbi.nlm.nih.
gov/pubmed/22743394.

Gardham, Duncan. "Brothers of ISIS Poster Child Ifthekar Jaman
Who Lived with Their Parents in Portsmouth While Helping
to Sneak Terrorists to Syria Are Jailed for Six Years Each." *Daily
Mail*, November 18, 2013. http://www.dailymail.co.uk/news/
article-3324198/Brothers-ISIS-poster-boy-Ifthekar-Jaman-
lived-parents-Portsmouth-helping-sneak-terrorists-Syria-
jailed-six-years-each.html.

Gendar, Alison, Scott Shifrel, and Larry McShane. "Iranian Plot
to Kill Saudi Ambassador to the U.S. Foiled: Attorney General
Eric Holder." *New York Daily News*, October 11, 2011. http://
www.nydailynews.com/news/national/iranian-plot-kill-sau-
di-ambassador-u-s-foiled-u-s-attorney-general-eric-holder-ar-
ticle-1.962033.

Glatter, Robert and Paul Biddinger. "Emergency Medical Response
to Terrorist Bombings: Lessons Learned From Boston and
Brussels." *Medscape.* April 11, 2016. https://www.medscape.
com/viewarticle/861613.

Global Counterterrorism Forum. "Initiative to Address the Life
Cycle of Radicalization to Violence, The Role of Families in
Preventing and Countering Violent Extremism: Strategic
Recommendations and Programming Options," no date.
https://www.thegctf.org/Portals/1/Documents/Toolkit-
documents/English-The-Role-of-Familes-in-PCVE.pdf.

Glover, Scott. The FBI Translator Who Went Rogue and Married
an ISIS Terrorist," CNN, May 1, 2017, https://www.cnn.
com/2017/05/01/politics/investigates-fbi-syria-greene/index.
html.

Greenwald, Glenn. "The Killing of Awlaki's 16-Year-Old Son." *Salon*, October 20, 2011. https://www.salon.com/2011/10/20/ the_killing_of_awlakis_16_year_old_son/.

Greenwald, Glenn. "Obama Killed a 16-Year-Old American. Trump Just Killed His 8-Year-Old Sister." *Intercept*, January 1, 2017. https://theintercept.com/2017/01/30/obama-killed-a-16-year-old-american-in-yemen-trump-just-killed-his-8-year-old-sister/.

Haaretz. "Israel's High Court Must Stop Collective Punishment of Terrorists' Families." April 4, 2016. https://www.haaretz.com/ opinion/high-court-must-stop-demolitions-1.5427115.

Hamade, Kassem. "The Ex-Wife: My Escape from the Highest Leader of ISIS." *Expressen*, March 31, 2016. http://www.expressen.se/geo/kassem-hamade/ the-ex-wife-my-escape-from-the-highest-leader-of-isis/.

Hasselle, Della. "Inmate Convicted in Deaths of 2 La. Deputies Released on Parole." *Advocate*, April 6, 2017. https://www.policeone.com/officer-shootings/articles/324771006-Inmate-convicted-in-deaths-of-2-La-deputies-released-on-parole/.

Hastings, Deborah. "Two Brothers Lose Legs in Boston Bombings, Were Standing Near 8-Year-Old Boy." *New York Daily News*, April 16, 2013, http://www.nydailynews.com/news/national/ brothers-lose-legs-boston-bombings-article-1.1318128.

Hawley, Samantha and Ake Prihantari. "Break the Cycle: From bombmaker, brother of Bali terrorists now fighting radicalization," *ABC News*, August 17, 2017. http://www.abc.net.au/ news/2017-08-17/former-bomb-maker-brother-of-bali-terrorists-fighting-radicalism/8814346.

Head, Jonathan. "Maute Rebel Group: A Rising Threat to Philippines." BBC News, May 31, 2017. http://www.bbc.com/news/world-asia-40103602.

Heightman, A.J. "Lessons Learned from EMS Response to the Orlando Pulse Nightclub Shooting." *Journal of Emergency Medical Services.* January 24, 2017. https://www.jems.com/articles/2017/01/lessons-learned-from-ems-response-to-the-orlando-pulse-nightclub-shooting.html?c=1.

Huggler, Justin. "German Teenager Who Stabbed Police Officer 'Told British Friend of Her Plans,'" *Telegraph*, June 18, 2016. https://www.telegraph.co.uk/news/2016/06/18/german-teen-who-stabbed-police-officer-in-isil-attack-told-briti/.

Huncar, Andrea. "Man Accused of Edmonton Jewelry Heist to Fund ISIS Funders," CBC, May 23, 2018. https://www.cbc.ca/news/canada/edmonton/edmonton-terrorist-u-s-extradition-fort-mcmurray-san-diego-court-1.4674994.

Huncar, Andrea. "3 ISIS Recruits from Edmonton Believed Killed," CBC, January 15, 2015. https://www.cbc.ca/news/canada/edmonton/3-isis-recruits-from-edmonton-believed-killed-1.2901146.

Hussain, Tom. "Florida al Qaida Commander was Betrayed by 'Mole': Pakistani Taliban," *McClatchy*, November 25, 2015. https://www.mcclatchydc.com/news/nation-world/world/article46463910.html.

Independent. "How a Taxi Dispatcher's Mistake May Have Prevented Even More Carnage in Brussels." March 23, 2016. https://www.independent.co.uk/news/world/europe/

brussels-attacks-airport-zaventem-suicide-bombing-taxi-explo-
sives-isis-terror-a6948366.html.

Interpol. "Counter-Terrorism Fusion Centre," no date.
https://www.interpol.int/Crime-areas/Terrorism/
Counter-Terrorism-Fusion-Centre.

Jason, Zachary. "And Now." *Boston College Magazine*, no date.
https://www.bc.edu/bc-web/bcnews/campus-community/
alumni/andnow.html.

Johnson, Carrie, Johnson and Spencer Hsu. "Terror Suspect Daniel
Boyd Seemed to Have Typical Suburban Life," *Washington Post*,
July 29, 2009, http://www.washingtonpost.com/wp-dyn/con-
tent/article/2009/07/28/AR2009072803193.html.

Klopowitz, Howard. "Read Las Vegas Shooter Jerad Miller's
Anti-Government Manifesto." *International Business Times*,
June 9, 2014. http://www.ibtimes.com/read-las-vegas-shoot-
er-jerad-millers-anti-government-manifesto-photo-1596345.

Koschade, Stuart. "A Social Network Analysis of Jemaah Islamiyah:
The Applications to Counter-Terrorism and Intelligence."
Studies in Conflict and Terrorism 29, no. 6 (2006): 559–75.
http://eprints.qut.edu.au/6074/1/6074.pdf.

Kozlowska, Hanna. "Meet the Female Terrorists Keeping Putin Up
at Night," *Foreign Policy*, January 22, 2014. https://foreignpolicy.
com/2014/01/22/meet-the-female-terrorists-keeping-putin-up-
at-night/.

Lay v. Tramwell, United States District Court for the Northern
District of Oklahoma, October 7, 2015. http://ok.findacase.
com/research/wfrmDocViewer.aspx/xq/fac.20151007_0000407.
NOK.htm/qx.

"Lebanon Monitored Australian Bomb Plot Suspects: Minister," *Reuters*, August 27, 2017. https://www.reuters.com/article/ us-lebanon-security-emirates-australia-idUSKCN1B11A0.

Leibowitz, Barry. "Bruce and Joshua Turnidge, Father-Son Bank Bombers, Convicted of Murdering Two Oregon Cops." *CBS News*, December 8, 2010. https://www.cbsnews.com/news/ bruce-and-joshua-turnidge-father-son-bank-bombers-convict-ed-of-murdering-two-ore-cops-in-08/.

Levy, Eyal. "What Deters Terrorists Most Is the Thought of What Will Happen to Their Families." *Jerusalem Post*, March 16, 2016. https://www.jpost.com/Arab-Israeli-Conflict/What-deters-terrorists-most-is-the-thought-of-what-will-happen-to-their-families-448140.

Linderman, Juliet. "Derrick Smith, One of 7 Original Suspects Charged in St. John Parish Deputy Ambush, Pleads Guilty." *New Orleans Times-Picayune*, May 22, 2013. http://www.nola.com/crime/index.ssf/2013/05/derrick_smith_one_of_7_origina.html.

Litchfield, John. "How My Hate-Filled Family Spawned Merah the Monster." *Independent*, November 12, 2012. http://www.independent.co.uk/news/world/europe/how-my-hate-filled-family-spawned-merah-the-monster-8307341.html.

LoBianco, Tom. "Donald Trump on Terrorists: 'Take Out Their Families.'" CNN, December 2, 2015. https://www.cnn.com/2015/12/02/politics/donald-trump-terrorists-families/.

Los Angeles Times. "Couple Appealing Death Sentence Claim Cop Killing Was Legal." September 8, 1996. http://articles.latimes.com/1996-09-08/news/mn-41695_1_death-sentences.

Los Angeles Times. "Hezbollah Fundraiser Sentenced to Prison." June 15, 2005. http://articles.latimes.com/2005/jun/15/nation/na-hezbollah15.

Malm, Sara. "Has Jihadi Junior Been Smuggled 2,000 Miles to Sweden for an Operation?" *Daily Mail*, June 6, 2016. http://www.dailymail.co.uk/news/article-3627039/Has-Jihadi-Junior-smuggled-2-000-miles-SWEDEN-operation-Reports-claim-four-year-old-moved-Syria-bungling-ISIS-doctors-failed-treat-illness.html.

"Man Arrested in Sydney Counterterrorism Raids Charged With Weapons Offense and Released on Bail," *9News*, August 6, 2017. http://www.9news.com.au/national/2017/08/03/11/23/alleged-terror-plot-detainees-to-be-charged.

McMillan, Robert. "Meet Apple's Security Headache: The GrayKey, a Startup's iPhone-Hacking Box." *Wall Street Journal*, June 14, 2018. https://www.wsj.com/articles/the-hacking-box-that-led-to-a-golden-age-of-iphone-investigations-1528996893.

Meisner, Jason. "Boilingbrook Man Given Almost 3½ Years to Join Islamic State." *Chicago Tribune*, November 18, 2016. http://www.chicagotribune.com/news/local/breaking/ct-islamic-state-terrorism-bolingbrook-man-met-20161118-story.html.

Meisner, Jason. "Boilingbrook Man Pleads Guilty to Terrorism Charge." *Chicago Tribune*, October 29, 2015. http://www.chicagotribune.com/news/local/breaking/ct-terror-case-bolingbrook-man-plea-20151029-story.html.

Mekhennet, Souad, and William Booth. "How a Dozen Young Men from a Small Town Secretly Plotted the Deadliest Terrorist Attack in Spain in More Than a

Decade." *Washington Post*, August 20, 2017. https://
www.washingtonpost.com/world/europe/how-a-dozen-
young-men-from-a-small-town-secretly-plotted-the-deadliest-
terrorist-attack-in-spain-in-more-than-a-decade/2017/08/19/
f3d775de-844a-11e7-9e7a-20fa8d7a0db6_story.
html?utm_term=.1d05ed74f2d2.

Miller, Greg. "Legal Memo Backing Drone Strike that Killed
American Anwar al-Awlaki is Released." *Washington Post*,
June 23, 2014. https://www.washingtonpost.com/world/
national-security/legal-memo-backing-drone-strike-is-re-
leased/2014/06/23/1f48dd16-faec-11e3-8176-f2c941cf35f1_
story.html?utm_term=.ba0dd1e5e50c.

Mills, Elizabeth Shown. "The Kinship Maze: Navigating it with
Professional Precision," *Association of Professional Genealogists
Quarterly*, 20(2) (2005), pp. 61-66. https://historicpathways.
com/download/navkinmaze.pdf.

Moloney, Aisling. "Who is the White Widow, Sally Jones and How
Did She Get Involved With ISIS," *Metro*, October 12, 2017.
https://metro.co.uk/2017/10/12/who-is-the-white-widow-sally-
jones-and-how-did-she-get-involved-with-isis-6994454/.

Murphy, Doyle. "KKK Wife Malissa Ancona Hoarded Cats, Popped
Pills, and Police Say, Murdered the Local Imperial Wizard,"
River Front Times, March 8, 2017. https://www.riverfronttimes.
com/stlouis/kkk-wife-malissa-ancona-hoarded-cats-popped-
pills-and-police-say-murdered-the-local-imperial-wizard/
Content?oid=3813315.

National Commission on Terrorist Attacks upon the United States.
The 9/11 Commission Report: Final Report on the National
Commission on Terrorist Attacks upon the United States.

Washington, District of Columbia: National Commission on Terrorist Attacks upon the United States, 2004. https://www.gpo.gov/fdsys/pkg/GPO-911REPORT/pdf/GPO-911REPORT.pdf.

National Counterterrorism Center. *Countering Violent Extremism: A Guide for Practitioners and Analysts* (May 2014): 20–21. https://www.documentcloud.org/documents/1657824-cve-guide.html.

National Crime Intelligence Resource Center. "Nationwide SAR Initiative," no date. https://nsi.ncirc.gov/.

National Counterterrorism Center. "Homegrown Violent Extremist Mobilization Indicators for Public Safety Personnel," 2017. https://publicintelligence.net/nctc-hve-indicators-2017/.

National Post, "A Quick Sketch of the Omar Khadr Family," July 24, 2017. https://nationalpost.com/pmn/news-pmn/canada-news-pmn/a-quick-sketch-of-omar-khadrs-family.

National Post. "Inside the Life of a 20-Year-Old Scottish Woman Who Ran Away to Become a Hardline Supporter of ISIS." January 24, 2015. http://nationalpost.com/news/inside-the-life-of-a-20-year-old-scottish-woman-who-ran-away-become-a-hardline-supporter-of-isis.

Nationwide SAR Initiative. "Suspicious Activity Reporting Indicators and Behaviors: Tools for Analysts and Investigators," Feb. 2016. https://nsi.ncirc.gov/documents/SAR_Indicators_One-Pager.pdf.

Newsweek. "Vegas Killers Hoped Shooting Would Be 'Beginning of the Revolution.'" June 10, 2014. http://www.newsweek.com/

vegas-killers-hoped-shooting-would-be-beginning-revolu-tion-254268.

New York Times. "Only Hard Choices for Parents Whose Children Flirt With Terror," April 6, 2016. https://www.nytimes.com/2016/04/10/us/parents-face-limited-options-to-keep-children-from-terrorism.html.

Ohio Homeland Security. Communities Against Terrorism flyers, no date. https://homelandsecurity.ohio.gov/printed_material.stm.

Orban, Jean-Christophe & Quintard, Hervé & Ichai, Carole. "ICU Specialists Facing Terrorist Attack: The Nice Experience." *Intensive Care Medicine.* October 2016. https://www.research-gate.net/publication/308993592_ICU_specialists_facing_terror-ist_attack_the_Nice_experience.

Pape, Robert, Lindsey O'Rourke, and Jenna McDermit. "What Makes Chechen Women So Dangerous?" *New York Times*, March 30, 2010. https://www.nytimes.com/2010/03/31/opin-ion/31pape.html.

Patrick, Robert, and Joel Currier. "Facing Charge of Murdering a Missouri KKK Leader, a Mother Turns on Her Son," *St. Louis Post-Dispatch*, October 28, 2017. https://www.stltoday.com/news/local/crime-and-courts/facing-charge-of-murdering-a-missouri-kkk-leader-a-mother/article_9f4e3630-6cb7-52e3-92b6-5d064b045697.html.

Pearce, Matt, John M. Glionna, and Matthew Walberg. "Las Vegas Shooters Saw Government as the Enemy." *Los Angeles Times*, June 9, 2014. http://www.latimes.com/nation/la-na-vegas-shooters-20140610-story.html.

Police Magazine. "Vegas Killers Wanted to 'Columbine,' the Police." June 10, 2014. http://www.policemag.com/channel/patrol/news/2014/06/10/vegas-killers-wanted-to-columbine-the-police.aspx?force-desktop-view=1.

Radicalization Awareness Network, European Commission. *Preventing Radicalisation to Terrorism and Extremism,* 2018. https://ec.europa.eu/home-affairs/sites/homeaffairs/files/what-we-do/networks/radicalisation_awareness_network/ran-best-practices/docs/ran_collection-approaches_and_practices_en.pdf.

Rasgon, Adam. "Who Was the Perpetrator of the Jerusalem Terror Attack?" *Jerusalem Post,* January 8, 2017. http://www.jpost.com/Arab-Israeli-Conflict/Who-was-the-perpetrator-of-the-Jerusalem-terror-attack-477833.

Readhead, Harry. "Paris Attacks." *Metro,* November 18, 2015. https://metro.co.uk/2015/11/18/paris-attacks-mother-and-grandmother-died-shielding-son-5-from-bullets-at-bataclan-5510961/.

Ressler, Steve. "Social Network Analysis as an Approach to Combat Terrorism: Past, Present, and Future Research." *Homeland Security Affairs,* July 2006. https://www.hsaj.org/articles/171.

Reuters. "The Mautes of the Philippines: From Monied Family to the Islamic State." June 22, 2017. https://www.reuters.com/article/us-philippines-militants-matriarch-idUSKBN19E0A9.

Ridley, Nicholas and, Dean Alexander. "Combating Terrorist Financing in the First Decade of the Twenty-First Century, *Journal of Money Laundering Control* 15(1),

pp. 38-57 (2012). https://www.emeraldinsight.com/doi/
abs/10.1108/13685201211194727.

Rubin, Alissa J., Patrick Kingsley, and Palko Karasz. "Barcelona
Attack Suspects Had Ties to Imam Linked to ISIS." *New York
Times*, August 20, 2017. https://www.nytimes.com/2017/08/20/
world/europe/spain-barcelona-attack-suspects.html.

Sageman, Marc. *Understanding Terror Networks*. Philadelphia, PA:
University of Pennsylvania, 2004. http://www.upenn.edu/penn-
press/book/14036.html.

Sellers, Francis Stead. "'I Was Walking on Blood': The Incredible
Work by Doctors to Help Paris Victims." *Washington Post*.
November 25, 2015. https://www.washingtonpost.com/world/
europe/i-was-walking-on-blood-the-incredible-work-by-doc-
tors-to-help-paris-victims/2015/11/25/291d9772-92db-11e5-
a2d6-f57908580b1f_story.html?utm_term=.d55a99bfb1e3.

Schafer, John, and Joe Navarro. "The Seven-Stage Hate Model."
FBI Law Enforcement Bulletin, March 2003. https://leb.fbi.gov/
file-repository/archives/mar03leb.pdf/view.

Schwartz, Yishai. "Israel's Home Demolition Policy Works."
New Republic, December 8, 2014. https://newrepublic.com/
article/120506/study-israels-home-demolitions-policy-works-
it-moral.

SecurityInfoWatch. "Guilty: Father and Son Convicted of Murder
of Bank Security Guard." September 27, 2005. http://www.
securityinfowatch.com/news/10594789/guilty-father-and-son-
convicted-of-murder-of-bank-security-guard.

Shepard, Michelle. "Court Rejects Abdullah Khadr Extradition
Request," *Toronto Star*, August 4, 2010. https://www.thestar.

com/news/world/2010/08/04/court_rejects_abdullah_khadr_extradition_request.html.

Siddique, Haroon. "London Attack: What We Know so Far." *Guardian*. March 24, 2017. https://www.theguardian.com/uk-news/2017/mar/22/attack-houses-parliament-london-what-we-know-so-far.

Soma, Gena. "Parents Despair for Son Who Chose Life of Terror." CNN, June 7, 2013. http://www.cnn.com/2013/06/07/us/us-somalia-family-despair/index.html.

Southeast Asia Regional Centre for Counter-Terrorism, no date. https://www.searcct.gov.my/about-searcct/introduction.

Stabley, Matthew. "Inexplicable Shooting Mortified Suspect's Family: Cousin." NBC Washington, November 5, 2009. http://www.nbcwashington.com/news/local/Fort-Hood-Gunman-Recently-Worked-at-Walter-Reed-Reports-69328622.html.

State v. Bixby, South Carolina Court of Appeals, December 17, 2010. http://law.justia.com/cases/south-carolina/court-of-appeals/2010/4768.html.

Sun-Sentinel. "Former Broward Resident Who Became al-Qaeda Operative Killed in Pakistan: Reports," December 7, 2014. http://www.sun-sentinel.com/local/broward/fl-al-qaeda-adnan-el-shukrijumah-killed-20141207-story.html.

Swann, Steve. "Brother Campaigns for 'Enemy Combatant,'" BBC, January 24, 2009. http://news.bbc.co.uk/2/hi/americas/7848515.stm.

Telegraph. "*Piecing Together the Shadowy Lives of the Hijackers*," *September 20, 2001.* https://www.telegraph.co.uk/news/

worldnews/northamerica/usa/1341136/Piecing-together-the-shadowy-lives-of-the-hijackers.html.

Times of Israel. "Israel Will Not Demolish the Homes of Families Who Turn in Terrorists." February 24, 2016. http://www.timesofisrael.com/israel-wont-demolish-homes-of-families-who-turn-in-terrorists/.

Times of Israel. "Trial of Toulouse Shooter's Brother Reveals Chaotic Family of a French Jihadist." October 19, 2017. https://www.timesofisrael.com/trial-of-toulouse-shooters-brother-reveals-chaotic-family-of-a-french-jihadist/.

Turque, Bill. "Suspect's Son Says He Is Sorry It Was Holocaust Museum Guard, Not Dad, Who Died." *Washington Post,* June 13, 2009. http://www.washingtonpost.com/wpdyn/content/article/2009/06/13/AR2009061302111.html.

United Nations Office of Counter-Terrorism. Counter-Terrorism Implementation Task Force. "About the Task Force," no date. https://www.un.org/counterterrorism/ctitf/en/about-task-force.

United Nations Office of Counter-Terrorism. United Nations Counter-Terrorism Center. "About UNCCT," no date. https://www.un.org/counterterrorism/ctitf/en/uncct/about.

United States of America v. Daniela Greene, Motion to Unseal and Substitute Redacted Versions of Some Documents. US District Court for DC, April 17, 2015. https://extremism.gwu.edu/sites/g/files/zaxdzs2191/f/Greene%2C%20Daniela%20-%20Motion%20to%20Unseal.pdf.

United States of America v. Mahmoud Youssef Kourani, Indictment. Eastern District of Michigan, Southern Division,

November 19, 2003. http://news.findlaw.com/cnn/docs/terrorism/uskourani111903ind.pdf.

United States of America v. Michael Todd Wolfe, Criminal Complaint. US District Court for the Western District of Texas, June 18, 2014. https://cchs.gwu.edu/sites/cchs.gwu.edu/files/downloads/Wolfe%20Criminal%20Complaint.pdf.

US Army Training and Doctrine Command. *Terrorist Organizational Models: A Military Guide to Terrorism in the Twenty-First Century.* Fort Leavenworth, KS: August 15, 2007. https://fas.org/irp/threat/terrorism/guide.pdf.

US Department of Homeland Security. "Chemical Facility Anti-Terrorism Standards (CFATS)." Last revised June 29, 2018. https://www.dhs.gov/chemical-facility-anti-terrorism-standards.

US Department of Justice."Aurora Cousins Sentenced to Lengthy Prison Terms for Conspiring to Provide Material Support to ISIL." US Attorney's Office, Northern District of Illinois, September 20, 2016. https://www.justice.gov/usao-ndil/pr/aurora-cousins-sentenced-lengthy-prison-terms-conspiring-provide-material-support-isil.

US Department of Justice. "Father of Would-Be Suicide Bomber Convicted of Obstructing Terrorism Investigation." US Attorney's Office, Eastern District of New York, July 22, 2011. https://archives.fbi.gov/archives/newyork/press-releases/2011/father-of-would-be-suicide-bomber-convicted-of-obstructing-terrorism-investigation.

US Department of Justice. "Federal Judge Hands Down Sentences in Holy Land Foundation Case." Office of Public Affairs, May

27, 2009. https://www.justice.gov/opa/pr/federal-judge-hands-downs-sentences-holy-land-foundation-case.

US Department of Justice. *Guidance for Federal Law Enforcement Agencies Regarding the Use of Race, Ethnicity, Gender, National Origin, Religion, Sexual Orientation, or Gender Identity.* December 2014. https://www.justice.gov/sites/default/files/ag/pages/attachments/2014/12/08/use-of-race-policy.pdf.

US Department of Justice. "No Cash for Terror: Convictions Returned in Holy Land Case." Federal Bureau of Investigation, November 25, 2008. https://archives.fbi.gov/archives/news/stories/2008/november/hlf112508.

US Department of Justice. "North Carolina Resident Daniel Patrick Boyd Sentenced for Terrorism Violations." US Attorney's Office, Eastern District of North Carolina, August 24, 2012. https://archives.fbi.gov/archives/charlotte/press-releases/2012/north-carolina-residentdaniel-patrick-boyd-sentenced-for-terrorism-violations.

US Department of Justice. "North Carolina Resident Found Guilty of Terrorism Violations," Office of Public Affairs, June 14, 2012. https://www.justice.gov/opa/pr/north-carolina-resident-found-guilty-terrorism-violations.

US Department of Justice. "Three Brothers Sentenced to Life Terms for Conspiring to Kill US Soldiers." US Attorney's Office, District of New Jersey, April 28, 2009. https://archives.fbi.gov/archives/philadelphia/press-releases/2009/ph042809.htm.

US Department of Justice. "US Army National Guard Soldier Pleads Guilty to Attempting to Provide Material Support to ISIL." Office of Public Affairs, December 14, 2015. https://

www.justice.gov/opa/pr/us-army-national-guard-sol-dier-pleads-guilty-attempting-provide-material-support-isil.

US Department of State. "National Consortium for the Study of Terrorism and Responses to Terrorism: Annex of Statistical Information: Country Reports on Terrorism 2016 and 2017." https://www.state.gov/j/ct/rls/crt/2016/272241.htm.

Wainwright, Martin. "Neo-Nazi Ian Davison Jailed for 10 Years for Making Chemical Weapon," *Guardian*, May 14, 2010. https://www.theguardian.com/uk/2010/may/14/neo-nazi-ian-davison-jailed-chemical-weapon.

Walberg, Matthew, and Michael Muskal. "Dad of Female Las Vegas Shooter Begged Her Not to Marry Jerad Miller." *Los Angeles Times*, June 9, 2014. http://www.latimes.com/nation/nation-now/la-na-amanda-jared-miller-father-las-vegas-shooting-20140609-story.html.

Walter, Stephen. "Westminster Terrorist Khalid Masood Told Family a Week Before Attack." *Telegraph*, April 16, 2017. https://www.telegraph.co.uk/news/2017/04/16/westminster-terror-ist-khalid-masood-told-family-member-week/.

Walt, Vivienne. "Nice Attack: Doctors Save Children Injured in the Atrocity." *Time*. July 15, 2016. http://time.com/4408598/nice-attack-eyewitness-survivors-hospital/.

Watts, Jonathan. "'These Boys Were Raised among Us': Terror Cell Town Reels after Catalonia Attacks." *Guardian*, August 22, 2017. https://www.theguardian.com/world/2017/aug/22/spain-at-tacks-these-boys-were-raised-among-us-the-town-where-ter-ror-cell-was-born.

WBUR. "Lawyer for Widow of Marathon Bomber Says 'Patriot's Day' Portrays Her Unfairly." December 23, 2016. http://www.wbur.org/morningedition/2016/12/23/katherine-russell-patriots-day.

Weinberg, David. "Analysis: Former al Qaeda Operative Freed, Sent Home to Qatar," *Long War Journal*, January 20, 2015, https://www.longwarjournal.org/archives/2015/01/former_al_qaeda_oper.php.

Weiser, Benjamin. "The Trade Center Verdict." *New York Times*, November 13, 1997. http://www.nytimes.com/1997/11/13/nyregion/trade-center-verdict-overview-mastermind-driver-found-guilty-1993-plot-blow-up.html.

Whitman, Elizabeth. "Amid Brussels Attacks, EMTs And Paramedics Face New Reality Of Terrorism And An Evolving Set Of Challenges." *International Business Times*. March 23, 2016. https://www.ibtimes.com/amid-brussels-attacks-emts-paramedics-face-new-reality-terrorism-evolving-set-2341419.

Wickman, Forrest. "Are Terrorists Often Brothers?" *Slate*, April 19, 2013. http://www.slate.com/articles/news_and_politics/explainer/2013/04/boston_bombing_suspects_dzhokhar_and_tamerlan_tsarnaev_how_often_are_brothers.html.

Williams, Pete, Tracy Connor, Erik Ortiz, and Stephanie Gosk. "Gunman Omar Mateen Described as Belligerent, Racist, 'Toxic.'" *NBCNews.com*. June 12, 2016. https://www.nbcnews.com/storyline/orlando-nightclub-massacre/terror-hate-what-motivated-orlando-nightclub-shooter-n590496.

Willsher, Kim. "Toulouse Attack: Brother of Islamist Convicted of Links to Terror Group," Guardian, November 2, 2017. https://www.theguardian.com/world/2017/nov/02/toulouse-attack-brother-of-islamist-convicted-of-links-to-terror-group.

Wood, Sam. "Philly's 'Young Lioness' Indicted on Terrorism Counts." *Philadelphia Inquirer*, April 23, 2015. http://www.philly.com/philly/news/Feds_indict_Phillys_YoungLioness_on_terrorism_charges.html.

Zeveloff, Naomi. "Does Aid to Palestinians Subsidize the Families of Terrorists?" *Forward*, August 23, 2016. https://forward.com/news/israel/348017/exclusive-does-aid-to-palestinians-subsidize-the-families-of-terrorists/.

ACKNOWLEDGMENTS

I would like to acknowledge and give gratitude for the insights and guidance of my father, Dr. Yonah Alexander, a pioneer in the study of terrorism. He is the director of the Inter-University Center for Terrorism Studies at the Potomac Institute for Policy Studies and the Inter-University Center for Legal Studies at the International Law Institute. He has published over a hundred books on security themes, founded and edited five international journals, and has his private collection of terrorism research at the Hoover Institution Library and Archives at Stanford University.

Current and former colleagues at Western Illinois University (WIU)—Dr. Christopher Bitner, Dr. Dennis Bowman, Dr. Glenn Daugherty, Dr. Niyazi Ekici, Professor Richard Janoski, Dr. Todd Lough, Dr. Thomas Meloni, Professor Jill Myers, Dr. Terry Mors, Dr. John (Jack) Schafer, and Dr. Vladimir Sergevnin—deserve special thanks for their very useful suggestions on the book. I am also appreciative of the aid that WIU students Adam Ahart, John Avelar, Justin Barnes, Montisa Clark, Nicholas Dejesus, Christopher Gonzalez, Jordan Green, Trev Hadachek, Kevin Harrington, Jerrod Kalinsky, Ayaaz Khan, Cory Lewis, Marlee Lindstrom, Johnathon Lynch, David Luna, Osbaldo Macias, Kelsey Maldonado, Shamia Murphy, Kyle Sandhaas, Tyler Smith, Bryce Taylor, and Austin Weyland provided me through their research or review of the work. Those who chose to stay anonymous provided other valuable insights.

While I am responsible for the content and views presented in this work, it is possible that errors and omissions may have occurred during the preparation of the book.

ABOUT THE AUTHOR

Dean C. Alexander, J.D., LL.M., is Director, Homeland Security Research Program and Professor at the School of Law Enforcement and Justice Administration at Western Illinois University. Since publishing on terrorism in 1991, Professor Alexander has published several books on the topic, including: *The Islamic State: Combating the Caliphate Without Borders* (Lexington, 2015), *Business Confronts Terrorism: Risks and Responses* (University of Wisconsin, 2004), and *Terrorism and Business: The Impact of September 11, 2001* (Transnational, 2002). He has trained law enforcement and military personnel in the United States and abroad on terrorism and counterterrorism issues at NATO's Center of Excellence Defense Against Terrorism (Turkey), Illinois Statewide Terrorism and Intelligence Center, Oregon Fusion Center, and Milwaukee Police Department, among many other institutions. His insights on terrorism have been featured in domestic and international media, such as: the *Washington Post, Voice of America, Tribune de Genève,* and *NHK.*